LET THERE BE LIGHT

UNLOCKING THE MYSTERIES

IN THE BOOKS OF GENESIS AND LUKE

OF THE HOLY BIBLE

BY DAN L. HOPPER

THE DANCY COMPANY
RENO, NEVADA

DEDICATION

This book is dedicated, with love, to my wonderful wife Nancy, for her total devotion and help in writing this book; and to my mother Ethel Hopper, and my mother-in-law Ruth Clausen, whose love, patience, encouragement, and support have helped to make this book a reality.

ISBN 0-9646124-0-2

Printed in the United States of America

Published By
THE DANCY COMPANY
941 W. Moana Lane
Reno, Nevada 89509

THERE IS A POWER WITHIN YOU

It can lift your life to its highest level.
It can change illness into health.
It can bring peace amid turmoil.
It can bring success out of failure, victory out of defeat.
It can bring companionship and happiness out of loneliness.

IT WILL RESPOND TO YOU

Ernest Holmes, *Science of Mind*

The Holy Bible contains both physical and spiritual material. This book is dedicated to unlocking the "hidden meaning" through the use of metaphysics. *Webster's New Riverside University Dictionary*, defines "metaphysics" as, "the things after physics, the title of Aristotle's treatise on first principles (so called because it followed his work on physics)... The branch of philosophy that systematically investigates the nature of the first principles and problems of ultimate reality..." What is beyond physics is God and the spiritual realm. Thus, this book uses the Holy Bible as the source of the first principle, and looks for a deeper meaning behind the physical words. Each word and name of the first three chapters of Genesis and Luke's Genealogy of Jesus are traced back to the original Hebrew meaning and compared to current literature on the meaning behind the symbols. The main research material used in this book was obtained from the following books:

* *Metaphysical Bible Dictionary*, Unity School of Christianity, Unity Village, MO 64065.

* *Dictionary of all Scriptures & Myths*, G. A. Gaskell, Gramercy Books, New York, Avenel, New Jersey.

* *Exhaustive Concordance of the Bible*, James Strong, MacDonald Publishing Company, McLean, Virginia 22102.

* *A Course In Miracles*, Foundation For Inner Peace, P.O. Box 1104, Glen Ellen, CA 95442.

I offer grateful acknowledgment to all who have been responsible for the generation and availability of these wonderful resources. Without these resources this book would not have been possible.

TABLE OF CONTENTS

PART IV PATHWAY TO CHRIST

LIST OF FIGURES

ACKNOWLEDGMENTS

With special gratitude I would like to acknowledge the students of my first seminars; Linda Albert, Charlotte Anderson, Vern Appleby, Jean Archer, Carolyn Bonin, Bob and Thelma Bowers, Marjorie Branden, Adom Lepe-Camacho, Ruth Clausen, Jean Cunningham, Barbara Cupit, Edward and Sandra Grant, Sunny Hand, Donna Hopkins, Floyd Jorgenson, Gee Gee Lenhart, Larry Lutzker, Bob and Virginia McKim, Nancy McGinnis, Joan Molinari, Suzan Rockwell, Rita Shelton and Zola Younger whose dedication, enthusiasm, interest, feedback and encouragement to publish the presented information inspired this book.

I would also like to acknowledge and extend appreciation to Rev. Sandy Jacobs, Darlene Madison, Evelyn Smith and Dr. David Thompson for the generosity with which they made available to us their time, energy, suggestions, and insights in the review of this book.

A very special thanks to my chief editor, Dr. Jacueline Langley, for all her literary and spiritual guidance in addition to all her help with general editing and organization. And last, but not least, I would like to acknowledge James Chlebda for his thorough proofing and editing.

PREFACE

It was a clear, sunny, summer day as I was walking by a stream in my favorite valley, high in the Sierras of California. The trees seemed unusually majestic as they caressed the blue sky, and only a hint of clouds painted thin streaks in the vastness. The warmth of the morning sun soothed both my body and soul, and I decided to lean back against a large boulder to take in the beauty of my surroundings. It was quiet except for the rustling of the leaves and the occasional squawking of a Steller Jay in the background. The light reflected off the waters of the stream as if the rays were doing a ballet to the graceful music of an orchestra.

Running water has always been very special to me. In fact, I built a waterfall in the backyard of every house I've owned. It adds a center of interest and beauty to the yard, and the sound of water trickling over the rocks is deeply soothing both to my ears and soul. So this particular spot in the mountains had the warmth of home and the feeling of being at one with the Creator.

As I sat there enjoying the running stream trickling over the rocks, I was full of gratitude for the animals, birds, and beauty of this spot. It was so quiet and peaceful that I let my mind wander and jump from one thought to the next. Suddenly, the volume of water in the stream began to decrease, and then it stopped all together! This was very alarming because I knew that this stream nurtured every living thing around it; the animals, the trees and bushes, the birds, the insects, and yes, even the human beings that were down stream from this location.

The rustling of a deer awakened me from the illusion of a dream, and I realized that the stream was still flowing as freely as ever. Yet the imagery continued to haunt me, and my mind screamed for answers to possible meanings. I instinctively realized that the stream was a symbol for Life. The trees were deeply connected to the ground, and yet, were still reaching out to the heavens. The animals and bird must, therefore, represent some form of thoughts.

Thus began my search for the meaning behind the words, or symbols, that we use daily in our lives. Because my dream had awakened an awareness of the spiritual dimension of my surroundings, by association I recognized that the Bible must be similarly encoded. With the right keys, surely it would be possible to discover, and spiritually decode, the vital meaning locked within the literal chronicles of an ancient history.

Formulated on the thesis that the Bible can thus be interpreted on the basis of both physical and spiritual dimensions, this book is dedicated to decoding its hidden, or spiritual meaning: to trace back and examine the literal, explicit, physical meaning of the Hebrew words of the first three chapters of Genesis and Luke's Genealogy of Jesus, and to reinterpret them in terms of their contemporary metaphysical meanings.

INTRODUCTION

In 1982, a search for material on the *Twelve Powers of Man* led me to a Religious Science bookstore. It was in this bookstore that my life was changed forever. Here, I found a wealth of information and, as I searched, more questions surfaced; my thirst for knowledge seemed unquenchable. It was here that the *Metaphysical Bible Dictionary* literally fell off the shelf into my hands. I realized that this was more than a coincidence so naturally, I bought it.

One of the first things that I was to look up in this Dictionary was my name. My legal name is Dan which, in Hebrew, means "rule of righteous judgment," and metaphysically represents the earliest expression of judgment before it is lifted to the spiritual plane. Dan, in my case is not short for the name Daniel, which in Hebrew means "God is my judge" and metaphysically represents spiritual judgment, or conscious integrity. I was struck by how well these definitions fit me. I had been judgmental all my life and was only recently beginning to shift to spiritual discernment, leaving judgment to Spirit. I was in the process of growing from Dan to Daniel; that is to say, my nature (name) is hopefully changing to that of Daniel.

Using my new *Metaphysical Bible Dictionary*, I began to look up other names and places and found them equally as fascinating. One day I began to look up all the names in Luke's Genealogy of Jesus (Luke 3:23 through 3:38), and those in the "Begatitudes" of Genesis (Genesis 5:5 to 47:28). In this process I began to realize that within the metaphysical interpretation of each word was a priceless clue to the inner, spiritual, message of each passage. This was a key that could unlock the mysteries of the Holy Bible.

Most Biblical scholars would agree that the Bible concerns itself with both the historical and spiritual evolution of man. The historical events and genealogy, or literal knowledge, of the Old Testament, for example, can be validated by science as far back as Abraham from 2,000 BC to 1500 BC. Science cannot validate the Biblical events from Adam to Abraham, yet Genesis provides detailed information on this missing data. Spiritual knowledge, that of "Divine origin," on the other hand, was encoded in the sacred scriptures through symbolic imagery not open to scientific interpretation.

Literal interpretations of the Bible, as diverse as its many interpreters, have been subject to a multiple of variables which include time, language and context. The Old Testament is four to six thousand years old and derived from the oral tradition passed on from generation to generation. Its purpose and language have survived and evolved through changing tribes, civilizations, lands and numbers. As a written document it has survived translation into every language and every cultural change; adapting to the nature of each. For example, the Hebrew language has no words with which to denote time (day, seasons, year), so English translators have had to interpret these concepts. Contextually, the Bible has evolved as a tool for teaching at all levels of learning throughout time. It includes information for the most basic of physical needs and the most advanced of spiritual levels.

At this point in his evolution, man, in general, does not recognize Spirit with his five senses. It makes sense, then, that it is difficult to describe the spiritual world with words of this world; and it accounts for the extensive use of the parable and analogy in Jesus' teachings to bring spiritual knowledge into man's domain. A *parable*, as defined by *Webster's Dictionary*, is "a simple story illustrating a moral religious lesson." For example, parables used in the Bible include: the lost sheep; the fallen sparrow; building a house upon rock; the mustard seed; and talents given to three servants. An *analogy,* according to *Webster's Dictionary,* is a "correspondence in some aspect between otherwise dissimilar things....a separation of an intellectual or substantial whole into its constituent parts for individual study." In his reply to the question, "Who is the greatest in the kingdom of heaven," Jesus answered, "except that ye...become as little children ye shall not enter into the kingdom of heaven," (Matthew 18:3). In this way, he explained in the terms of his disciples, a concept that could only be understood from their experience; children are innocent and pure, as heaven is innocent and pure.

Introduction

Spiritual interpretation of the Bible depends on a very different frame of reference, a different perception of reality; one that looks beyond the literal interpretations and can see the difference between **content** and **context.** Content is the thing itself, while the context is how we perceive it. Content always remains the same, while context is subject to change. In the past, for example, it was believed that the earth was flat, that it was the center of the universe, and that the atom was the smallest particle known to man. With new scientific knowledge we see these beliefs with a different frame of reference: the world is round, the center of the universe is the sun, and the smallest particle known to man is a quark (and even that knowledge is being challenged). Through increased knowledge our context has changed.

Perception depends on the perceiver. Each man interprets his experience through the lens of his own mental map. Seldom has he been aware of the uniqueness of his map, let alone questioned its accuracy. As a result, man's attitudes and behaviors are defined by his mindset; one that is based on physical input rather than spiritual knowledge. Only a change of perception can alter the perceiver.

New Thought, or metaphysical perception, teaches that Spirit is within each physical body (as well as everywhere else). By extension, each word of the Bible represents a spiritual concept. The ancient word, the sacred scriptures, are held to be of divine origin, whose words convey spiritual messages or ideas to the physical, lower, mind in the form of images, parables, and analogies. I believe the Bible is a record of the experience and development of the human soul; a treatise on man's relationship to God. I have consequently chosen to dedicate this book to the search for the spiritual messages encoded in selected verses of the Bible: the first three chapters of Genesis and Luke 3:23 through 3:38. Literally, these chapters delineate a tribal ancestry back to Adam in very specific detail. They appear at first reading to be little more than a precise lineage. It is my purpose to trace each word, or name, back to the original Hebrew word, and its associated meanings, and search for the greater spiritual meaning encoded therein. In doing so, I rely heavily on the symbology of other religions, and on metaphysics.

ENCODED HISTORY

It will be of some significance here to explore the purpose of such a spiritual encoding. To do so will require a review of the early history of the Israelites, who were placed in bondage by four different nations. With each captivity there was a profound loss of religious freedom and an associated change in lifestyle and beliefs.

Moses led the Israelites from bondage under Egypt (1450 to 1410 B.C), and it is here that the first set of Spiritual Laws were given to the Israelites. The twelve tribes of Jacob operated more or less independently from each other until David became king. David was a sensible and able politician and was able to unite the twelve tribes into the single nation of Israel. David's selection of Jerusalem as the capital offended no tribe and minimized any impression that he intended to favor Judah. David's second action was to appoint two chief priests in Jerusalem, one from the north and one from the south. The Kingdom of Israel prospered under the leadership of David.

King Solomon, David's son, is famous for his wisdom. The Biblical picture of him is that he maintained a strong, prosperous kingdom through diplomatic and economic skill rather than on the battlefields as his father had done. Solomon outdid David in "marriage diplomacy". However, because of his outlandish spending habits and the resulting high taxation to pay for the temple in Jerusalem, Israel became divided and split into two countries after his death. Rehoboam became king in the South, and Jeroboam became king in the North. The two kingdoms of Israel were related by a common language, shared traditions, and had similar but not identical forms of religion. The northern kingdom was destroyed by Assyria in 722 B.C. Judah was captured by Babylon and the temple in Jerusalem was destroyed in 587 B.C.

It is assumed that all religious records were destroyed when the temple in Jerusalem was burned and ravished by the Babylonians. This theory is confirmed in II Chronicles 36:19 and 20 which indicate that the temple was burned, all the goodly vessels destroyed, and the people that survived were carried away and became servants in Babylon. In addition, II Chronicles 36:21 and Ezra 1:1 tell us that the prophet Jeremiah fulfilled the word of the Lord by *mouth*, which suggests that written material was not available to the Israelites.

It was Ezra, a priest and scribe of the Jews, and Nehemiah, a onetime cup-bearer to the king of Persia under the decree of King Cyrus, that brought order, returned the children of Israel back to Jerusalem and rebuilt the temple and the walls of Jerusalem. Ezra 7:6 and 7:10 tells us that Ezra was "a ready scribe in the law of Moses", and that he had "prepared his heart to seek the law of the Lord and teach Israel the statutes and judgments". This is the second confirmation that the religious records were destroyed by the Babylonians. Finally, in Nehemiah 8:1 through 8:6 the people gathered together and requested that Ezra bring the book of the law of Moses, which the Lord had commanded to Israel. "And Ezra the priest brought the law before the congregation..." This is the first indication that the law of Moses might have survived the Babylonian destruction. However, based on the above references, the most logical conclusion is that Ezra, being pure of Spirit, re-transcribed the law of Moses from memory, and gave it to the people of Israel.

Therefore, it is my theory that it was Ezra who encoded the Old Testament. Being a priest, he passed the decoding down to other priests. They maintained this tradition, until the total destruction of the temple of Jerusalem and the loss of its priests in the Roman-Jewish war, where the decoding technique was lost forever.

Why did Ezra encode the Old Testament? It is my theory that the answer lies in the fact that the people of Israel spent several hundred years in captivity to Egypt, Assyria, and Babylon. Egypt, metaphysically, represents *ignorance*, Assyria represents intellectual or *mental reasoning* and Babylon represents a state of *confusion*. Thus, the Israelites were in bondage to ignorance, mental reasoning and confusion for several hundred years. Without understanding and knowledge it was difficult for them to adhere to the Spiritual Laws. However, the priests, schooled in the ways of Spirit, could understand the encoded message and pass the information along when souls entrusted to them had evolved sufficiently to handle spiritual information.

The knowledge of the relationship between Universe and man is part of the secret wisdom of Kabbalism, which teaches that in the chain of being everything is magically contained within everything else. Such is part of the wisdom which is said to be implicit and revealed under the vail of allegory in the Torah. All is, however, deeply concealed under successive veils of allegory, symbols and metaphorical history.

This is made clear in Matthew 13:10 through 13:13, after Jesus told the parable of the sower. "And the disciples came, and said unto Him, Why speakest thou unto them in parables? He answered and said unto them, *Because it is given unto you to know the mysteries of the kingdom of heaven*, but to them it is not given. For whosoever hath, to him shall be given, and he shall have more abundance: but whosoever hath not, from him shall be taken even that he hath. Therefore speak I to them in parables: because they seeing see not; and hearing they hear not, neither do they understand." In Matthew 13:16 & 13:17 Jesus confirms that the disciples have the keys to the mysteries of the kingdom of heaven; "But blessed are your eyes, for they see; and your ears hear. For verily I say unto you, That many prophets and righteous men have desired to see *those things* which ye see, and have not seen *them*; and to hear *those things* which ye hear, and have not heard *them*." These words indicate intelligence is to be separated from ignorance, and to understand Spirit one needs know the "keys" to unlocking the mysteries of the spiritual realm. Understanding the "keys" opens the spiritual mind to spiritual seeing and hearing.

Thus, encoding the Bible protects the spiritual intelligence from being confused by physical ignorance, while at the same time provides parables and allegories that will illustrate the moral or religious lessons of otherwise dissimilar things. Many prophets and righteous men, were not given the "keys" inspite of their lofty positions in the physical world, and, thus, did not understand the spiritual message. Only when a person has achieved a certain level of conscious awareness are the "keys to the mysteries of the kingdom of heaven" given them.

It is my theory that the "keys to the kingdom of heaven" were guarded by the chief priest, or a select few, and released through merit only. This capability was lost with the destruction of the temple of Jerusalem and its leaders in the Roman-Jewish War after the death of Jesus. This war brought an end to the Israelite Nation and its Hebrew traditions. At this point the Christian tradition is brought forth by Roman and Greek influences.

Perhaps the keys were never really lost, and the world has just now evolved to a point where the spiritual information can be understood and effectively used.

PURPOSE

This book documents the portion of my research, over the last fifteen years, that focused on selected verses of the Books of Genesis and Luke in the Holy Bible. The purpose is to discover the sub-text, or spiritual message encoded within.

It has been my purpose to expose the divinely inspired messages within the sacred scriptures which have not traditionally been accessible in the interpretation commonly found as the basis of Western, Christian religions.

Having been raised a Protestant Christian, the Bible has been at the center of my religious life. Over the years, however, many questions began to surface that remained unanswered by my traditional religion. My subsequent search eventually led me to *A Course in Miracles* and the teachings of the Science of Mind in the Religious Science Church. At first, it seemed that these teachings were different from the Bible and traditional Christianity in some respects, but on closer examination I found that, at the important or spiritual levels, what appear on the surface as differences are really different ways of saying the same thing. So, rather than destroy my original beliefs and faith, these interpretations actually expanded and strengthened them; my beliefs were reinforced as the Bible passages were decoded in the following research.

It is hoped that this book will help to bridge the gap between New Thought, Protestant, Catholic, and other religions of the world: that it will confirm apparent differences as differences only at the lower levels of consciousness. We are all the Sons of the same God. (We are all one.) Although the physical words in the Bible are subject to changing interpretations, the underlying spiritual meaning remains constant. *It is within us to change our perception that we are different and separate from each other.* This book is dedicated to exposing the Spiritual Truth for each individual, and humanity as a whole.

VOCABULARY OF FREQUENTLY USED WORDS

The following words are used in the body of this book as a working vocabulary of commonly used terms, and in some cases may have a different interpretation or meaning than that commonly used:

Astral plane - Is that plane which exists between the physical and mental plane and is the formative, or idea, source of all physical manifestation.

Christ - Is the Higher Self, and the fundamental principle underlying the idea or personal Godhood. It is the consciousness of God with us and in us, and is the highest level of consciousness attainable by the physical world.

Consciousness - Is the passive aspect of Spirit on the mental plane.

Evolution - Is the process of movement towards reunification with God. It is the ascent of Spirit through matter, and progressively moves from the outer to the higher inner values and ideals.

Faith - Is an unconditional acceptance of Spirit - A perception that all is perfect and in process to perfection, or the Source.

Firmament - Represents understanding. It is the higher mental plane which separates heaven and earth; Spirit and illusions.

God - Is the central principle of Being, the only reality, and the source of the transitory manifestation of the external universe. The Source, the Divine Consciousness, and the Divine Mind are synonymous with God.

He - Will be used as a term to represent an individual, and is not intended to denote gender.

Heaven - Is a state of consciousness in which the soul and body are in harmony with God. It is also called the upper or Divine Consciousness

Holy Spirit - Is the feminine aspect of the Divine Trinity and proceeds directly from the Godhead; the infinite source of all. It is the Universal Presence, in which we all live and which manifests Itself through us.

Illusion - An appearance devoid of reality in itself.

Intellect/Intelligence - The mental principal capable of disclosing differences and perceiving similarities; This choosing faculty introduces will.

Intuition - Is the wisdom of the heart; and is much surer than the intellect. Faith awakens the so-called sixth sense, or divine knowing.

Involution - Is the descent of Spirit into matter.

Mind - A conscious state that has the same meaning as Spirit. It is the subjective reaction of thought, or the Law of Mind in action.

Outer manifestation - Is the physical manifestation of the images of the lower mind, or earth.

Perception - Is an impression in the mind of something received by the physical senses marked by understanding and discernment.

Psychic- Is the subjective life of oneself, or the race consciousness revealing *human* rather that *Divine* Truth.

Pure or purity - Is the removal of every trace of extraneous matter. To be pure is to have only Spiritual thoughts, because they are based on Truth and Reality.

Reality - Is the central principal, the Source.

Soul - Is man's consciousness of himself, as an individual entity.

Spirit - Is a symbol of the positive energetic force; the qualitative and formative aspects of God.

Truth - Is the emanation of God, (the Source).

Trust - Is having complete confidence in Spirit.

Sea - Is a symbol of the astral plane; a state of unrest.

Water - In its different aspects represents unformed thoughts, mental potentiality, cleansing and, in some cases, life or vital energy. It is the symbol of the mental potential and represents Truth. Based upon Truth it purifies the physical matter. Truth and water seek the course of least resistance.

Unformed thoughts - Are illusions based on ignorance, untruths, fear and guilt. Through spiritual involution they are transformed to formed Truth, or Spiritual thoughts, and action.

PART I

THE FIRST STORY OF CREATION

CHAPTER 1:

LET THERE BE LIGHT

Why start with the Book of Genesis? Genesis is the first book of the Bible and describes the creation of manifest man and the manifest universe. It specifically *deals with the creative power of thought.* Thought is the law that governs Cause and Effect. The other books of the Bible illustrate the way in which the law of thought works in different circumstances, but Geneis is the foundation. Without understanding the message of Genesis the understanding of the evolution of man is lost as well as the deeper spiritual message of the Bible. The importance of Genesis has been known since the beginning of time, and is best described by the following 19th century quote; "This (spiritual) order of evolution is found in the first and second chapters of Genesis, if one reads it in its true esoteric sense; for chapter 1 contains the history of ... (his development) up to the moment when Man is called to *conscious* life by the Elohim of Wisdom." - H. P. Blavatsky, *Secret Doctrine*, Vol. II, p. 190.

Thus, to unlock the esoteric sense and mysteries of Genesis I have used the following format:

Text - The Bible verse quotation from the *Authorized King James Version.*

Decoding - The Hebrew meaning of each major word, and a metaphysical meaning of the word where available. The Hebrew meaning is derived from the *Exaustive Concorance of the Bible* and the metaphysical meaning is derived from the *Metaphysical Bible Dictionary,* or the *Dictionary of all Scriptures & Myths*.

Translation - The one to one word correlation of the Hebrew and/or metaphysical meaning of the text.

Interpretation - Observations and explanations of the deeper meaning of what the text is indicating in the words and symbols of our present day language.

Chapter 1 and the first three verses of chapter 2 of Genesis constitute a summary of the laws that governs thought. It is a treatise on the Spiritual evolution of man. Day and night, for example, in the Scriptures are symbols describing degrees of unfoldment, where night is ***ignorance*** and day is ***understanding***. Thus, the completion of each cycle of unfoldment is indicated by the words, "And the evening and the morning," which are symbolic of the in-drawing and out-going forces of manifestation. Each day consists of an evening which has witnessed the decline of spiritual energy (darkness); and a morning which initiates the process of a spirital energy (light) (verses 1:5, 1:8, 1:13, 1:19, 1:23, 1:31, and 2:2).

Thus, the detailed investigation of each symbol, or word, that is presented in the first chapter of Genesis of the Bible, proceeds on a day-by-day basis.

FIRST DAY - GENESIS 1:1-5

Gen. 1:1 "In the beginning God created the heavens and the earth."

"In the beginning" is not consistent with the theory of the life cycle, which has no beginning or ending. From the ego's (the personal consciousness) point of view, there is a beginning and an ending, starting with birth and terminating at death. However, the Bible and most of the spiritual writings of the world, indicate that death is an llusion. **Beginning** comes from the Hebrew word *reshiyth* (ray-sheeth') which means time, place, order, or principal thing.

God in Hebrew is *Elohiym* (el-o-heem') which has a plural meaning denoting power and strength, while in the New Testament it is derived from the Greek word *Theos,* meaning deity. Metaphysically, God is a general term for the Divine Mind.

Created in Hebrew is *bara* (baw-raw') which means to cut down, dispatch, do, or make.

Heaven in Hebrew is *shameh* (shaw-meh') which means to be lofty, sky, or higher ether where the celestial bodies revolve. Heaven then, is the state of consciousness which is above the mental plane. Metaphysically, heaven is an ideal state of consciousness in which the ideas are in complete harmony with the Divine Mind. Heaven, then, represents the Divine Consciousness; sometimes called the upper mind. Jesus evidently experienced difficulty in making Himself understood on this subject, which accounts for the numerous parables and analogies that He used to describe heaven. Never did Jesus describe heaven as a place located in some distant realm.

Earth in Hebrew is *erets* (eh'-rets) which means to be firm, field, ground, or land. Earth is a symbol for matter which, when acted upon by Spirit, takes on the form and qualities for manifestation. That is, this is where the ideal thought is manifested. It is the lower condition of the Divine Mind. The primordial elements, Spirit and Matter, are differentiated from that condition which is itself neither, but which is potential to both. Metaphysically, earth is the outer manifestation of the Divine Mind, and is sometimes referred to as the lower mind.

Metaphysically, this verse might read: "**In principal, Divine Mind dispatched an ideal state of consciousness above the mental plane and the outer manifestation to take the form and qualities of Divine Mind.**"

This indicates that God envisioned two universal states of consciousness in the mind. One state is the realm of pure ideals (heaven) and the other is the form of thought (earth). God did not create the visible universe directly, but created the ideas, which are used by its intelligent "images" and "likeness" to make the universe. God's creations are always Spiritual. However, man's creations are both material and spiritual, according to man's understanding.

Gen 1:2 "And the earth was without form, and void; and darkness was upon the face of the deep. And the

Spirit of God moved upon the face of the waters."

Earth is a symbol of matter which, when acted upon by Spirit, takes the form and qualities of manifestation. Earth is where the ideal thought is to be manifested, and is the lower and outer condition of the Divine Mind.

Form in Hebrew is *tohu* (to-hoo) which means worthless thing, confusion, empty place, without form, or wilderness. The words **without form** indicate that the outer manifestation, or lower mind, was without shape, structure, color, texture, or density; because Spirit is not yet permeating and forming matter, and the process of involution has not begun.

Void in Hebrew is *bohuw* (bo'-hoo) which means an indistinguishable ruin, empty, or to be empty. According to Webster's Dictionary, void means to make empty, and is not occupied. Therefore, the earth, or the outer manifestation, was not occupied.

Darkness in Hebrew is *choshek* (kho-shek') which means the dark, misery, destruction, death, ignorance, or wickedness. Metaphysically, darkness is the inability to understand spiritual concepts and values.

Face in Hebrew is *paneh* (paw-neh') which means a part that turns, edge, forefront, or presence. Face is a symbol of the mental aspect of being.

Deep in Hebrew is *tohu* (same meaning as without form above). Deep is a symbol of the lower nature of darkness which is below the higher nature.

Spirit in Hebrew is *ruwach* (roo'-akh) which means resemblance of breath, or rational being. Metaphysically, Spirit means God, and is the breath of life.

Water in Hebrew is *shaqah* (shaw-kaw') which means to irrigate, furnish, influence, or give to. Metaphysically, water is a symbol of the astral plane, that of illusions, the inverted or distorted reflection of truth, or the Spirit. Metaphysically, water represents the mental potential of the Universal Mind.

Metaphysically, this verse might read: **"And the outer manifestation was without shape and was not occupied; and the inability to understand spiritual values was of the lower nature of darkness. And the breath of life moved into the presence of the distorted reflections of Truth."**

This indicates that God envisioned that ideal thought would be manifested in the lower, or outer condition of the Divine Mind. The lower mind would be the receptacle of Spirit and would consist of matter, as opposed to the*Spiritual understanding* of the upper mind. Because Spirit had not yet permeated and formed matter, the process of *involution* had not begun; the outer condition was unformed and not occupied, and ignorance was present in the outer manifestation. Yet the spiritual consciousness in the I AM (God) was in the mental potential that was there. The spiritual consciousness is always in the mental aspects of being, regardless of unformed thoughts.

Gen. 1:3 "And God said, let there be light and there was light."

> **God** is a general term for the Divine Mind, or Spirit.
> **Light** in Hebrew is *owr* (ore) which means illumination, glorious, shine, or sun. Light is a symbol of Truth as the *consciousness* is united with Spirit and Matter at the commencement of manifestation. Metaphysically, light is the symbol of intelligence.

Metaphysically, this verse might read: **"And Divine Mind said, let there be intelligence and there was intelligence."**

The Divine Mind wills "light," or the union of Spirit and Matter. First a simple and pure spiritual light was created, which is the material of Souls. The Light material is from the upper mind (heaven) from which the souls descend. It is also called Reason, or the Light of God. Intelligence (light) will always overcome ignorance (darkness); as turning on the light in a room will always get rid of the darkness. Intelligence is of God, and is freely given to us. All we have to do is ask, or be willing to accept it.

Gen. 1:4 "And God saw the light, that it was good; and God divided the light from the darkness."

God is a general term for the Divine Mind.

Light is the symbol for intelligence.

Good in Hebrew is *towb* (tobe) which means beautiful, cheerful, or pleasant. Good in this context is a symbol of the perfect production of qualities and forms for purposes of manifestation upon the lower mind in the cycle of evolution.

Divided in Hebrew is *badal* (baw-dal') which means to separate, or distinguish.

Darkness is the inability to understand spiritual concepts.

Therefore, metaphysically, this verse might read: **"And Divine Mind saw the intelligence, that it was beautiful, and Divine Mind distinguished the intelligence from the inability to understand spiritual concepts."**

This indicates that God saw that what was produced through involution was perfect for the purposes of manifestation in the lower plane. Furthermore, Intelligence must be distinguished from ignorance, because if the two are mixed together it will create a state of confusion in the consciousness. Intelligence and ignorance are mutually exclusive.

Please note that the Divine Mind only creates the good. Never is anything judged as bad or evil. This is strictly a man-generated concept.

Gen. 1:5 "And God called the light day, and the darkness he called night."

God is a general term for the Divine Mind.
Light is the symbol for intelligence.
Day in Hebrew is *yowm* (yome) which means to be hot, or sunrise to sunrise. Day is symbolic of a period of spiritual activity. Metaphysically, day means understanding.
Darkness, metaphysically, means the inability to understand spiritual concepts.
Night in Hebrew is *layiah* (lah'-yel-aw) which means twisted away from the light, adversity, or spiral step; and is symbolic of periodic ignorance. Metaphysically, night represents ignorance.

Metaphysically, this verse might read: "**And Divine Mind called the intelligence understanding, and the failure to understand he called ignorance.**"

Intellect is the mental principle which involves choice in uniting with, or rejecting, spiritual concepts. It is this choosing faculty that makes man (individuality) as God. It is the function of the intellect to discern differences and perceive similarities, but without intuition it can never reveal the perfect truth. Intellect, having the capacity for uniting with that which it perceives, becomes the formative factor in the soul, but it tends to contract and limit that which it operates on. Intelligence is knowing that you know, and removes choice from the consciousness, because it is of Spirit. Therefore, intelligence, being of Spirit, will light understanding, while darkness, or the inability to understand, will have the nature of ignorance and be devoid of spiritual qualities.

Figure 1 Illustrates The First Understanding in Genesis 1:3 - 5.

MENTAL ASPECTS OF BEING - (GEN, 1:1-2)
Distorted Reflections of Truths

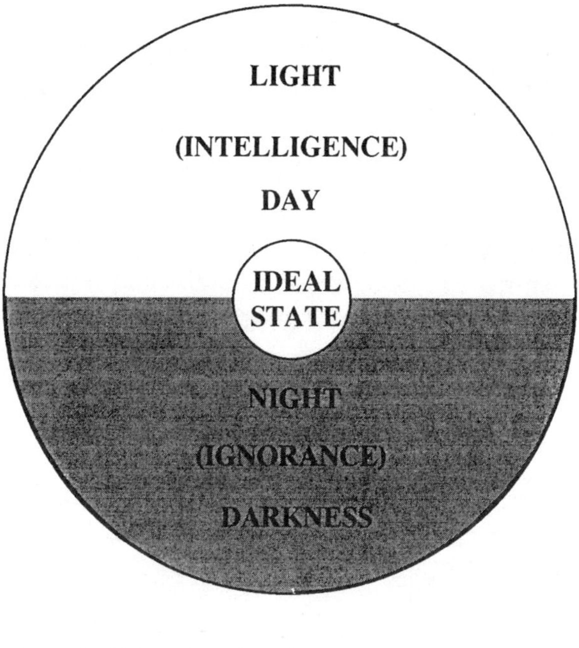

SEPARATION OF INTELLIGENCE FROM IGNORANCE (GEN. 1:3-5)

FIGURE 1 - FIRST UNDERSTANDING - (GENESIS 1:3-5)

SUMMARY OF THE FIRST UNDERSTANDING

The first day of creation is describing the formation of two states of consciousness. The first is an ideal state of consciousness that is in complete harmony with the Divine Mind, and the second is the outer manifestation of these ideals. The outer manifestation consists of a mental plane and realm of physical forms. These two states of consciousness provide the essential qualities for choice, and the ability to separate intelligence from ignorance. Without this apparent duality, choice would be impossible. This indicates that God intended man to choose his experiences, and in so doing grow into the spiritual ideal that God envisioned.

Secondly, the ideal state of consciousness (heaven) is of a higher consciousness than the mental potential, which is above the outer manifestation of forms (earth). However, at this point the lower mind is without shape and not occupied with spiritual concepts. Yet, the breath of life is present in the distorted reflections of truth. Note that verse 1:2 is indicating that the spiritual light is distorted reflections of the Truth, until the ignorance has been removed. Thus, the illusions of the physical world can be transformed by Truth, which truly makes them beautiful in the image of the God.

CHAPTER 2:

LET THERE BE A FIRMAMENT

From the beginning the Divine Mind created two different thought systems. One state is the realm of pure ideals and the other state is the manifestation of thought. Man has misintrepreted this event to represent the duality of good and evil, rather than viewing it as all good. Divine Mind's creations are always Spiritual. However, man's creations are both material and spiritual according to man's understanding.

The ideal thought is manifested in the lower mind or outer manifestation of the Divine Mind. The lower mind is the receptacle of Spirit and consists of matter as opposed to Spiritual understanding. At first, the outer manifestation is without Spiritual influence and the thoughts are unformed until the process of involution transforms them to the true mental potential that is there. The Divine Mind then wills the union of Spirit and matter by giving the lower mind pure spiritual light. This spiritual light is from the upper mind (heaven) from which the soul descends. This Spiritual light is intelligence given freely from the Divine Mind. Intelligence will always expose ignorance and transform it to understanding. Intelligence must be separated and distinguished from ignorance, because if the two are mixed together it will create a state of confusion. Man tends to confuse intellect with intelligence. Intellect is the mental principle that provides choice. Choice is the choosing part of the mind that unites, or rejects, spiritual concepts. Intellect is based on perceptions, while intelligence is knowing that you know. Thus, the outer manifestion needs a firm, unwavering, understanding of spiritual concepts.

SECOND DAY - GENESIS 1:6-8

Gen. 1:6 "And God said, Let there be a firmament in the midst of the water, and let it divide the waters from the waters."

> **God** is a general term for the Divine Mind.
> **Firmament** in Hebrew is *raqiya* (raw-kee'-ah) which means expanse, firmament, or visible arch of the sky, and is a symbol of the higher mental plane as the firm foundation of creation. It divides the upper planes of Reality from the lower planes of illusion. Metaphysically, firmament means faith, or understanding of mind power; a firm unwavering place in consciousness.
> **Midst** in Hebrew is *tavek* (taw'-vek) which means to sever, the center, among, between or half.
> **Water** in Hebrew is *shaqah* (shaw-kaw') which means to irrigate, furnish, influence, or give to. Water is a symbol of the astral plane that contains errors and illusions which are the inverted or distorted reflections of truth. Metaphysically, water in its different aspects represents unexpressed possibilities, weakness and negativity, mental potential, and in some cases, life.
> **Divide** in Hebrew is *badal* (baw-dal') which means to separate, distinguish or divide.

Metaphysically, this verse might read: **"And Divine Mind said, let there be a firm foundation in the middle of unexpressed possibilities, and let it distinguish the weakness and negativity from the mental potential."**

This indicates that there is a firm, unwavering place in consciousness that divides the upper planes of Reality from the lower planes of illusion. This firm place in consciousness is called faith, or understanding, and is the first step to spiritual knowing. Understanding is a perception of the ideal of that which is coming in evolution. It is a sense of that which is superior to knowledge, that is, the intuition of Truth which is under law, reason, cause and effect. Understanding in the power of Divine Mind, in the middle of unformed and unexpressed thoughts, separates the weak and negative thoughts from the spiritual potential that is there.

Gen. 1:7 "And God made the firmament, and divided the waters which were under the firmament from the waters which were above the firmament; and it was so."

> **God** is a general term for the Divine Mind, or Spirit.
> **Firmament,** metaphysically, represents understanding of mind power, a firm unwavering place in consciousness where the higher mental plane of creation divides the upper planes of Reality from the lower planes of illusion. The phrase **under the firmament** is a symbol of the lower mental plane where there is great confusion because of the struggle between the analytical illusions of the intellect, and the intuition, or inspiration (intelligence) of Reality, which presents the Truth. The phrase **above the firmament** symbolizes the higher mental planes of consciousness which separate Spirit from illusion.
> **Water** means to irrigate, furnish, influence, or give to. Water is a symbol of the astral plane that contains errors and illusions which are the inverted or distorted reflections of truth. Metaphysically, water in its different aspects represents unexpressed possibilities, weakness and negativity, mental potential, and in some cases, life.

Metaphysically, this verse might read: "**And Divine Mind made the firm unwavering place in consciousness, and distinguished the unexpressed possibilities, which were in the lower mental plane, from the mental potential, which is of a higher mental plane; and it was so.**"

In the lower mind, or subconscious, there is a great deal of confusion and disturbance. It arises from the struggle between the analytical faculties, which differentiate and define (the intellect), and the intuition and inspiration (intelligence), which present the truth from within the soul to the mind. The formed spiritual thoughts (Reality) can replace the unformed thoughts (illusions) of the intellect. The formed Spiritual ideals can, therefore, be separated from the unformed ideals until the firm unwavering understanding in the power of the mind has transformed them to spiritual ideals. Without this separation the consciousness will become confused.

Gen. 1:8 "And God called the firmament Heaven:"

God is a general term for the Divine Mind.
Firmament, metaphysically, means understanding of mind power, a firm, unwavering place in consciousness.
Heaven is an ideal state of consciousness in which the idea is in complete harmony with the Divine Mind.

Metaphysically, this verse might read: **"And Divine Mind called the firm unwavering place an ideal state of consciousness."**

Understanding is of the mental and the material. Spiritual knowing is the foundation whereby human concepts distinguish between Truth and error. In order for this understanding to be accomplished there must be a firm and unwavering place in consciousness that is free of the constantly changing illusions and thoughts of the lower mind. The firm unwavering place is called an ideal state of consciousness, because this is where the Truth can be found, and the, "Truth shall set you free."

Figure 2 illustrates the Second Understanding - Let There Be A Firmament.

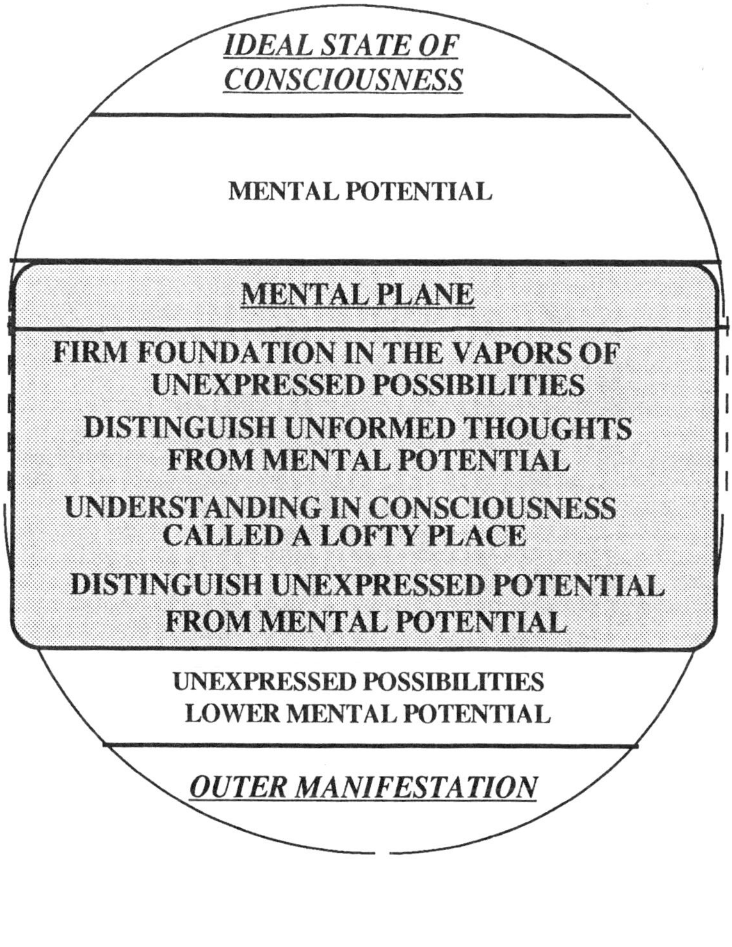

FIGURE 2 - SECOND UNDERSTANDING - GENESIS 1:6-8

SUMMARY OF THE SECOND UNDERSTANDING

The second day of creation, is the placing of a firm foundation of understanding in consciousness. It is strong and unwavering to distinguish between the unformed thought activity of the lower mind and the mental potential of the upper mind. Truth separates out mental and physical thoughts, or illusions, that exist in the lower mind as physical forms. The unformed, or unexpressed, possibilities of thought reside in the subconscious mind, while the formed mental potential of all things resides in the conscious mental mind. Illusions, being affected by weak and negtive thoughts, are only reflections of the Spiritual Truths, and are not based on intelligence. The physical world, therefore, is the direct reflection of our thought process, and mirrors the interpretation of its mental perceptions. Without superior knowledge, or intition, it would be impossible to understand and grow to spiritual intelligence. It is Truth that transforms the unformed illusions to Spiritual Truth. The constantly changing and unexpressed possibilities of the lower mind are to grow and express the mental potential of the ideal state of consciousness. This firm place in consciousness is called understanding the power of the mind, and understanding is the first step to spiritual knowing. To me this is the true meaning behind the Bible statement, "The truth shall set you free."

CHAPTER 3:

LET THE EARTH BRING FORTH ACTIVITY

So far we have been told that the ideal state of consciousness is called heaven, and the outer manifestation is called earth. The outer manifestation has two components, a mental potential and a realm of forms. Truth and intelligence are of the ideal state of consciousness, while the mental potential and the realms of form reflect distortions of theTruth until transformed to the true, formed, spiritual ideals. It follows, then, that it is important what thoughts be allowed to reside in our individual minds. Please note that the individual mind is not separated from the Divine Mind and is, in fact, an integral part of the Divine Mind. The individual mind first expresses unformed thoughts. Through evolution and involution, the individual mind learns to distinguish the unformed illusions from the spiritual Truth.

THIRD DAY - GENESIS 1:9-13

Gen. 1:9 "And God said, let the waters under the heaven be gathered together unto one place, and let the dry land appear; and it was so."

God is a general term for the Divine Mind.
Water, metaphysically in this context, represents mental potential.

Heaven is an ideal state of consciousness in which the ideas are in complete harmony with the Divine Mind.
Gathered in Hebrew is *qavah* (kaw-vaw') which means to bind together.
Dry in Hebrew is *yabbashah* (yab-baw-shaw') which means dry ground, or land. Metaphysically, **land** represents a state of consciousness that will unfold into awareness at different levels of consciousness.

Metaphysically, this verse might read: **"And Divine Mind said, let the mental potential under the ideal state of consciousness be bound together in one place, and let the consciousness at different levels of awareness appear; and it was so."**

The pure ideals and thoughts of the Divine Mind are separated from the unformed thoughts of the lower mind until they have been transformed to understanding by the power of the mind, which is of the upper mind. The consciousness, unfolding at different levels of awareness, is the true meaning of Jacob's Ladder. There must be a firm understanding of each existing level, or rung, before the next level of understanding can be accomplished.

Gen. 1:10 "And God called the dry land Earth; and the gathering of the waters called the Seas; And God saw that it was good."

God is a general term for the Divine Mind.
Dry land represents a state of consciousness that will unfold into awareness at different levels of consciousness.
Earth is where the ideal thought is to be manifested, and is the lower condition, or outer manifestation of the Divine Mind.
Gathering in Hebrew is *miqveh* (mik-veh) which means something waited for (i.e. confidence), a collection, abiding, or gathering together.

Water, metaphysically in this context, represents mental potential.
Sea in Hebrew is *yam* (yawm) which means breaking into a noisy surf, large body of water, or artificial basin. Metaphysically, sea represents the universal mind of unexpressed and unformed thoughts that contains all potential. Sometimes we think of sea as a state of unrest.

Metaphysically, this verse might read: **"And Divine Mind called the state of consciousness that will unfold into awareness the lower mind, and the collection of the mental potential was called the Universal Mind; and Divine Mind saw that it was good."**

The Universal Mind is the great basin of unexpressed and unformed thoughts and ideas that contain all potential. Because the thoughts are unformed, this state of consciousness unfolds at different levels of awareness until the spiritual ideals have transformed the mental potential there. Thus, this state of consciousness is constantly in a state of unrest that must be centralized and coordinated so that preparations can be made for physical matter (dry land) to appear. God considered this state of consciousness to be good. Only Man believes that ideas, or thoughts, might be otherwise. Even the lowest of low thoughts in the lower mind can be transformed to spiritual thoughts by the power of Spirit.

Gen. 1:11 "And God said, Let the earth bring forth grass, the herb yielding seed, and the fruit tree yielding fruit after its kind, whose seed is in itself, upon the earth; and it was so."

God is a general term for the Divine Mind.
Earth is the lower mind, or the outer manifestation of the ideal thought.

Grass in Hebrew is *deshe* (deh'-sheh) which means a sprout, green, or tender herb, and is the symbol of the condition of awakening of the Divine life in the lower nature of the soul.

Herbs in Hebrew is *eseb* (eh'-seb) which means to glisten, grass, tender shoot, or herb. Herb is symbolic of the natural laws of growth and increase in the development of desires, affection, and faculties of the soul. Herbs are plants and were gathered for flavor, aroma, or medical value (2 Kings 4:39). Used at the Passover, herbs were symbols of suffering (Exodus 12:8 and Numbers 9:11). Herbs, however, could provide a modest meal.

Seeds in Hebrew is *zera* (zeh'-rah) which means fruit, plants, sowing time, or prosperity; and symbolizes the manifesting God as the source of all things. Seeds are the productive components of a plant. Since thoughts are the productive component of the mind, I believe that seeds represent ideas or thoughts that spring from a parent thought.

Fruit tree is the symbol of the law linking life and form, and the potencies within, which are ready to unfold. Thus, fruit tree represents the soul that contains all that it needs within it to enable it to unfold and expand its own nature.

Fruit in Hebrew is *periy* (per'ee) which means bring forth, increase, or cause to be, and is the symbol of action, either good or bad. It is the Effect of the Law of Causation in the soul's progress. Fruit is the spiritual consciousness direct from the source (Fountainhead of God).

Metaphysically, this verse might read: "**And Divine Mind said, Let the lower mind bring forth the condition of Divine life, the natural law of growth yielding the Divine Mind as the source of all things, and the law of**

life and form yielding action after its kind, whose prosperity is in itself, and on the lower mind; and it was so."

This verse is indicating that the physical, or natural law of growth is being set in operation. In other words, there is an awakening of the divine life in the lower mind which brings forth desires and affection; which gives rise to higher states of awareness. These aspirations are to bear fruit on a higher plane of consciousness. The Divine Mind directs from the very beginning what the Divine life shall proceed to manifest. The phrase "whose seed is in itself" is indicating that the ideas, or thoughts, of the Divine Mind are always in the lower mind, or outer manifestation.

Within the human soul is the eternal divine essence, the being of God himself. Every soul is like a seedling in which is wrapped a mysterious potency of life which may take long to unfold, but cannot be destroyed. As a giant oak is hidden away in every acorn, so is the life of God latent within the spirit of man waiting for unfoldment. *Man is to evolve, or unfold, through the involution of Spirit.*

Gen. 1:12 "And the earth brought forth grass, and the herb yielding seed after it kind, and the tree yielding fruit, whose seed was in itself, after its kind: and God saw that it was good."

Earth is the lower mind, or the outer manifestation of the ideal thought.

Grass is the symbol of the condition of awakening of the Divine life in the lower nature of the soul.

Herbs is symbolic of the natural law of growth, and increases the development of desire and affection of the soul.

Seeds symbolize the manifesting of God as the source of all things.

Tree in Hebrew is *ets* (ates) which means firmness; and is the symbol of man as a replica of the Divine Being in whose image man is made. As God is a Tree of Life, so

is man. Metaphysically, tree represents the thinking that is rooted in the earth, but reaches toward the heaven, or expressed thoughts of unity. It symbolizes the connection between the lower and upper minds.
Fruit is the symbol of action and is the Effect of the Law of Causation in the soul's progress. Fruit is the spiritual consciousness direct from the source (Fountainhead of God).

This verse is similar to the above and, metaphysically, might read: "**And the lower mind brought forth the awakening of the Divine Life, and the law of natural growth yielding God as the source of all things after its kind, and the connection of the Divine Being yielding spiritual consciousness, whose manifestations were within itself, after its kind; and Divine Mind saw that it was good.**"

Note the similarity of the last two verses. The difference is the word "tree" as opposed to "fruit tree". "Tree" represents the Tree of life, while the "fruit tree" represents the law linking life and form, and the potencies within, which are ready to unfold. Thus, what was manifested in this verse is **Life** and not the potential within (thought), that is ready to unfold. "The kingdom of God is like unto a grain of mustard seed, which a man took and cast into his own garden; and it grew and became a tree, and the birds of the heaven lodged in the branches thereof" (Matthew 13:31). The "Tree" is the best analogy that could be given for the "Kingdom" as above and so is it below. For, as a diagram of the evolution of the Divine Life, the growth from the seed to the sprout and roots, a trunk grows, branches sprout, leaves are generated, and then flowers and fruit are produced all mirroring the entire cosmic process.

Figure 3 illustrates the Third Understanding - Let The Earth Bring Fourth Activity (Genesis1:9 to 1:12).

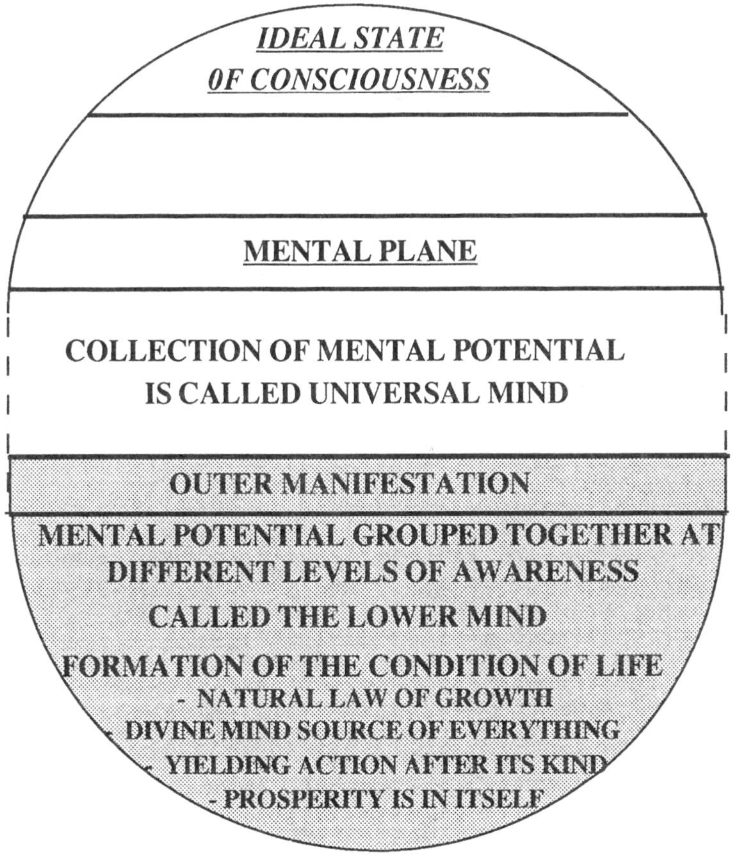

FIGURE 3 - THIRD UNDERSTANDING - GENESIS 1:9-12

SUMMARY OF THE THIRD UNDERSTANDING

The mental potential, or Universal Mind, is an aspect of the outer manifestation that is below the ideal state of consciousness, and binds together all unformed and unexpressed thoughts into a consciousness that will unfold at different degrees of awareness. Thus, the outer manifestation is in a constant state of change (as indicated by the word sea), as opposed to the firm unwavering place of understanding in the ideal state of consciousness. These unformed thoughts need to come under the dominion of the formative power of the upper mind if these thoughts are to become spiritual.

The collection of the mental potential is called Universal Mind. *Webster's Dictionary* defines Universal as "the whole of something." Thus, the whole individual mind is under the **Natural Law of Growth** and brings forth conditions of Divine Life, and yields the Divine Mind as the source of all things. *The purpose of evolution is to know that the Divine Mind is all there is, and to become perfect as the Divine Mind is perfect.* Finally, these unformed and unexpressed thoughts are free to bring forth thoughts after their own kind. That is, spiritual consciousness yields spiritual thoughts and material consciousness yields thoughts after its kind.

CHAPTER 4:

LET THERE BE INTELLIGENCE

The Universal Mind is the great basin that contains all potential of ideas and thoughts. Because these thoughts are unexpressed and unformed, they are constantly in a state of change, until they are expressed and formed by Spirit. Spirit comes to the lower mind in the form of a consciousness that unfolds at different levels of awareness. It is the Natural Law of Growth that awakens the consciousness to the Divine Life in the lower mind, which brings forth desire and affection that will bear fruit on a higher plane of consciousness.

FOURTH DAY - GENESIS 1:14-19

Gen. 1:14 "And God said, Let there be lights in the firmament of the heavens to divide the day from the night; and let them be signs, and for seasons, and for days, and years."

God is a general term for the Divine Mind.

Light, metaphysically, is a symbol for intelligence.

Firmament in Hebrew means a firm foundation and, metaphysically, means understanding in mind power; a firm unwavering place in consciousness.

Heaven in Hebrew is a lofty or high place and, metaphysically, is an ideal state of consciousness in which the ideas are in complete harmony with the Divine Mind.

Divide in Hebrew means to separate, distinguish, or be divided.

Day in Hebrew means to be hot, and is symbolic of spiritual activity. Metaphysically, "day" represents under-

standing.
Night in Hebrew represents adversity or periodic ignorance. Metaphysically, it represents ignorance.
Sign in Hebrew is *owth* (oth) which means a signal, flag, beacon, omen, or evidence and signifies an event, act, or other manifestation that indicates God's presence or intention. Thus, signs are outward forms, subjectively selected, to indicate inward conditions or processes of the Divine life in the soul of the universe. Signs may be miraculous and spectacular, as in the those performed by Moses before the people of Israel to demonstrate that God had sent him to them (Exodus 4:1-9,17, 30). On the other hand, a natural phenomenon, such as a rainbow or a sunset, may be called a sign (Genesis 9:13). Therefore, a sign is a symbol that represents an abstract concept and interprets it in concrete terms.
Season in Hebrew is *yowm* (yome) and represents cycles of manifestation (sunset to sunset, days, etc.). The word "season", from the Latin word *satio,* means sowing time and is a period of the year marked off by prevalent climatic conditions. Years and day are symbols for time.
Years in Hebrew is *shaneh* (shaw-neh') which means an evolution of time, change, repeat, or return.

Metaphysically, this verse might read: **"And Divine Mind said, Let there be intelligence in the understanding of a firm foundation in the ideal state of consciousness to distinguish understanding from ignorance; and let there be beacons and cycles of manifestations, for understanding the evolution of time."**

This indicates that intelligence will separate understanding from ignorance. Man was given beacons as an outward manifestation of the inner intentions. These beacons, or signs, are presented to the lower mind as cycles of periodic change so that man can understand the evolution of time. In the physical world, these signs are the sun, moon and stars which give us the periodic changes of day, night, month, year, and millennium.

Please note that there are no specific words for time, millennium, season, year, month or day in the Hebrew language. Therefore, these words are used to depict cycles or changes and were inserted to illustrate the intent, as envisioned by the writer of Genesis, or the scholar that translated the Bible from Hebrew to English.

Gen.1:15 "And let them be for lights in the firmament of the heaven to give light upon the earth; and it was so."

Them in this case is indicating the signs of the previous verse.

Light, metaphysically, is the symbol of intelligence.

Firmament in Hebrew means a firm foundation and, metaphysically, means faith, or understanding in mind power; a firm unwavering place in consciousness.

Heaven in Hebrew is a lofty or high place and, metaphysically, is an ideal state of consciousness in complete harmony with the Divine Mind.

Earth in Hebrew means firm and, metaphysically, is the lower mind, or the outer manifestation of the ideal thought.

Metaphysically, this verse might read: **"And let signs be for intelligences in the firm understanding of the ideal state of consciousness to give intelligence to the outer manifestation; and it was so."**

Intelligence is of God, but is extended to the lower mind, or outer manifestation, for its use in spiritual understanding and for the fulfillment of God's ideal. It is easy to understand from this verse how astrology and psychic thoughts can be interpreted to be spiritual. These forms of thought are not of themselves spiritual, but can help man to understand spiritual principles. This is because the origin of the light, or understanding, comes from spiritual concepts (similar to the sun's light being the origin of the moon's reflected light. Of its self, the moon has no light.)

There does seem to be evidence that our solar system and its cyclic movements do correlate to man and his spiritual unfolding. For example, approximately every two thousand years the north pole points to a different constellation, or astological sign, each of which appears to represent an aspect of man's spiritual progress. For example, we are just completing the Piscean Age. Pisces is a water sign, and the constellation resembles a fish. Jesus, the spiritual leader of this age, was referred to by many as the **Ichthus**, meaning, 'the fish'. The fish was the sign used by the early Christians. In fact, Jesus selected his disciples from fishermen, traditional Catholics ate only fish every Friday, and the Pope's Crown resembles the mouth of a fish. This same correlation seems to hold true for other ages as well. Interested readers are encouraged to read *A Spiritual Approach to Astrology*, by Myrana Lofthus, for greater details.

Gen. 1:16 "And God made two great lights; the greater to rule the day, and the lesser to rule the night, He made the stars also."

God is a general term for the Divine Mind.

Made in Hebrew is *asah* (aw-saw') which means to do, accomplish, bestow, bring forth, or commit.

Great in Hebrew is *gadol* (gaw-dole') which means mighty, noble, great, or proud thing, and is a symbol of the Absolute, God, or source of all.

Light, metaphysically, is the symbol of intelligence.

Rule in Hebrew is *memshaliah* (mem-shaw-law') which means dominion, power, or a ruler, and is a symbol of Spirit descending through the mental activities that control the lower emotions and desires.

Day in Hebrew means symbolic spiritual activity, and metaphysically means understanding.

Night in Hebrew means adversity, or periodic ignorance, and, metaphysically, means ignorance.

Star in Hebrew is *kowkab* (ko-kawb) which means shining, blazing, or a star and, metaphysically, is the rise of knowledge, or great inner intelligence that guides us to the new born Christ. Therefore, stars represent revelation of Truths that are yet remote. Stars are sometimes likened to psychic thoughts.

Metahphysically, this verse might read: **"And the Divine Mind brought forth two mighty intelligences; the greater to guide understanding and the lesser to guide ignorance, He brought forth the rise of inner knowledge also."**

The Hebrews believed the sun, moon and stars moved across or were fixed in the firmament. Metaphysically, the *sun is spiritual intelligence*, and the *moon is the personal intelligence,* which is supplied light from the spiritual intelligence (similar to the moon receiving its light from the sun), and the *stars are revelations of Truths that as yet are remote*. So, the influx of spiritual energy has regular periods of flooding the consciousness similar to the increased energy that we receive from the sun at the height of the growing season or the moon when it is full.

Gen. 1:17 "And God set them in the firmament of the heavens to give light upon the earth."

God is a general term for the Divine Mind.

Them in this case is the great lights in the previous verse (sun, moon and stars).

Firmament in Hebrew means a firm foundation and, metaphysically, means understanding in mind power; a firm unwavering place in consciousness.

Heaven in Hebrew means a high or lofty place and, metaphysically, is an ideal state of consciousness in which the ideas are in complete harmony with the Divine Mind.

Light in Hebrew means luminary and, metaphysically, is the symbol of intelligence.

Earth is the lower mind, or the outer manifestation of the ideal thought.

Metaphysically, this verse might read: **"And Divine Mind set them in the firm foundation of the ideal state of consciounsness to give intelligence to the outer manifestation."**

The firmament is a symbol of a higher mental plane, that is a firm unwavering foundation, where spiritual intelligence is projected to the lower mind, or outer manifestation. The thoughts in the outer manifestation are always in the process of changing (cyclic changes such as seasons, days and years). Thus, this verse implies that the thoughts of the outer manifestation, are transformed from changing forms of ignorance to stable spiritual intelligence, an inner knowledge as yet remote to the lower mind. Man is to use these intelligences on his evolutionary path from the desires and passions of the physical world to the ideal state of consciousness that is in complete harmony with the Divine Mind.

Gen. 1:18 "And to rule over the day and over the night, and to divide the light from the darkness; and God saw that it was good."

> **Rule** in Hebrew means dominion, power, or a ruler, and is a symbol of Spirit disciplining through the mental activities that control the lower emotions and desires.
> **Day,** metaphysically, means understanding.
> **Night,** metaphysically, means ignorance.
> **Divide** in Hebrew means to separate, distinguish, or be divided.
> **Light,** metaphysically, is the symbol of intelligence.
> **Darkness** is the failure to understand.
> **God** is a general term for the Divine Mind

Metaphysically, this verse might read: **"And intelligence is to rule over understanding and over ignorance, and to distinguish intelligence from the failure to understand; and Divine Mind saw that it was good."**

The lower mind receives intelligence, and gains understanding, which is obtained from spiritual intelligence (sun). It overcomes ignorance through personal intelligence (moon); and distinguishes the Christ intelligence (stars) from the failure to understand that also comes from the personal intelligence.

Figure 4 illustrates the Fourth Understanding - Let There Be Intelligence In The Firm Foundation.

SUMMARY OF THE FOURTH UNDERSTANDING

Intelligence is the firm understanding in the ideal state of consciousness (heaven). Intelligence distinguishes between understanding and ignorance. Intelligence manifests as beacons and cycles of manifestation, and unfolds at different evolving levels of understanding. Thus, the Divine Mind provides beacons as outward manifestations of inner intentions. These beacons, or signs, are presented as cycles of periodic change in order for man to understand the evolution of time, because there are no time or spatial concepts in the spiritual realm.

It is important to be very clear on this concept and not confuse what is being said with concepts of astrology or psychic thoughts. Although astrology and psychic thoughts can be used to describe the spiritual nature of things, they are simply reflected truths or illusions. In our example, the moon of itself does not generate light; the light that is seen is only the reflection of the sun. In a similar manner, when man seeks outside of himself for his purpose he can more easily understand the principles of astrology, than those of Spirit, and misperceives them as the source, rather than the constantly changing information that it is.

The Divine Mind provides three types of light, or intelligences, for man to use. The first and foremost is Spiritual Intelligence symbolized by the sun; it is the ruler over understanding. Understanding is of the intellect and is transformed by Truth to

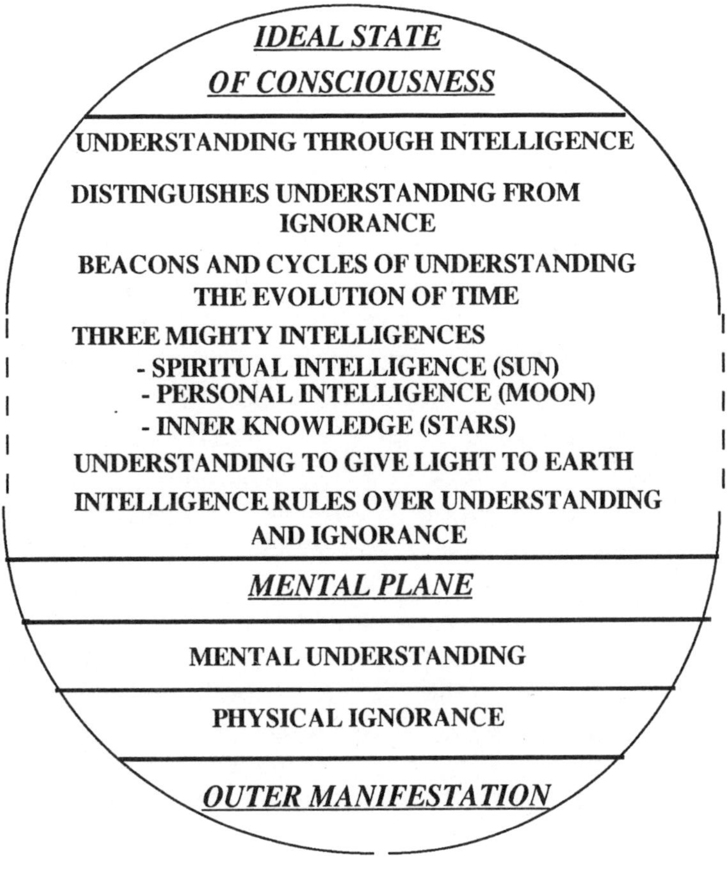

FIGURE 4 - FOURTH UNDERSTANDING - GENESIS 1:14-19

yield Spiritual Intelligence. The second source is Personal Intelligence symbolized by the moon. It is the unawakened consciousness, or the failure to understand. Thus, the Personal Intelligence is the ruler of ignorance. The third source is the Spiritual revelation that is as yet remote to the consciousness, symbolized by the Stars. This will unfold at different levels of awareness, with the highest level of awareness being the Christ Consciousness as we will discover in Part IV of this book. This unfoldment is under the direction of the Holy Spirit. *Thus, the fourth understanding is addressing the Trinity: The Father, Son and the Holy Spirit.*

CHAPTER 5 :

LET THE MENTAL POTENTIAL BRING FORTH

In the last chapter we saw where man is given three intelligences to guide him on the evolutionary path. These lights, or intelligences, are like beacons that come in cycles of periodic change in order for man to understand the evolution of time. They are used by man to count days, months, years, and millenniums. Days are numbered as the sun rises in the east and sets in the west. Months are counted from one full moon to the next, and the growing season defines four different cycles (fall, winter, spring and summer) that equates to a year. The North Pole points to a new constellation, or Zodiac sign, approximately every 2,000 years. Thus either the North or South Poles point to a new constellation every 1,000 years, or millennium. Each millennium presents a different Spiritual force that affects our lives in various ways. These are all visible-physical signs of the concept of the Natural Law of Growth.

FIFTH DAY - GENESIS 1:20-23

Gen. 1:20 "And God said, Let the waters bring forth abundantly the moving creatures that hath life, and fowl that may fly above the earth in the open firmament of heaven."

God is a general term for the Divine Mind.

Water, metaphysically in this context, represents mental potential.
Moving creatures, metaphysically, represent active thoughts of various kinds.
Life in Hebrew is *chay* (khah'-ee) which means alive, flesh, or be whole.
Fowl, metaphysically, represents conscious thoughts in the mind that are free to express.
Earth is the lower mind, or the outer manifestation of the ideal thought.
Firmament, metaphysically, means understanding of mind power; a firm unwavering place in consciousness.
Heaven, metaphysically, is an ideal state of consciousness in which the ideas are in complete harmony with the Divine Mind.

Metaphysically, this verse might read: **"And Divine Mind said, Let the mental potential bring forth abundantly various active thoughts that have life, and thoughts that are free that they may rise above the outer manifestation in the open full understanding of the ideal state of consciousness."**

The mental potential of the lower mind brings forth various thoughts that have spiritual activity that will take the unformed material thoughts of the lower mind, and transform them to the formed spiritual thoughts of the higher mind. The Bible uses the word "seed" to describe this process and, I believe, that the seed is the mental potential and contains all that is necessary to bring forth spiritual activity.

This verse implies that the consciousness (soul) is free to choose which power it wishes to follow. It would appear that God wants us to choose the Spiritual realm of our own free will. Inherent in this verse is the concept of individual freedom to evolve beyond the limitations of the outer manifestation.

Gen. 1:21 "And God created great sea monsters, and every living creature that moveth, which the waters

brought forth abundantly, after their kind; and God saw that it was good."

Created in Hebrew is *bara* (baw-raw') which means root, select, choose, or create, and is the symbol of the potential and unmanifested becoming the actual and manifested.

Great in Hebrew means mighty, noble, great, or proud thing, and is a symbol of the Absolute, or source of all.

God is a general term for the Divine Mind.

Sea in Hebrew is *yam* (yawm) which means to roar, large body of water, or an artificial basin; and, metaphysically, represents the unformed state of mind.

Monsters in Hebrew is *tanniym* (tan-neem') which means marine or land monster, sea serpent, dragon, or serpent; and, metaphysically, represents undirected and undisciplined emotions needing the guidance of the mind to direct them. Webster's Dictionary indicates monsters are frightening, bizarre shaped and arouse horror.

Creatures in Hebrew is *sherets* (sheh'-rets) which means swarm, active mass, or move; and, metaphysically, represents active thoughts of various kinds.

Water, metaphysically in this context, represents weak and negative thoughts of the mental potential.

Metaphysically, this verse might read: **"And Divine Mind selected mighty unformed, undirected and undisciplined thoughts and emotions, and swarms of active thoughts that live, which the mental potential brought forth abundantly after their kind; and Divine Mind saw that it was good."**

This verse is indicating that the consciousness of the outer manifestation, or lower mind, has the potential to create ideas and thoughts. The mind of desires (sea monsters) then judges them to be real. They are unformed, undirected and undisciplined and will create more of the same, unless they are transformed by Spirit into formed, spiritual thoughts. Thus, the thoughts in the lower mind will be in a state of constant change until all the thoughts in the consciousness have been lifted up to the higher level. This is the evolution of man's thought process, and the Divine Mind says that it is good. This indicates that man is to *reap the good directly proportional to his thoughts.*

Gen. 1:22 "And God blessed them saying, 'Be fruitful, and multiply, and fill the waters of the sea, and let fowl multiply in the earth.'"

God is a general term for the Divine Mind.

Blessed in Hebrew is *barak* (baw-rak') which means kneel, bless, or adoration; and, metaphysically, represents Divine Will operating through the human consciousness.

Them in this case is the unformed, undirected, and undisciplined thoughts.

Fruitful in Hebrew means bring forth, cause, or grow; and, metaphysically, means to be full of spiritual consciousness.

Multiply in Hebrew means abundance, enlarge, be full of, or increase; and, metaphysically, means for the soul to increase its experiences, faculties, capacities and higher qualities.

Fill in Hebrew is *mala* (maw-law') which means accomplish, confirm, be at an end, or have fully. According to Webster's Dictionary, "fill" means to occupy.

Water, metaphysically in this context, represents weak and negative thoughts of the mental potential.

Sea, metaphysically, represents the unformed state of mind.

Fowl, metaphysically, represents conscious thoughts in the mind that are free to express.

Earth is the lower mind or the outer manifestation of the ideal thought.

Metaphysically, this verse might read: **"And Divine Mind blessed them saying, 'Be full of spiritual conscious-**

ness, and grow, and bring to an end the weak and negative thoughts in the unformed state of consciousness, and let free conscious thoughts increase in the outer manifestation.'"

The traditional religious interpretation of this verse has led man to believe that the Divine Mind intended him to be fruitful and multiply, by sexual means. However, when decoded, this verse indicates that the spiritual thoughts are to bring to an end the weak, negative, and unformed thoughts of the lower mind. These thoughts can only be freed by exposing the weak and negative thoughts to the intelligence that is extended from the upper mind. Thus, man grows in spiritual consciousness by discerning the spiritual from the illusion of the physical world. Man progresses from the lower, unformed sense thoughts to the formed and directed thoughts that Jesus the Christ demonstrated.

This indicates that it was always the plan that the unformed and unexpressed thoughts of the lower mind would evolve to spiritual ideas. I believe that this was the original purpose for human experience, but man became beguiled by the physical world and was led by the personal consciousness at the expense of his spiritual consciousness. *We, therefore, evolve to Spiritual consciousness by being aware of our thoughts, experiencing the result of our actions, and choosing thoughts consistent with Spiritual ideals.*

Figure 5 illustrates the Fifth Understanding - Let The Mental Potential Bring Forth Activity.

SUMMARY OF THE FIFTH UNDERSTANDING

The mental potential is to bring forth various thoughts that have life, and each type of thought will create thoughts after its kind. That is, material thoughts will manifest material thoughts and objects, and spiritual thoughts will create the spiritual good in our lives. The various mental thoughts are free to rise above the limitations of the outer manifestation to the ideal state of con-

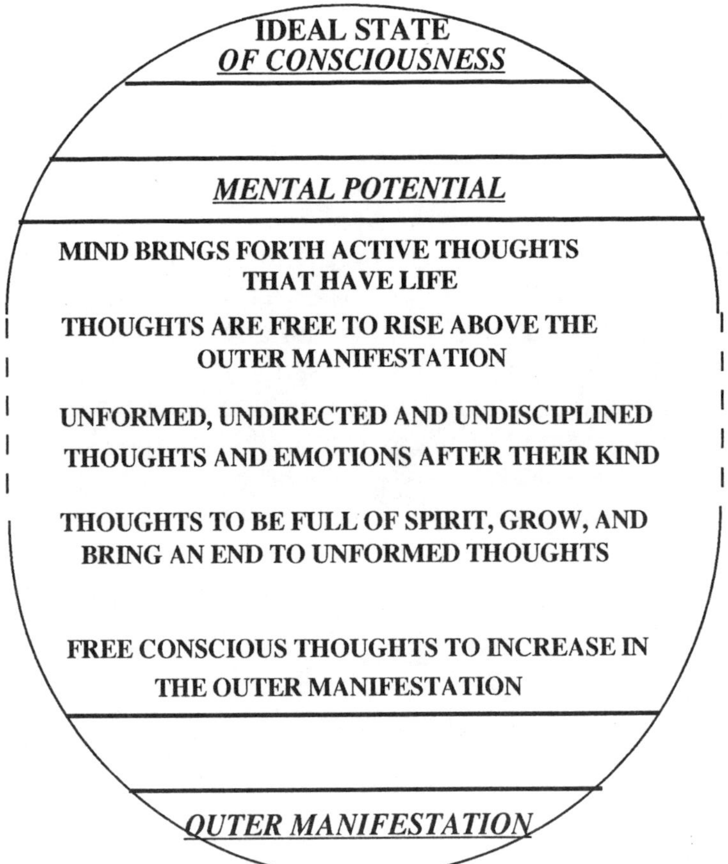

FIGURE 5 - FIFTH UNDERSTANDING - GENESIS 1:20-23

sciousness (heaven), which *implies choice.* The individual mind must make this choice between Spirit and the ignorant illusions of the physical world. This so called duality has created a thought system where there is an opposite to God, or the Divine Mind. In reality, this is *impossible*, because God is all there *is*. All thoughts were created to *assist man* in becoming Spiritual like the Divine Mind. The concept of a devil is, therefore, a man-generated term. It is interesting that the word "devil" does not appear in the Bible until Matthew 4:1, and is, therefore, a New Testament term. The Old Testament uses the term "evil", which means, "morally bad or wrong," according to Webster's Dictionary. In Hebrew "evil" is *ra* (rah) which means bad, adversity, or affliction, and comes from the root word *raa* (raw-ah') which means to spoil. This indicates that when we think weak or negative thoughts, it will spoil the dream of being completely happy. However, the object of life is to learn from these mistakes, and grow away from the weak and negative thoughts. Therefore, thoughts that have been spoiled can be changed to the fresh thoughts of the Holy Spirit, which knows both the physical and spiritual worlds and can help guide our choice. "Ask, and it shall be given you; seek, and ye shall find; knock, and it shall be opened to you;" (Matthew 7:7).

CHAPTER 6:

THE REASONING AND ANALYZING MIND

Thus far, the story of creation has told us that the Divine Mind created two states of consciousness; one the ideal state of consciousness and the other the manifestation of thought in the realm of forms. Within the ideal state of consciousness it is possible to distinguish unexpressed, unformed negative and weak thoughts from the mental potential which is strong and formed in the upper mind. Secondly, the lower mind brings forth conditions of the Divine Life through the Natural Law of Growth. Every thought in the lower mind has life and creates thoughts after its kind, and each type of thought is free to rise above the limitations of the outer manifestation. The only thing left to define is the reasoning and analyzing mind that will use the understandings of the previous five creations.

SIXTH DAY - GENESIS 1:24-31

Gen. 1:24 "And God said, Let the earth bring forth the living creature after his kind, cattle, and creeping thing, and beast of the earth after his kind: and it was so."

God is a general term for the Divine Mind.

Earth is the lower mind, or the outer manifestation of the ideal thought.

Living Creatures in Hebrew is *chay* (khah'ee) which means raw life, living thing, beast, or creature; and, metaphysically, represents subtle, or difficult thoughts to detect, that have life. Creatures are any animate being whose existence is dependent upon God (Geneses 1:20, 24). At this point of the story, the "creatures" are outgoing desires and passion thoughts which feed upon instincts and sensations.

Cattle in Hebrew is *behemowth* (be-hay-mohth') meaning a dumb beast, any large quadruped or animal; and, metaphysically, represents lower emotions that are under the control of higher desires. Cattle symbolize obedience and docility to a higher rule, and were used by the Hebrews for food, sacrificial offerings, and as pack animals. Thus cattle in this connotation is referring to thoughts that are domesticated or tame.

Creeping things is from the Hebrew word *remes* (reh' mes) meaning reptile, any rapidly moving animal, or creeping thing; and, metaphysically, represents cunning, greed, subtlety, mischief, or destructiveness. Such creatures were considered unclean by the Hebrews (Leviticus 22:5). Therefore, creeping things refer to unclean thoughts of the lower instincts of desire and passion.

Beast, metaphysically, represents the unruled passions of sensuous or material thoughts. Beasts are wild and dangerous thoughts.

Metaphysically, this verse might translate to: **"And Divine Mind said, Let the outer manifestation bring forth various thoughts that are difficult to detect that have life after their kind, obedient, and passionate thoughts, and material thoughts of the outer manifestation after their kind; and it was so."**

Please note that the animals mentioned in the original Bible verse move in a prone position with the body close to the ground. This indicates that they are influenced by the physical things of the earth; and are slow and limited, and thus are not free. These creatures represent the emotions of the lower nature which feed on instincts and sensations. The Divine Will directs the lower nature to bring forth that which is first in order; that is, the natural qualities, or animal forces. Man is to stand firm, draw away from, and keep down the lower mind passions. If he is able to do this, the will and the mind ascend into an ideal state of consciousness, and the passions die away. Please note that the foul, unclean thoughts represent the vices of the consciousness, and the clean, obedient thoughts represent joy.

The thoughts and emotions described in this verse are of the Sense Consciousness.

Gen. 1:25 "And God made the beast of the earth after its kind, and the cattle after their kind, and everything that creepeth upon the earth after its kind; and God saw that it was good."

God is a general term for the Divine Mind.

Made in Hebrew is *asah* (aw-saw') and means to accomplish, appoint, bestow, bring forth, or make. In Webster's Dictionary "made" means to produce artificially.

Beast, metaphysically, is sensuous or material thoughts.

Earth is the lower mind, or the outer manifestation of the ideal thought.

Cattle, metaphysically, means obedient, domestic or tame thoughts.

Creepeth in Hebrew is *remes* (reh'-mes) and means reptile or other rapidly moving animal, to glide, or to crawl. Metaphysically, "creepeth" symbolizes the lower instincts of desires and emotions; such as cunning, greed, subtlety, mischief, cruelty, or destructiveness, and represents subtle thoughts that are unclean.

Metaphysically, this verse might read: "**And Divine Mind artificially produced the material thoughts of the outer manifestation after their kind, and obedient domestic thoughts after their kind, and cunning and destructive thoughts that move on the outer manifestation after their kind: and Divine Mind saw that it was good.**"

Note that the word "made" is used as opposed to created. "Made," according to Webster's Dictionary, is past tense, and implies something produced artificially and, thus, not natural. This is the first time that the word *made* has been used in the story of creation, and appears to be a mistake until it is further analyzed. The thoughts that are produced here, are constantly changing, and, thus, cannot be spiritual thoughts. Therefore, the word *made* is used as a flag to denote that something different is happening here, that is, unnaturally produced and not of Spiritual quality. The intelligence of Spirit must transform these thoughts before they can become the firm, unchangeable thoughts of Spirit. Thus, to change requires physical or mental activity to move from one phase, or level, to another. It is up to man to choose to transform these thoughts to higher spiritual values. Thus, the manifestations on the earthly plane are only temporary, while the spiritual thought is eternal.

Why did God make these thoughts? Man was given the ability to choose, and to choose freely, which implies that there must also be an opposite. Without the ability to choose, there would be no action, and thus, no purpose to life. Without choice, there would be no experience, and no opportunity to learn and grow. The only constant in the physical world is *change*. Thus, the Divine Mind artificially produced the physical sensations as an aide to obtaining the ideal state of consciousness, and instructed us to, "Be ye perfect, as your Father in Heaven is perfect."

The thoughts and emotions described in this verse are of the Physical Consciousness.

Gen. 1:26 "And God said, Let us make man in our image, after our likeness; and let them have dominion over the fish of the sea, and over the fowl of the air, and over the cattle, and over all the earth, and every creeping thing that creepeth upon the earth."

God is a general term for the Divine Mind.

Make in Hebrew is *asah* (aw-saw') which means accomplish, appoint, become, bestow, or bring forth.

Man in Hebrew is *adam* (aw-dawm') which means ruddy, to show blood, flesh, a human being, or mankind. As used here, man is a symbol for the conscious or directive mind within each of us. It is that part of the spiritual mind that reasons and analyzes. Metaphysically, man also means spirit.

Image in Hebrew is *tselem* (tseh'-lem) which means to shade, a phantom, illusion, or resemblance. According to Webster's Dictionary, it means imitation or representation.

Likeness in Hebrew is *demuwth* (dem'-ooth) which means resemblance, model, shape, fashion, or manner. According to Webster's Dictionary, likeness means the state, or quality, of being similar.

Fish in Hebrew is *dagah* (daw-gaw') and means to move rapidly, moving by the vibratory action of the tail, fish, or to become numerous. Metaphysically, fish represents ideas of multiplication, or a great possibility of increase. Therefore, fish are ideas drawn out of the deep.

Sea in Hebrew is *yam* (yawm) which means to roar, large body of water, or artificial basin. Metaphysically, sea represents the unformed thoughts and ideas that contain all potential.

Fowl in Hebrew is *owph* (ofe) which means a bird, covered with feathers, or flying. Metaphysically, fowl represent conscious thoughts in the mind that are free to express.

Air in Hebrew is *shameh* (shaw-meh') which means to be lofty, sky, the higher ether where celestial bodies revolve, or heavens and, metaphysically, is a symbol of the mental plane, or mind.

Cattle, metaphysically, are obedient, domestic, or tame thoughts that are based on sensation or animal strength.

Earth is the lower mind, or the outer manifestation of the ideal thought.

Creeping things is from the Hebrew word *remes* (reh'-mes) meaning reptile, any rapidly moving animal, or creeping things; and, metaphysically, represents cunning, greed, subtlety, mischief, or destructiveness. Such creatures were considered unclean by the Hebrews (Leviticus 22:5). Therefore, creeping thing is referring to unclean thoughts of the lower instincts of desire and passion.

Creepeth in Hebrew is *remes* (reh'-mes) and means reptile or other rapidly moving animal, to glide, or to crawl. Metaphysically, "creepeth" symbolizes the lower instincts of desires and emotions; such as cunning, greed, subtlety, mischief, cruelty, or destructiveness and represents subtle thoughts that are unclean.

Metaphysically, this verse might read: **"And Divine Mind said, Let us appoint a spiritual mind that reasons and analyzes in our imitation and resemblance; and let it have dominion over the numerous ideas of the unformed thoughts, and over the conscious thoughts of the mental mind, and over the sensational thoughts, and over all the outer manifestation, and the cunning and destructive thoughts that glide on the outer manifestation."**

"Let us" is plural, yet most religions teach that God is one, or singular. So how can this verse be correct? The Hebrews used the word *Elohim* as the name of God. Other names of God, such as YHWH, Yahweh, Jehovah, Divine Mind, and Adonai are all singular nouns. Elohim is the only one that is plural, which indicates to me that this verse was translated correctly, and I believe that "Let us" is describing the infinite consciousness, or the collective consciousness. The infinite consciousness is the collective images of all consciousness. We recognize our own images of the likeness of God, as ourself. That is, we have similar elements of personality to those of God. *Thinking* (Gen. 2:19-20, & 38), *Feeling* (Gen. 3:6), and *Willing* (Gen. 3:6-7) are just a few of the similar elements of personality. Our image and likeness to God is of the *same Mind*, and has nothing to do with a likeness of our physical bodies. I believe that "Let us make" is a flag to denote that the spirit (man) that is being made is not of the same level and characteristics as the Spirit of the Divine Mind.

The Spiritual mind of man, that reasons and analyzes, is clearly a mind that is not the same as the Divine Mind. The Divine Mind is absolute, and does not need to reason and analyze, because these are intellectual terms. However, the mind of man has various levels of consciousness, and must discern between intellectual analysis and reasoning to obtain the Truth, as opposed to knowing Spiritually. At this stage of involution, Divine Mind projects a likeness of itself to the lower mind, and the lower mind is to have dominion over feelings, ideas, actions, and the entire nature, including the lower instincts of desires and emotions (such as cunning, greed, subtlety, mischief, cruelty, and destructiveness). Therefore, the collective consciousness of verse 26 is plural, and cannot be stated in any way other than in a plural way.

Man is free to choose any idea that his intellectual consciousness can discern and analyze. The word "free" is extremely important, because without free will, man would not be able to choose the ideals of the Creator. However, the choice of any thought other than the Spiritual Thought will manifest thoughts after its own kind. Thus, the intellectual consciousness will manifest thoughts (effects) that are directly related to the cause (idea).

This verse is describing the Individual Consciousness. These thoughts are not spiritual until intelligence and Spirit have transformed them.

Gen. 1:27 "So God created man in his own image, in the image of God created he him, male and female created he them."

God is a general term for the Divine Mind.
Man, as used here, is a symbol of the conscious, or directive mind within each of us. It is that part of the Spiritual Mind that reasons and analyzes.
Image in Hebrew is *tselem* (tseh'-lem) which means to shade, a phantom, illusion, or resemblance. According to Webster's Dictionary, it means imitation or representation.
Male in Hebrew is *zakar* (zaw-kawr') meaning a male sexual form (man or animal); and, metaphysically, is similar to man, which is the thinking part of the mind.
Female in Hebrew is *neqebah* (nek-ay-baw') which means female sexual form, bore, curse, express, or pierce; and, metaphysically, is the receptive or feeling component of the mind.
Created is Hebrew and means to create, select or choose; and, metaphysically, represents becoming the actual and manifest in the scheme of being in which the spiritual and mental precede the astral and physical. It is the fact in thinking out the thought.

Metaphysically, this verse might read: **"So Divine Mind created a spiritual mind that reasons and analyzes in its own imitation, in the imitation of Divine Mind it created them, thinking and feeling it created them."**

Note that the word "created" was used, which indicates that the mind being created is of the Divine Mind, and is eternal. Therefore, this is the spirit of man, which is invisible, that is being created. The two aspects, are being created. The two aspects, male and female, united together, are essential to the making of man as a spiritual being. It is the thinking portion that will evolve to spiritual *Wisdom*, and the feeling component will evolve to *Love,* which will eventually produce the Divine consciousness. And so, the Divine Will caused to be created the Archetypical Man in the image of the Divine fullness as the dual expression of Truth-Wisdom.

The male and female components must be united, because no perfect image of the Divine Mind can be completely expressed separately. Thus, this verse is describing the Mental Consciousness.

Gen. 1:28 "And God blessed them, and God said unto them, Be fruitful, and multiply and replenish the earth, and subdue it; and have dominion over the fish of the sea, and over the fowl of the air, and every living thing that moveth upon the earth."

God is a general term for the Divine Mind.

Blessed in Hebrew is *barak* (baw-rak') which means an act of adoration, praise, or salute; and, metaphysically, represents the Divine Will operating through the human consciousness. According to Webster's Dictionary, "blessed" means holy, sacred, or consecrated.

Fruitful in Hebrew is *parah* (paw-raw') which means reward, to bear, to bring forth, or cause to be; and, metaphysically, is a symbol of results of action that bring forth good through spiritual cultivation. That is, the spiritual consciousness comes directly from the source (Fountainhead of God). Therefore, fruitful means to be full of spiritual consciousness.

Multiply in Hebrew means abundance, enlarge, be full of, increase; and, metaphysically, means for the soul to increase in experiences, faculties, capacities and higher qualities. According to Webster's Dictionary, it means to cause to increase.

Replenish in Hebrew is *mala* (maw-la') which means to fill, accomplish, or be at an end.

Earth is the lower mind, or the outer manifestation of the ideal thought.
Fish, metaphysically, represents ideas of multiplication in which there is great possibility of increase. Therefore, fish are ideas drawn out of the deep.
Sea, metaphysically, represents the unformed thoughts and ideas that contain all potential.
Fowl, metaphysically, represent conscious thoughts in the mind that are free to express.
Living thing in Hebrew is *chay* (khah'ee) which means alive, or life; and, metaphysically, represents spiritual activities on the higher plane that correspond to manifestations at the lower thought level.

Metaphysically, this verse might read: "**And Divine Mind blessed them, and Divine Mind said to them, Be full of spiritual consciousness and increase, and fill the outer manifestation, and subdue it, and have dominion over the ideas of multiplication and over the unformed thoughts that live upon the outer manifestation.**"

This verse is indicating that man is blessed with a spiritual nature (Holy Spirit), and is instructed to multiply and fill the unexpressed potential of the lower mind, and let free thoughts multiply and extend to the lower mind. He is further instructed to subdue the animal passions and thoughts of the lower mind and have dominion over them. To have dominion means to control the passion and desire of the subconscious mind by bringing them to the conscious mind (Mental Consciousness) where they are free to be converted to spiritual thoughts, and thus, rise above the limitations and restrictions of the outer manifestation.

The Mental Consciousness, of the previous level, is based on an intellect that reasons and analyzes everything that it senses. In so doing, it interprets what it senses, and the results may not be of a spiritual nature. Therefore, Spirit must enter into the consciousness before it can become intelligence. It is the intuition, or the female, the feeling component of consciousness, that converts the intellect to intelligence. In other words, the thinking (male) and the feeling (female) components are united, and the result is intelligence. Please note that at this level the thinking component of consciousness has not yet obtained Wisdom and the feeling component has not yet reached the level of Love; so the ideal state of consciousness has yet to be created.

Thus, this verse is describing the Intellectual Consciousness.

Gen. 1:29 "And God said, Behold, I have given you every herb bearing seed, which is upon the face of all the earth, and every tree, in the which is the fruit of a tree yielding seed; to you it shall be for meat."

God is a general term for the Divine Mind.

Herb in Hebrew is *eseb* (eh'-seb) which means to be green, grass, or any tender shoot; and, metaphysically, represents the natural laws of growth.

Seed in Hebrew is *zera* (zeh'-rah) which means to sow, plant, bear, conceive, posterity, or sowing time; and is the productive component of a plant. Metaphysically, seed symbolizes the manifesting of God, and is the source of all things.

Face in Hebrew is *paneh* (paw-neh') which means turn, to face, appear or look; and, metaphysically, symbolizes the mental aspect of being, where knowledge is acquired either through the senses or intuition. It is the expression of truth from within.

Earth, metaphysically, is where the ideal thought is to be manifested, and is the outer manifestation of the Divine Mind.

Tree in Hebrew is *ets* (ates) which means firmness, stock, or timber; and, metaphysically, represents the thinking that is rooted in the earth but reaches toward the heaven. Metaphysically, trees are expressed thoughts of unity that connect the earth and heaven.

Fruit is the spiritual consciousness direct from the source.

Meat in Hebrew is *oklah* (oklaw') which means food, consume, devour, or eat; and, metaphysically, is a symbol of knowledge and higher emotions.

Metaphysically, this verse might read: "**And Divine Mind said, Behold, I have given you every natural law of growth bearing the source of all things, which is upon the expression of Truth within, and every expressed thought of unity, in which is the spiritual source of a firmness yielding a spiritual consciousness; to you it shall be for knowledge and higher emotions.**'"

This verse is indicating that the physical, or natural law of growth, was set in operation in the lower mind. There is to be an awakening to the divine life in the lower nature (earth) and the desires and affection of this lower nature are to rise to higher states of knowledge and emotion. These aspirations are to bear fruit on higher levels of consciousness, and are preparing for the forthcoming evolution of the soul to Divine Mind's perfection.

Fruit is a symbol of the results of action, which can either be good or bad depending upon the thought that is being manifested. We harvest what we sow. When we harvest bad fruit, we have undesirable experiences, and we grow by this experience and obtain knowledge that, hopefully, will keep us from repeating the experience. Thus, we grow to the Divine Consciousness by our mental activity, and with this, the intellect is transmuted to intelligence. This is the Law of Cause and Effect in operation. Thus, Divine Mind acquaints the Soul with the fact that it has expanded its own nature. This unfolding proceeds through the lower nature, and every emotion. The emotion, as a seed, is capable of becoming exalted, and providing growth to the soul. Thus, this growth will serve as sustenance. This is the basis of the statement, "Food for thought."

Thus, Divine Mind gives us every thought on the surface of the earth, and every thought that connects heaven and earth yielding a Spiritual Consciousness after its own thoughts, and all these thoughts are the sustenance of life. Therefore, it is the thought that is eternal. Even the undesirable thoughts that we call "negative" are given us by the Divine Mind in order that the consciousness can discern, through experience, that these thoughts do not serve the good.

This verse is describing a Spiritual Consciousness.

Gen. 1:30 "And to every beast of the earth, and to every fowl of the air, and to every thing that creepeth upon the earth, wherein there is life, I have given every green herb for meat: and it was so."

Beast represents sensuous or material thoughts.

Earth is the lower mind, or outer manifestation of the ideal thought.

Fowl represents conscious thoughts in the mind that are free to express.

Air in Hebrew means to be lofty, sky, heavens, or the higher ether where celestial bodies revolve; and, metaphysically, is a symbol of the mental plane, or mind.

Creepeth in Hebrew means reptile or other rapidly moving animal, to glide, or to crawl. Metaphysically, "creepeth" symbolizes the lower instincts of desire and emotion; such as cunning, greed, subtlety, mischief, cruelty, or destructiveness; and represents subtle thoughts that are unclean.

Life in Hebrew is *chay* (khah'-ee) which means alive, flesh, or be whole. "Flesh", metaphysically, represents the lower nature of desires and passions.

Herb in Hebrew means to be green, grass, or any tender shoot; and, metaphysically, represents the natural laws of growth.

Meat in Hebrew is *oklah* (oklaw') which means food, consume, devour, or eat; and, metaphysically, is a symbol of knowledge and higher emotions.

Metaphysically, this verse might read: **"And to every sensuous thought of the outer manifestation, and to**

every conscious thought that is free of the mental plane, and to everything that desires passionate thoughts upon the outer manifestation, where there is desire and passion, I have given every natural law of growth for knowledge and higher emotions: and it was so."

The spiritual activities on the higher planes correspond to the relationships on the lower planes, which exist as growth-producing ideals, and are kept alive by the personal consciousness. The male and female principles are the dual aspects of the qualities which always present themselves in the evolution of the soul. These "seeds" are the ideal physical, mental and spiritual thoughts brought over from the previous cycles of manifestation. Thus, Divine Mind gives us natural material thoughts, conscious and free thoughts of the mental plane, and every desire and passion of the lower instincts, so that we can grow to higher planes of divine consciousness. This verse is indicating that non-spiritual thoughts also manifest into the outer manifestation. All of these thoughts of the lower mind are natural, and must be balanced by spiritual thoughts. When all lower levels of consciousness have been balanced, the thinking component becomes Wisdom, and the feeling component becomes Love. Then the consciousness has reached the ideal state that the Divine Mind envisioned.

Thus, this verse is describing the Christ Consciousness.

Gen. 1:31 "And God saw every thing that he had made, and, behold, it was very good."

God is a general term for the Divine Mind.

Made in Hebrew means to accomplish, appoint, bestow, bring forth, or make. In Webster's Dictionary, "made" means to produce artificially.

Behold in Hebrew is *hinneh* (hin-nay') which means lo, see, or expressing surprise.

Good in Hebrew is *towb* (tobe) which means in the widest sense, beautiful, bountiful, cheerful, joyful, pleasant, or precious. Webster's Dictionary indicates "good" to mean effective, efficient, or producing favorable results.

Metaphysically, this verse might read: **"And Divine Mind saw everything that it had accomplished, and, lo, it was very good."**

All thoughts that were produced were pronounced to be very good, that is, perfect for purposes of the forthcoming manifestation upon the lower planes of the mind in cycles of evolution. Please note that all the various thoughts that God created are good. Only man is capable of creating thoughts that are "not good", when his thoughts are not in complete harmony with the Divine Mind. Since the mental picture of these thoughts is good, it is *unnatural* for man to create the "monsters" of his individual mind. However, man is given free will to create either the "good or the bad," depending upon his understanding. It is through the cycles of evolution that the Spirit is revealed, and it is this that sets us free from the negative monsters of our minds.

Figure 6 illustrates the Sixth Spiritual Understanding - The Reasoning And Analyzing Mind.

SUMMARY OF THE SIXTH UNDERSTANDING

The Sixth Spiritual Understanding is describing the thoughts and emotions associated with each of seven levels of consciousness. The seven levels of consciousness define the Universal Mind, or the whole mind. This indicates that Divine Mind intended that man develop spiritually, by experiencing thoughts and emotions through an unfolding consciousness to obtain an awareness of the Spiritual understanding in degrees. The consciousness unfolds from the outermost physical level to an inner spiritual consciousness. The outermost level, the Sense Consciousness, brings forth thoughts and experiences of passion and desire of our basic animal tendencies. These thoughts and experiences were considered unclean, because they are dir-

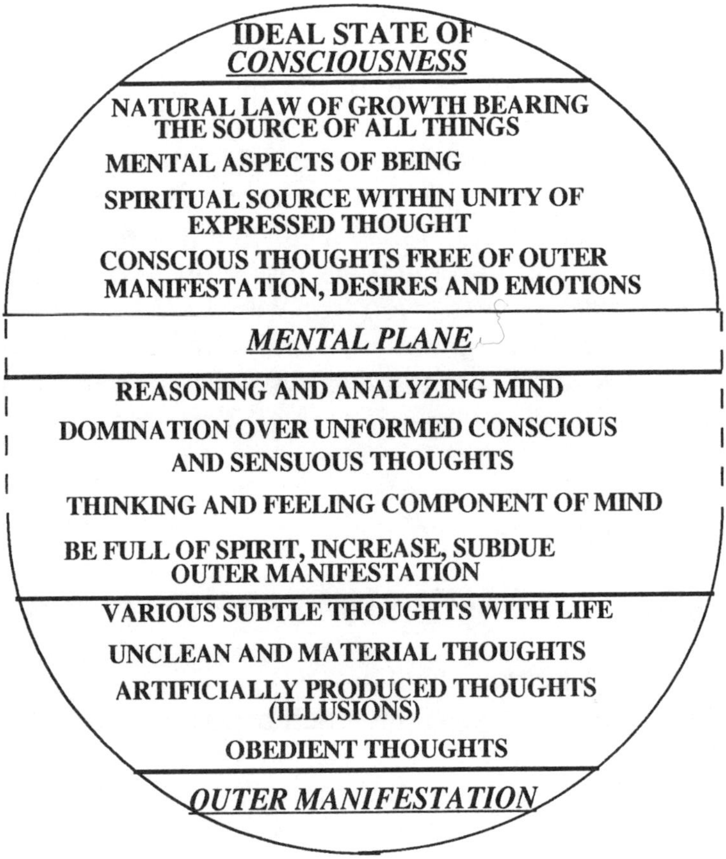

FIGURE 6 - SIXTH UNDERSTANDING - GENESIS 1:24-31

ected by our natural animal force as opposed to spirit. The second level, the Physical Consciousness, gives thoughts and experiences that are based on the illusions of the physical world. The illusions are unformed thoughts. Thus, the first two levels identify with the physical world, and lead us to believe that we are our bodies.

The third level, the Individual Consciousness, presents a reasoning and analytical mind to the consciousness. This mind resembles and imitates the Divine Mind in that both are of the same mind. However, the Individual Consciousness is a mind that is based on intellect while the Divine Mind is of intelligence. The fourth level, the Mental Consciousness, brings in the spiritual element by introducing a feeling component to the thinking component of the Individual consciousness. The fifth level, the Intellectual Consciousness, increases spiritual thoughts to the consciousness in order to subdue and dominate the unformed thoughts of the lower levels of mind. Thus, levels three, four and five deal with the identification of the mental aspects of our Being.

The sixth level, the Spiritual Consciousness, gives the consciousness the Natural Law of Growth in order that it may know that the Divine Mind is the source of all things. The Natural Law of Growth will yield a firm spiritual consciousness that gives knowledge and higher emotions. The seventh level, brings equilibrium by balancing the previous six levels, and the domination of these thoughts and experiences by Divine Mind ideals. Jesus the Christ demonstrated these ideals, so this level is called the Christ Consciousness. Thus, levels six and seven deal with the Spiritual component of Being.

Therefore, from the very beginning, the Divine Mind envisioned a Being that would consist of three components; body, mind, and spirit working as a single unit. This is the basis of the Christian Trinity of Father, Son, and the Holy Ghost.

CHAPTER 7:

MENTAL ASPECTS OF BEING AT REST

The Divine Mind, at this point, has created an ideal state of consciousness; the outer manifestation where the Spiritual ideals will manifest as forms; a firm understanding in consciousness to give intelligence to the unformed ignorance of the outer manifestation; a consciousness that will unfold at different levels of awareness; the Natural Law of Growth to bring forth Divine Life that yields the Divine Mind as the source of all things; and a reasoning and analyzing mind that will have free choice to raise the limited, unformed thoughts of the lower mind to the unlimited, formed thoughts of Spirit. It has defined the seven levels of growth to bring the consciousness from its natural animal passions and desires to the ideal state of consciousness. Now the Divine Mind rests from its mental efforts before starting the next phase of creation.

SEVENTH DAY - GENESIS 2:1-3

Gen. 2:1 "Thus the heavens and the earth were finished, and all the host of them."

> **Heaven,** metaphysically, is an ideal state of consciousness in which the ideas are in complete harmony with the Divine Mind.
>
> **Earth** is the lower mind, or the outer manifestation of the ideal thought.

Finished in Hebrew is *kalah* (kaw-law') which means to cease, to finish, to complete, accomplish or consume. **Host** in Hebrew is *tsbaath* (tseb-aw-aw') which means to mass, assemble, perform, appointed time or waiting upon. According to Webster's Dictionary, "host" means to initiate or preside over a gathering. "Preside" means to be in the position of authority, or control.

This verse, metaphysically, might read: **"Thus the ideal state of consciousness and the outer manifestation were complete, and all in the appointed time of them."**

This verse states that the various ideas, or thoughts, that the Divine Mind produced have an appointed time in which they will evolve in consciousness. The ideal state of consciousness (heaven) has a different authority, than that of the outer manifestation (earth), because the Divine Consciousness is more highly evolved than that of either the outer manifestation or mental planes. The difference is one of understanding and knowledge of Spiritual concepts. I believe that the Holy Spirit is the authority and the intelligence in the mental plane and the ego, or individualized consciousness, has the authority in the outer manifestation, or lower mind. The Holy Spirit is able to translate physical illusions to Spiritual concepts, because it understands both worlds. The individual consciousness, on the other hand, understands only physical concepts and illusions. The mental possibilities in the consciousness can be under the control of either, depending upon the level of the individual's understanding. However, only one can control the consciousness at any given time. The choice is entirely up to the spiritual mind which will be created in the next phase of creation.

Gen. 2:2 "And on the seventh day God ended his work which he had made; and he rested on the seventh day from all his work which he had made."

Seventh in Hebrew is *shebiyiy* (sheb-ee-ee') which means seventh time. Metaphysically, seven is a perfect number representing the completeness in the world of phenomena. Seven always refers to the divine law of perfection for the divine-natural man. Therefore, seventh day means the seventh or perfect level of physical unfoldment.

Day, metaphysically, represents a degree of unfoldment in consciousness, i.e., understanding.

God is a general term for the Divine Mind.

Ended in Hebrew is *kalah* (kaw-law') which means to cease, be finished, accomplished, leave off, or bring to pass.

Work in Hebrew is *melakab* (mel-aw-kaw') meaning employment, business, or ministry. According to Webster's Dictionary, "work" is physical or mental effort to make something.

Rested in Hebrew is *halah* (kaw-law') meaning to cease, be finished, accomplish, or fulfill.

Metaphysically, this verse might read: **"And on the seventh level of understanding, Divine Mind ceased its mental effort which it had brought forth; and it finished on the perfect level of physical understanding from all its mental efforts which it had brought forth."**

At this stage the Divine nature rests, since the mental involution of the Divine Mind has been completed. In Hebrew the period of involution is signified by the six days of Divine activity preceding the Sabbath Day of rest, or inactivity. After this the universe and the soul awaken to the new life process of Evolution, as described in the second chapter of Genesis. According to Webster's Dictionary, "rest" is peace of mind, emotional calm, or tranquility; which implies that all the different thought systems created are in a state of equilibrium, and consistent with the ideals of the Divine Mind. Therefore, rest is a state of mind that man enters, or acquires, when he goes into the silence of his own soul, or into the realm of Spirit. There he finds true rest and peace. Under the old Jewish law, no one was allowed to work on the seventh day (Exodus 20:8-11).

Gen. 2:3 "And God blessed the seventh day, and sanctified it, because that in it he had rested from all his work which God created and made."

God is a general term for the Divine Mind.

Blessed in Hebrew means an act of adoration, praise, or salute; and, metaphysically, represents the Divine Will operating through the human consciousness. According to Webster's Dictionary, "blessed" means holy, sacred, or consecrated.

Seventh day, metaphysically, means completeness of the divine understanding.

Sanctified in Hebrew is *qadash* (kaw-dash') meaning make, pronounce, observe, consecrate, proclaim or sanctify. According to Webster's Dictionary, it means to make holy.

Rested in Hebrew means to cease, be finished, accomplish or fulfill.

Work in Hebrew means employment, business, or ministry. According to Webster's Dictionary, "work" is physical or mental effort to make something.

Created in Hebrew means to create, formative process, choose or dispatch.

Made in Hebrew means to accomplish, appoint, bestow, bring forth or make. In Webster's Dictionary, "made" means to produce artificially.

Metaphysically, this verse might read: **"And Divine Mind blessed the completeness of the divine understanding, and proclaimed it, because in it, it had ceased from all its mental effort which Divine Mind had created and made."**

The seventh day, or perfect, stage of spiritual unfoldment, is sanctified because the Universal Consciousness has fulfilled the divine law in both thought and act. It is at this state of mind that man finds true rest and peace. (Please note that this is the natural state of Spirit.) This verse presents in concise words a law that pervades the universe. According to some geologists, the rock-ribbed earth beneath our feet bears a record of six great creative periods, with a seventh in process. It has also been said that Jesus was born during the sixth millennium. The seventh millennium will commense in the next 15 to 29 years, and with it will bring 1,000 years of peace. Seven movements of the creative law are the foundation of the world about us. The seven colors of the visible spectrum, the seven principal tones of music, and the seven senses of man (two not yet universally used), all point to these degrees, or days, of action and rest.

"I rest in God." This thought will bring to you the rest and quiet, peace and stillness, and the safety and the happiness you seek."I rest is God." This thought has the power to wake the sleeping truth in you, whose vision sees beyond to wake the same truth in you, to that same truth in everyone and everything there is. Here is the end to suffering for all the world, and everyone who ever came and yet will come to linger for a while. Here is the thought in which the son of God is born again, to recognize himself." (ACIM Work Book 193)

This seventh stage of unfolding can be enjoyed at any hour. Man shows his ignorance and limits his happiness by confining the Sabbath to any one day of the week. If God ordained a certain day for rest, and rested on that day Himself, He certainly would have left some evidence of it in His Creations; but He did not. The fact is, the Divine Mind rests in a perpetual Sabbath, and that which seems work is not work at all.

Figure 7 illustrates the Seventh Spiritual Understanding - Mental Aspects Of Being At Rest.

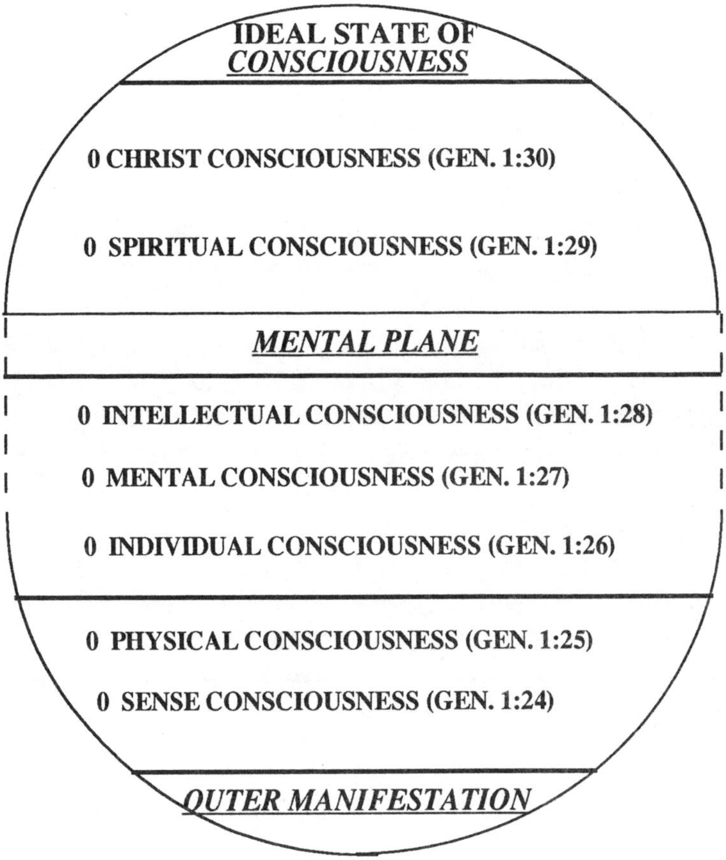

FIGURE 7 - SEVENTH UNDERSTANDING - GENESIS 2:1-3

SUMMARY OF THE SEVENTH UNDERSTANDING

At the completion of the ideal state of consciousness, the outer manifestation, and the associated levels of consciousness that unfold at different levels of awareness, the Divine Mind rests from all its mental activity. This rest occurs at the perfect stage of understanding, which is the Christ Consciousness. Then the Divine Mind blessed the completion of understanding. Each of the various created thought forms have their appointed time in which to evolve to full consciousness. Two separate thought systems are created to provide free choice to the consciousness. However, at this stage of creation, all the various levels of consciousness are at rest, or in a state of balance or equilibrium.

Rest is the suspension of activity, which is necessary before starting another and distinct movement forward in the creation process. Therefore, rest is a state of mind that man enters, or acquires, when he goes into the silence of his own soul, or into the realm of Spirit. There he finds True rest and peace. I believe that man is to work and evolve the first six understandings of creation and master the effects of matter, and then rest in the knowledge that Spirit is all there is. This is the true meaning behind the words, "Let go, and let God".

PART II

THE SECOND STORY OF CREATION

CHAPTER 8:

CREATION OF MAN

The first Chapter of Genesis describes the creation of the Universal Mind and its relationship with the Divine Mind. The spirit of man within this universe, has the same likeness and qualities as the Divine Mind. On the earth plane the spiritual man is to evolve to higher consciousness through experiencing the results of its thoughts. This evolution consists of mental movements through seven different levels of understanding. It progresses from the lowest Sense Consciousness to the Divine Mind qualities of the Christ Consciousness. Now the stage has been set, and all that is needed is a spiritual mind that reasons and analyzes to set the evolutionary process into motion.

The second Chapter of Genesis describes a second creation, that is, the formation of a spiritual being that has qualities like those of the Divine mind, but must evolve to a oneness with the Divine Mind through the Law of Cause and Effect, or the Natural Law of Growth. To understand this Spiritual Being, we will analyze and decode Genesis verses 2:4 to 2:24.

Gen. 2:4 "These are the generations of the heavens and the earth when they were created, in the day that the Lord God made the earth and the heavens."

Generations in Hebrew is *towldah* (to-led-aw') which means descent, family, history, or birth. Metaphysically, generations are a symbol of the stages of history in the development of the human consciousness.

Heaven in Hebrew is *shameh* (shaw-meh') which means to be lofty, sky, or higher ether where the celestial bodies revolve. Heaven then, is the state of consciousness which is above the mental plane. Metaphysically, heaven is an ideal state of consciousness in which ideas are in complete harmony with the Divine Mind. It is sometimes referred to as the upper mind.

Earth in Hebrew is *erets* (eh'-rets) which means to be firm, field, ground, or land. Earth is a symbol of matter which, when acted upon by Spirit, takes the form and qualities of manifestation. Metaphysically, earth is the outer manifestation of the Divine Mind, and is sometimes referred to as the lower mind.

Created in Hebrew is *bara* (baw-raw') which means to cut down, dispatch, do or make.

Day in Hebrew is *yown* (yome) which means to be hot, or sunrise to sunrise. Day is symbolic of a period of spiritual activity. Metaphysically, day means understanding.

Lord God in Hebrew is *yhovah* (yeh-ho-vaw') which means self-Existent, or Eternal. It comes from the root word *hayah* (haw-yaw') which means to exist, breathe, be or become. It is the Directive Intelligence which works upon the various form levels. Jehovah is the Jewish national name for God, and is sometimes referred to as Jehovah the Lord.

Therefore, this verse, metaphysically, might read: **"These are the stages of history in the development of the ideal state of consciousness and of the outer manifestation when they were dispatched, in the understanding that the Eternal made the outer manifestation and the ideal state of consciousness."**

This verse is setting into motion the idea of the evolutionary process. This is the genetic power of the in-dwelling Self in the soul, in which the interactive spiritual-material creative function produces form. It is by these forms that the growth of consciousness is rendered possible. These forms are transmuted, that is, changed, from the original primitive form to something of a higher quality, or level. It is the astral-mental function of mind and desires by which ideas and lower emotions are produced. They are no longer used in the blind, or natural, way of outer manifestation. Instead they are raised and consecrated to the highest uses, giving rise to higher emotions and concepts of truth. This is the ideal state of consciousness. Therefore, this growth function evolves from the lower primitive form to the higher spiritual state of the I AM, or Christ Consciousness. This is consistent with Genesis 1:26, in which there are seven different "levels of qualities" of the Universal Consciousness as presented in Chapter 6 of this book.

This verse makes clear that it was the Lord God that created the outer manifestation and the ideal state of consciousness. It is the descent of Spirit into matter for the purpose of reunification with the Divine Mind. This process is called *involution*. The Spirit ascends through matter, and progressively moves from the outer levels of matter to the higher inner values and ideals. This process is called *evolution*. Note that this is the first time that LORD God is used. LORD is another name for spiritual man. As LORD, spiritual man is ruler of himself. The LORD consciousness is one of dominion. It is the I AM or the Christ Consciousness. The change from God to LORD God denotes a change from the universal consciousness to the dominion of one consciousness. I believe the double meaning of "I AM, I AM" is intended as a flag to denote a major change is occurring from that of the creation in Gen. 1:1-30 & 2:1-3.

Gen. 2:5 "And every plant of the field before it was in the earth, and every herb of the field before it grew; for the Lord God had not caused it to rain upon the earth, and there was not a man to till the ground."

Plant in Hebrew is *siyach* (see'-akh) which mean to ponder, converse, declare, meditate, prayer, a shoot, shrubbery, bush, or shrub. Plants are symbols of simple instincts and feelings growing upward to the light. The mind and emotion-principles undergo a transformation from simple feelings and instincts into human ideals and emotions. And so, the human race was launched upon its evolutionary path.

Field in Hebrew is *saday* (saw-dah'ee) which means to spread out, country, ground, land, or soil. Field is a symbol of the lower nature, or the arena within which the soul's evolution takes place. It includes all the planes of manifestation; the mental facilities, the emotions, the desires, the passions and the sensations in all their varieties as the means of soul-development. The human organism on the lower planes is the field of experience. To know it all is to rise above it and become one with the Higher Self.

Earth is a symbol of matter which, when acted upon by Spirit, takes the form and qualities of manifestation. Metaphysically, earth is the outer manifestation of the Divine Mind, and is sometimes referred to as the lower mind.

Herb in Hebrew is *eseb* (eh'-seb) which means to glisten, grass, tender shoot, or herb. Herbs symbolize the primitive desires and affections which are aroused by the activities of the senses.

Grew in Hebrew is *tsamach* (tsaw-makh') which means to sprout, bear, bring forth, bud, or spring forth.

Lord God means self-Existent, Eternal, or breathe; and represents the Directive Intelligence which works upon the various form levels.

Caused in Hebrew is *nathan* (naw-than') which means to give, appoint, ascribe, bestow, commit, deliver, bring forth, lift up, or make.

Rain in Hebrew is *matar* (maw-tar') and is a symbol of the downpouring of truth.

Man in Hebrew is *adam* (aw-dawm') which means to show blood, red (ruddy), a human being, an individual, or person. As used here, man is a symbol for the conscious or directive mind within us. It is that part of the spiritual

mind that reasons and analyzes. It signifies the mental qualities. Metaphysically, man also means spirit.
Ground in Hebrew is *adamah* (ad-aw-maw') which means soil, country, land, or earth. Ground is a symbol of the lower nature of the soul, which requires "tilling" and "sowing" to produce good "fruit".

This verse, metaphysically, might read: "**And every meditated thought of the lower nature before it was in the outer manifestation, and every primitive desire and affection of the lower nature before it sprouted, for the Directive Intelligence had not given it to downpour truth upon the outer manifestation, and there was not a conscious or directive mind to work the lower nature.**"

This verse states that at this early period of the Universal Mind, no desire has as yet appeared upon the outer manifestation; and no sign of awakening life has taken place. The Directive Intelligence of the spiritual mind has not yet caused the forthcoming of stimulative ideas. Therefore, evolution is only an idea in the Divine Mind and has not yet been set into motion, because there was no mental faculty that was actively functioning in the outer manifestation. That is to say, the spiritual mind has been created, but has not as yet come into contact with the concept of material form.

Gen. 2:6 "But there went up a mist from the earth, and watered the whole face of the ground."

Mist in Hebrew is *ed* (ade) which means enveloping, fog, or vapor.
Earth is a symbol for matter which, when acted upon by Spirit, takes the form and qualities of manifestation. Metaphysically, earth is the outer manifestation.
Watered in Hebrew is *shaqah* (shaw-kaw') which means to irrigate, or furnish a potion to, influence, drink, drown, water, or moisten. Water, metaphysically, represents the mental potential, and is the symbol of Truth,

or the eternal Reality, and source of all manifestation.
Face in Hebrew is *paneh* (paw-neh') which means a part that turns, edge, countenance, appearance, front, or heaviness. Face is a symbol of the mental aspect of being. This represents knowledge acquired either through the senses or the intuition.
Ground means soil, country, land, or earth. Ground is a symbol of the lower nature of the soul, which requires "tilling" and "sowing" to produce good "fruit".

This verse, metaphysically, might read: "**But there went up a vapor from the outer manifestation, and Truth influenced the whole mental aspect of being of the lower nature of the soul.**"

Mist implies that a water vapor covered the lower nature of the soul. Water, metaphysically, represents the mental potential, or purifying unity of Truth that is outpouring and cleansing the outer manifestation. Truth gives knowledge that can be acquired either through the senses (material) or by intuition (spirit). "Face of the ground" implies knowledge of appearance, or the surface of things of the lower nature. The lower self, or personality, is brought to realize that it can no longer depend upon the lower knowledge for subsistence or satisfaction. The soul does not yet know the Higher Self, or source, of its inspiration.

Gen. 2:7 "And the Lord God formed man of the dust of the ground, and breathed unto his nostrils the breath of life; and man became a living soul."

Lord God means self-Existent, Eternal, or breathe; and represents the directive intelligence which works upon the various form levels.
Formed in Hebrew is yatsar (yaw-tsar') which means to press, squeezing into shape, to mold into a form, fashion, or make. 'Form', according to Webster's Dictionary, means "the shape or outline of anything; excluding color, texture, and density."

Man means to show blood, red (ruddy), a human being, an individual, or person. As used here, man is a symbol of the conscious or directive mind within us. It is that part of the spiritual mind that reasons and analyzes. It signifies the mental qualities. Metaphysically, man also means spirit.

Dust in Hebrew is *aphar* (aw-fawr') which means powdered or gray; hence clay, earth, mud, ashes, ground, or mortar. Dust is defined as " fine pulverized particles of earth." This implies that it can easily be blown by the winds of turmoil, which suggest that it is temporary. 'Dust ' also means confusion or disintegrating thoughts, according to Webster's Dictionary.

Ground means soil, country, land, or earth. Ground is a symbol of the lower nature of the soul, which requires "tilling" and "sowing" to produce good "fruit".

Breathed in Hebrew is *naphach* (naw-fakh') which means to puff, inflate, blow hard, or breath.

Nostrils in Hebrew is *aph* (af) which means the nose or face, and occasionally a person, and is symbolic of volition and free will.

Breath of life in Hebrew is *nshamah* (nesh-aw-maw') which means a puff, wind, vital breath, Divine Inspiration, intellect, soul, or spirit. Breath has a deep inner meaning, as it represents the most important precondition of life as we know it. Without breath there is no life. To the Essenes, breath represented the unity between man and the cosmic oceans of life and thought. The "breath of life" is a symbol of the spiritual essence, or the Divine Spark, which is immortal.

Man is that part of the spiritual mind that reasons and analyzes. It signifies the mental qualities. Man is Spirit, absolute and unconditioned; and becomes an individual consciousness into which God breathes the breath of life.

Soul in Hebrew is *nephesh* (neh'-fesh) which means a breathing creature, body, desire, ghost, mind, mortally, person, self, or will. The soul is symbolic of spirit and matter in relation to the Divine process of manifestation. First there is Involution and then Evolution. The soul represents man's consciousness, both conscious and subconscious.

Metaphysically, this verse might read: **"And the Directive Intelligence pressed into shape a spiritual mind that reasons and analyzes the confusion of the outer manifestation, and blew into his free will the spiritual essence; and the spiritual mind that reasons and analyzes became a living consciousness."**

Note that the word 'formed' was used as opposed to "create" or "make". This implies that the Divine Mind molded the spiritual mind that reasons and analyzes, as opposed to artificially producing it. The molded spiritual mind that reasons and analyzes is, therefore, similar in likeness and quality to that of the Divine Mind.

'Dust' at first glance is an uncomplimentary term. However, the Essenes believed that the earth was a symbol of "Life". 'Dust' to them represented the end as well as the beginning of all material life on the planet (dust to dust). Thus, "dust of the ground" is a symbol of the lower mind which is unstable and subject to every wind of doctrine and opinion that obscures the truth. Free will is established to provide choice, and the spiritual mind that reasons chooses which doctrine and opinion will lead to the Truth. This is the process of Evolution by which we learn through experience which doctrine and opinion leads us to the Spiritual qualities of life.

The "breath of life" is the symbol of the spiritual essence. Into the lower mind, or astral-mental body, was projected the Divine spark, and the spiritual mind that reasons and analyzes became a creature capable of responsible, independent existence. Without the Divine Spark, the spiritual mind that reasons and analyzes could not overcome the confusion of the outer world and could not grow in a responsible manner. Thus, the soul becomes a living consciousness that has developed out of Spirit as well as the impression it receives from the outer world. Dust could also be a symbol for man's soul, which contains both Spirt and Matter. Dust is lighter than the Matter of the lower nature and heavier than Spirit. Thus the soul becomes a living being and is a symbol of spirit and matter in relation to the Divine process of manifestation.

SUMMARY OF THE CREATION OF MAN

Genesis 2:4 through 2:7 provides further details about creation and the formation of man (spirit-mind), and his role in the creative process. There is a power in the soul, where the interactive spiritual-material creative function (thought) produces form. It is the astral-mental function of the mind and desires, by which ideas and lower emotions are produced. These are freed of the blind and natural ways of an ignorant lower mind and are raised to the higher emotions and concepts of Truth.

Prior to the formation of man, the Universal Mind had no desire and no sign of awakening life, because the Divine Mind had not caused the stimulative ideas to proceed. Thus, evolution was only an idea in the Divine Mind. There was no mental faculty that was actively functioning in the outer manifestation, or lower mind. That is, the spirit-mind, or, man had been created, but had not come into contact with the concepts of material form. Before a spiritual mind can be placed in the lower mind, there must first be a purification process of Truth that is outpouring and cleansing. Truth provides knowledge that can be acquired either by the physical senses or by the intuition of Spirit. Thus, the lower self, or individual personality, begins to realize that it can no longer depend upon the lower knowledge for subsistence and satisfaction.

The spiritual mind that reasons and analyzes, or man, is formed by the Directive Intelligence. Formed implies that the Spirit-Matter is molded into a spirit-mind that is of like qualities to that of the Divine Mind. This spirit-mind is formed from the dust of the lower mind, which implies it is unstable and subject to every wind of doctrine and opinion that obscures the Truth. However, the spiritual essence, or Divine Spark, is breathed into it, and it becomes a creature capable of responsible and independent existence. The breathing of spiritual essence provides Free Will and the ability to choose between things of Spirit and Matter. Thus, the soul becomes a living consciousness that is developed out of Spirit as well as the impressions it receives from the lower mind, or outer manifestation. The spiritual mind can now use its reasoning and analytical capabilities to choose which doctrine and opinion to follow, and experience which qualities will lead to the good experiences of life. Thus, the evolutionary process of the soul is set into motion, where the soul is a symbol of spirit and matter in relation to the Divine process of manifestation.

Evolution is the gradual ascent of Spirit through matter towards reunification with the Divine Mind, and progressively moves from the outer to the higher inner values and ideals. Involution, on the other hand, is the descent of Spirit into Matter. Involution always comes first into existence before Evolution, because if the Universal-soul were produced first, no experience or evolution would be necessary. The life of the Universal-soul is the means whereby the form is energized into activity. Therefore, Spirit pre-exists, and Matter subsists.

Manifestation involves duality. First comes the limitation of Spirit in form (Involution); and second is the Resurrection, or the liberation, of Spirit from captivity in matter (Evolution). Both beget ideals enabling the Self to subsequently manifest and eliminate the illusions of the lower mind. The Divine purpose in manifestation is to evolve all things in matter, that they may return again by evolution after having accomplished the end for which they existed; namely, the growth and exaltation of the myriad souls of humanity.

CHAPTER 9:

PREPARATION OF EDEN FOR MAN

The Universal Mind has been created and the idea of a spirit-mind has been formed. However, before the spiritual mind can be placed in the lower mind, and the process of Evolution set into motion, there must be a place to put it. In other words, a place must be prepared to receive the spiritual mind and the structure for its use must be established before the spiritual mind can reside there. Thus, Genesis 2:8 through 2:14 describes the environment where the formed spiritual mind will grow in spiritual activities.

Gen. 2:8 "And the LORD God, planted a garden eastward in Eden; and there he put the man whom he had formed".

LORD God means self-Existent, Eternal, or breath; and represents the directive intelligence which works upon the various levels.

Planted in Hebrew is *nata* (naw-tah') which means fix, to plant, or fastened.

Garden in Hebrew is *gan* from the root word *ganan* (gaw-nan') which means to hedge about, protect or defend, and is any organized sphere of activity. Garden symbolizes the spiritual body in which man dwells after the creation of the spirit and the formation of the soul.

Eastward in Hebrew is *qedmah* (kayd'-maw) which means eternal, forward part, or east, and is from the root word *qadam* (kaw-dam') which means to protect, precede, or to anticipate. Metaphysically, east means within.

Eden in Hebrew is *heden* (ay'-den) which means pleasure, delight, time, season, or a place in Mesopotamia. Eden, metaphysically, is a pleasant, harmonious, productive state of consciousness in which all possibilities of growth are found.

Man is that part of the spiritual mind that reasons and analyzes. It signifies the mental qualities. Man is Spirit, absolute and unconditioned; and becomes an individual consciousness into which God breathes the breath of life.

Formed means to press, squeezed into shape, to mold into a form, fashion, or make. 'Formed', according to Webster's Dictionary, means "the shape or outline of anything; excluding color, texture, and density."

Metaphysically, this verse might read: **"And the Directive Intelligence fixed a spiritual body within a pleasant, harmonious, productive state of consciousness; and there it put the spiritual mind which it had formed."**

When man is expressing in harmony with the Divine Mind, he brings forth the qualities of Being in divine order, and he dwells within Eden, or in a state of bliss in a harmonious body. The "garden" symbolizes the spiritual body in which man dwells when he brings forth his thoughts after the original Divine Ideas. This Garden is the substance of God (Eden) or a state of perfect relation of ideas in Being.

Note that this is a different man than that created in Gen. 1:27. This spirit is formed (not created) out of dust. Thus, this spirit is the soul, or the spiritual mind, that is being formed. The soul is placed in a state of perfect relation of ideas (God's thoughts) to Being (manifestation). Man at this point has both a spirit and a soul.

Gen. 2:9 "And out of the ground made the LORD God to grow every tree that is pleasant to the sight, and

good for food; the tree of life also in the midst of the garden, and the tree of knowledge of good and evil."

Ground means soil, country, land, or earth. Ground is a symbol of the lower nature of the soul, which requires "tilling" and "sowing" to produce good "fruit".

Made in Hebrew is *asah* (aw-saw') which means to do, accomplish, advance, appoint, bestow, or bring forth.

LORD God means self-Existent, Eternal, or breath; and represents the directive intelligence which works upon the various levels.

Tree in Hebrew is *ets* (ates) which means firmness, wood, stock, or timber. Tree signifies the connecting link between earth and heaven (between body and mind, the formless and the formed).

"Every tree that is pleasant to the sight" pertains to the perceptive faculty of mind. It is always pleasant to perceive Truth.

"Good for food" pertains to the substance of spiritual thought which is "food" that is good.

"Tree of life in the midst of the garden" represents the absolute life principle established in man's consciousness by Divine Mind.

"Tree of knowledge of good and evil" represents the discerning capacity of mind. Man first perceives Truth; then he must discern the relation of ideas before perfect activity is set up within him.

Metaphysically, this verse might read: **"And out of the lowest nature, the Directive Intelligence brought forth to grow every perceptive faculty of mind that is pleasant to the sight and substance of spiritual thought; the absolute life principle established in man's consciousness; and the discerning capacity of mind."**

This verse is bringing forth all the mental activities that will eventually be used by the spiritual mind in the lower mind; and includes pleasant sensual thoughts, spiritual thought which is the absolute life principal, and the discerning capability to distinguish between the two.

The generative center, in the loins of man, is the point at which the physical man contacts life, but when the consciousness has been redeemed and man has placed himself in the "garden" through the I AM, or Jehovah, he contacts the "tree of life" at the solar plexus region, or heart center. From the heart center he exercises authority and dominion over the whole current of life in the organism.

The spiritual body contains the spiritual mind that produces every sensual thought that can be perceived, spiritual thoughts which are the absolute life principle established in consciousness, and the discerning capacity of the mind. This sets up the condition where a choice between sensual thoughts and spiritual thoughts must be made. The discerning capacity of the mind chooses between illusion and Truth.

Gen. 2:10 "And a river went out of Eden to water the garden; and from thence it was parted, and became four heads".

River in Hebrew is *nahar* (naw-hwr') which means to sparkle, a stream, or a running stream. River, metaphysically, represents a current of thought or a current of vital forces of life in the organism.

Eden in Hebrew is *heden* (ay'-den) which means pleasure, delight, time, season, or a place in Mesopotamia. Eden, metaphysically, is a pleasant, harmonious, productive state of consciousness in which all possibilities of growth are found.

Water in Hebrew is *shaqah* (shaw-kaw') which means irrigate, to cause, drink, or moisten. Metaphysically, water represents weakness and negativity, cleansing, mental potential, and in some cases, life or vital energy.

Garden symbolizes the spiritual body in which man dwells after the creation of the spirit and the formation of the soul.

> **Heads** in Hebrew is *resh* (roshe) which comes from the root word *appar* which means to shake the head, forefront, lead, principle, or ruler. 'Head', according to Webster's Dictionary, means godhead.

Metaphysically, this verse might read: **"And a current of thought went out of the harmonious state of consciousness, to cleanse the spiritual body; and from that place it was separated, and became four principles."**

A spiritual thought, or a current of vital forces of life, went out of the harmonious state of consciousness to cleanse the spiritual body of weakness and negativity and it separated into four principles. A river is a symbol of the course of the soul's evolution from the material to the spiritual life in the world of experiences. The comparison between human life and a river is very clever and quite accurate. The best analogy between human life and a river is provided by R. J. Campbell in his sermon, *The Ceaseless Quest,* as follows: "Our course starts far from our divine goal, and sometimes seems to be leading us away from it; it is long before we even catch a glimpse of what it is; but the currents of our being gradually deepen and broaden as we near the full oceans of the life of God, and at the last stage of our winding journey the ocean tide comes up to meet us, gathers us into its bosom, and bears us away to our eternal home. As the river never stops flowing 'till it gets to the ocean, so man can never stop seeking 'till every part of his being is perfectly at one with God. The flow of our desires is first in one direction and then in another, but it can never cease and never pause 'till it comes to rest, and every part and particle of it comes to fulfillment in the infinitude of God."

At first the river takes the course of least resistance, but as it broadens and deepens, it becomes established, and has no alternative but to follow its course. However, the events of life can and do alter our course. For example, a beaver may choose to follow his course and build a dam in the river's path. The water from the river finds resistance, because the dam is blocking its natural flow. This resistance continues to build until the water breaks free of its banks and creates a new course. The spiritual Mind (man) is like the river in that it has power and chooses its path.

Gen. 2:11 "The name of the first is Pishon; that is it which compasseth the whole land of Havilah, where there is gold;"

Name in Hebrew is *shem* (shame) which means a mark or memorial of individuality, authority, nature or character.

Pishon (pi-shon) is Hebrew and means dispersive. Metaphysically, Pishon represents Spirit at work in man's consciousness, Spirit diffusing its ideas of intelligence and light, and the activity of divine ideas in their fullness.

Land in Hebrew is *erets* (eh'-rets) which means the earth, country, field, ground, land, world, or wilderness. Land represents the consciousness unfolding at different levels of awareness.

Havilah in Hebrew is *chaviylah* (khar-ee-law') which comes from the root word *chuwl* (kheel) which means to twist or whirl (in a circular or spiral manner), dance, to writhe in pain, or sorrow, and represents the struggle of elemental life born of trial.

Gold in Hebrew is *zahab* (zaw-hawb') which means to shimmer, something of gold color, or fair weather (golden); and is the symbol of spiritual treasures locked up in the body temple. These treasures are released by the inflow of spiritual work. It is at the higher consciousness level that Wisdom and Truth are clearly perceived.

Metaphysically, this verse might read: **"The authority of the first is Spirit at work: that is, it which circles around the whole consciousness, unfolding at different levels of awareness of the struggle of life, where there is treasure of Spirit."**

The nature of the first (head/principle) is Spirit diffusing ideas of intelligence and light that completely surround man's consciousness. This consciousness unfolds at different levels of awareness. In unfolding, there are trials that are necessary to bring into manifestation the inner spiritual possibilities that lie back of and are wrapped up in the seemingly material organism. In this unfolding consciousness there is the struggle of elemental life, born of trial. The quote, "There is gold in the land," implies that locked up in our body temple are all the treasures of Spirit. Gold is the symbol of the spiritual qualities of Divine Wisdom and Truth and is found in the higher state of consciousness where Wisdom and Truth are clearly perceived. Solomon said, "There is treasure to be desired and oil in the dwelling of the wise; but a foolish man spendeth it up. He that followeth after righteousness and mercy findeth life, righteousness and honour." (Prov. 21:20 & 21). *Thus, the first vital life principle (river) is Spirit (Intelligence, Wisdom, and Truth).*

Gen. 2:12 "And the Gold of that land is good; there is bdellium and the onyx stone".

Gold is the symbol of spiritual treasures locked up in the body temple. These treasures are released by the inflow of intelligence.

Land represents consciousness unfolding at different levels of awareness.

Bdellium in Hebrew is *bdolach* (bed-o'-lakh) which means something in pieces, gum, or a pearl. Bdellium comes from the root word *bahal* (baw-dal') which means to divide, separate, or distinguish. 'Bdellium', according to Webster's Dictionary, is an aromatic gum resin similar to myrrh.

Onyx in Hebrew is *shoham* (sho'-ham) which means a gem (probably beryl because of its pale green color). 'Onyx', according to Webster's Dictionary, is a mystical stone that occurs in colored bands and is used as a gemstone (semiprecious gem).

Stone in Hebrew is *eben* (eh'-ben) which means to build, make, repair, or set up. Stone refers to the indwelling Christ, which is the key to man's character.

Metaphysically, this verse might read: "**And the spiritual treasures of the consciousness unfolding at different levels of awareness are good; there is aromatic gum and gems to build the in-dwelling Christ.**"

The spiritual treasures that come with the unfolding consciousness to the Truth are considered to be good by the Directive Intelligence. Bdellium is an aromatic gum resin similar to myrrh, and is produced by various trees of the genus *Commiphora* of western Asia and Africa. A tree is the symbol of the connecting, or uniting, link between the physical and the spiritual, and represents wisdom that is obtained through knowledge, and experience. A stone is a symbol of Spirit, because it is a substance unreceptive, resistant to impression, and firm; and is the opposite of matter which is receptive, takes impressions, and is unstable. Spirit alone is substance, and matter is a manifestation of Spirit. Therefore, bdellium and onyx are symbols of wisdom and power on the Christ level of consciousness.

Gen. 2:13 "And the name of the second river is Gihon; the same is it that compasseth the whole land of Ethiopia."

Name is a symbol of a mark, or memorial of individuality, authority, or character.

River represents a current of thought or a current of vital forces of life in the organism.

Gihon in Hebrew is *gichown* (ghee-khone') which means short, or a river of paradise. Gihon is a symbol of the lower mental nature, a current of life on the lower planes. Metaphysically, Gihon represents the formative movement. It represents the breath of God inspiring the bursting forth of the joyous life and Truth that flows through the darkened consciousness.

Land represents consciousness unfolding at different levels of awareness.

> **Ethiopia** in Hebrew is *kuwsh* (koosh) which means Cush. Cush is the name of a son of Ham and his territory that is now known as Ethiopia. Ethiopia means burned faces or country of the burning. Metaphysically, it means darkened or material thought to which man has held his body and its activities. (Ham is the physical in man, given over to sensuality.) It is the mortal or physical part of man, as opposed to the Truth. The result is error thinking in the body.

Metaphysically, this verse might read: **"And the authority of the second current of vital forces of life is the formative movement of the lower mental plane; the same as that which circles around the whole consciousness unfolding at different levels of awareness of the darkened consciousness of body activity."**

The second current of thought is the formative movement of the lower mental nature that encompasses the consciousness from the darkened body thoughts. This verse is defining a lower mental nature which includes all of the activities of the astral-mental nature, which in turn includes all of the material and body activities. The lower mental nature is given the capability of differentiation from the higher mental plane of Spirit (Pishon). The body consciousness changes as man perceives the Truth and holds in mind the perfect-body idea. The darkness will disappear, and every cell of the body will shine in spiritual light and life. *Thus, the second vital life principle is the mind.*

Gen. 2:14 "And the name of the third river is Hiddekel; that is it which goeth toward the east of Assyria. And the fourth river is Euphrates"

> **Name** is a symbol of a mark, or memorial of individuality, authority, or character.
> **River** represents a current of thought or a current of vital forces of life in the organism.

Hiddekel in Hebrew is *chiddeqel* (khid-deh'-kel) and is the name of a river that is now known as the Tigris. 'Hiddekel' means universal generative fluid that symbolizes the spiritual nerve fluid that God is propelling throughout man's whole being; giving him the invigorating, steady, power of the Holy Spirit.
East is the symbol of the within.
Assyria in Hebrew is *ashshur* (ash-shoor') which means to be straight, be honest, prosper, lead, or relieve. Assyria, Metaphysically, represents the psychic realm of the soul, and is a symbol of the dawn of the personality on the astral-plane.
Euphrates in Hebrew is *perath* (per-awth') which means to break forth, rushing, to bear fruit, grow, or to increase. Euphrates represents that which is the fructifying (bears fruit) cause. Metaphysically, it represents the circulatory system. (As the blood stream receives and distributes the nutrients contained in the food we eat.)

Metaphysically, this verse might read: **"And the authority of the third current of vital forces of life is the universal invigorating power of the Holy Spirit; that is, that which goes toward the within of the psychic realm of the soul. And the fourth current of vital forces is receiving and distributing nutrients."**

The third current of thought in the astral-plane, on which the individual personality develops, is the universal invigorating power of the Holy Spirit that comes from within the psychic realm of the soul. The river Hiddekel symbolizes the spiritual nerve fluid that God is propelling throughout man's whole being continually, as the electromagnetic center of every physically expressed atom. This stream of fluid finds its way over all nerves in man's body temple, giving him the invigorating, steadying power of the Holy Spirit. The nerve fluid, the most attenuated and volatile fluid of the body, breaks down into flares at the ends of the nerves, giving rise to various kinds of psychic and mental action, forming the character of the soul. The mind uses the nerve flares to express its ideas. *Thus, the third vital life principle is the Holy Spirit.*

The fourth current of vital forces of life is the fructifying causes that bear fruit and receive and distribute the nutrients. Fructifying is the symbol of the Divine life within the lower nature embodied through the process of involution. The Spirit energizes the consciousness within and, from below the awareness of the senses, rises to a higher nature. Thus, the liberation of the life within, through response to the impacts from without, evokes the consciousness to move to a higher level.

The blood stream receives and distributes the nutrients contained in the food we eat. Every part of the organism is supplied with substance through the blood stream. Since blood is the symbol for the body, *the fourth vital life principle is the body.*

Figure 8 illustrates the four vital life forces of the spiritual body. Note that the individual consciousness, or ego, that unfolds at different levels of awareness is completely surrounded by the *First Vital Life Principle* of Wisdom and Truth. Wisdom and Truth are the Treasures of Spirit. It is the work of Spirit that brings out the inner spiritual possibilities that lie back of, and are wrapped up in, the seemingly material organism. Things of Spirit always extend, so Wisdom and Truth are extended to the unfolding consciousness and the darkened body consciousness. The darkened body consciousness is the *Second Vital Life Principle* which is the Mind. It is the mind that must differentiate between the intelligence of the upper mind and the intellect of the lower mind. Thus, the darkened body consciousness is transformed to a spiritual mind through Spirit diffusing ideas of intelligence, Wisdom and Truth. The *Third Vital Life Principle*, the invigorating power of the Holy Spirit, being of Spirit, also extends to both the mind and the body. It is the Holy Spirit that translates the sensual passions, desires and emotions of the body to more spiritual qualities and extends this information to the individual mind. Only the Holy Spirit is capable of this transformation, because it understands Spirit as well as the material realm.

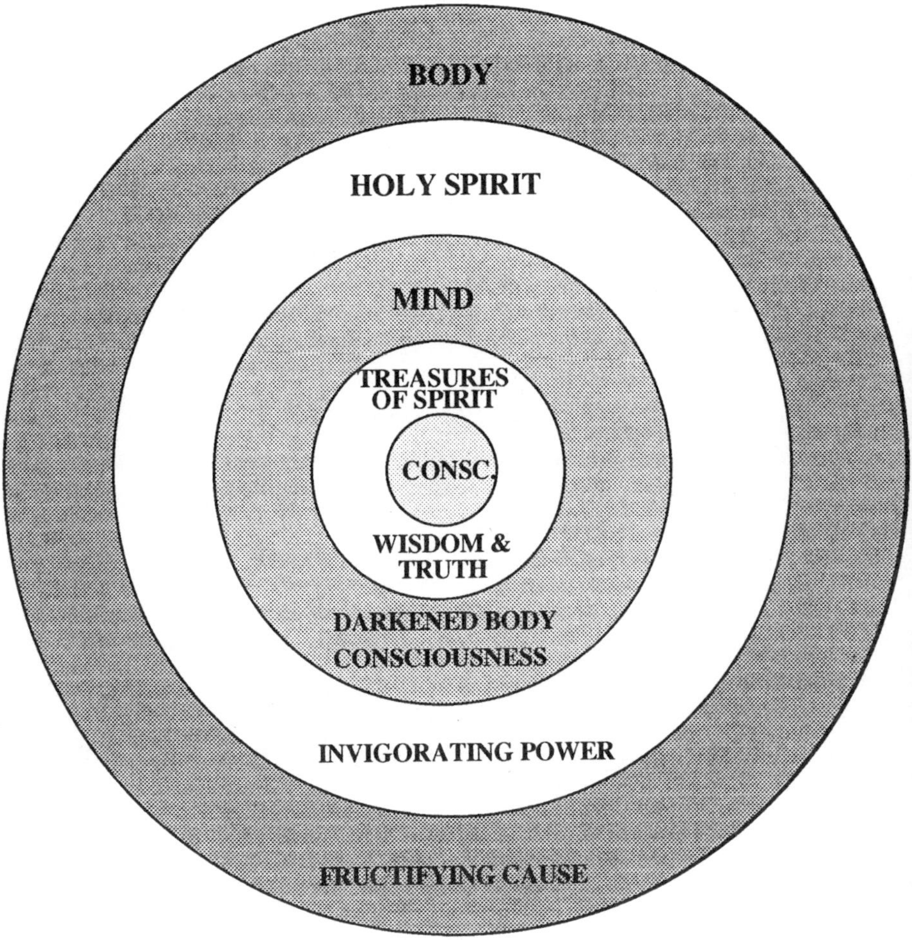

FIGURE 8 - VITAL LIFE PRINCIPALS

And finally, it is the body, the *Fourth Vital Principle*, that completely surrounds the Holy Spirit, mind, Spirit, and the unfolding consciousness, which is the fructifying cause that receives and distributes the nutrients. Fructifying is the symbol of the Divine Life within the lower nature embodied through the process of involution.

SUMMARY OF THE PREPARATION OF EDEN

The spiritual mind, or soul, is placed in a state of perfect relation of ideas (God's thoughts) to Being (manifestation). Man at this point has both a spirit and a soul. In the spiritual body grows every sensual thought that can be perceived by the mind, spiritual thoughts which are the absolute life principle in the consciousness, and the discerning capability of the mind. The spiritual body sets up the condition where a choice between Spirit and Matter must be made. The discerning capacity of the soul must choose between Truth and illusions.

A spiritual thought, or vital life principle, went out of the harmonious state of consciousness to cleanse the spiritual body of weakness and negativity and it separated into four principles. These four principles are used in the soul's evolution from the material to the spiritual life in the world of experiences.

The *First Principle is Spirit diffusing ideas* of intelligence and understanding that completely surround the consciousness. As the consciousness unfolds to the Spiritual Truth, there are trials that are necessary to evolve from material thoughts to those of Spirit. In this unfolding there are the struggles with material life, and Spirit is born of trial. However, there are treasures of Intelligence, Wisdom and Truth locked up in the spiritual body to minimize this trail. The spiritual mind has only to seek them out.

The *Second Principle* is a *mind* that is capable of growth, development and transformation (formative movement). This mind is of the lower nature, includes all of the material and body activities, and receives the ability of differentiation from the higher Spiritual Mind. The darkness of body consciousness transforms as the spiritual mind perceives that Truth holds the perfect-body idea. Then darkness disappears, and every cell of the body shines in spiritual understanding and life.

The *Third Principle* is the *universal invigorating power* of the Holy Spirit, which the individual personality develops out of the psychic realm of the soul. This invigorating power manifests in the spiritual body as a stream of fluids over the nerves, giving the spiritual body the invigorating, steady power of the Holy Spirit. The nerve fluids break down into flares at the ends of the nerves, which produce various kinds of psychic and mental actions. It is the electromagnetic center of every expressed atom.

The *Fourth Principle* is the *body,* which is the fructifying cause that bears fruit, receives, and distributes nutrients. Fructifying is the symbol of the Divine life within the lower nature embodied through the process of involution. The Spirit energizes the consciousness within and, from below the awareness of the senses, rises to a higher nature. Thus, the liberation of the life within, through the response to the impacts from without, evokes the consciousness to move to a higher level. Thus, the body is the vehicle in which we experience Matter and raise it to the higher ideals of Spirit.

CHAPTER 10:

RULES OF THE SPIRITUAL BODY

Now that a spiritual body has been prepared, the next step is to inhabit it with living beings to "work it and keep it"; and bring forth the ideals that the Divine Mind envisioned. Rules and regulations must be established and obeyed by the residents to insure that a harmonious and productive state of consciousness is maintained. Thus, Genesis 2:15 through 2:20 details the inhabiting of the spiritual body and a simple rule required to insure an harmonious state of being.

Gen. 2:15 "And the LORD God took the man, and put him into the garden of Eden to dress it and to keep it."

LORD God means self-Existent, Eternal, or breath; and represents the Directive Inelligence which works upon the various levels of consciousness.

Took in Hebrew is *laqach* (law-kakh') which means to take, bring, carry away, fetch, or place.

Man in Hebrew is *adam* (aw-dawm') which means ruddy, a human being, an individual, or a person. Man is the universal symbol of mind in two aspects; a higher and lower mind. It signifies intellect, reason, intelligence, or mental qualities.

Put in Hebrew is *yanch* (yaw-nakh') which means to deposit, bestow, cast down, or place.

Garden symbolizes the spiritual body in which man dwells after the creation of spirit and the formation of the soul.

Eden in Hebrew is *heden* (ay'-den) which means pleasure, delight, time, season, or a place in Mesopotamia. Eden, metaphysically, is a pleasant, harmonious, productive state of consciousness in which all possibilities of growth are found.
Dress in Hebrew is *abad* (aw-bad') which means to work, serve, till, execute, bring to pass, or transgress.
Keep in Hebrew is *shamar* (shaw-mar') which means to hedge about, to protect, attend, take heed, observe, or preserve.

Metaphysically, this verse might read: **"And the directive intelligence took the mental qualities, and put them into the spiritual body of the harmonious state of consciousness to work it and observe it."**

The mental qualities, placed in the spiritual body, consist of two parts, a higher nature and a lower nature. The higher nature has the substance of Divine Mind (intelligence and Truth) and is unchanging and real; while the lower nature is based on perceptions from the material senses and desires, which constantly change and are thus unreal. The lower nature proceeds from the higher nature, but is always deficient as a copy of the higher nature, and is always in the process of becoming perfect. The lower nature cannot understand the higher nature, because the greater can contain the lesser, but lesser cannot contain the greater. The mental qualities have the faculties of intellect, reason and intelligence. The intellect is offended by the intelligence of the upper nature. It is stubborn, proud and unable to make an effort to progress and inherit the things of eternal life. The intellect is the formative factor and tends to limit its own activity, and so, cannot expand of itself sufficiently. Therefore, the effort of Spirit from above is needed to assist it. But the intellect, as is its nature, argues, discusses and must grow, or evolve, to its higher intelligent nature.

The Directive Intelligence places the mental qualities in an harmonious, productive state of consciousness to work the lower nature and observe it, that it may evolve to the intelligence of the upper nature of the mental qualities. At this point, the mental qualities are one with the Divine Mind. The higher and lower natures are *symbols* of the mental qualities of the human mind.

Gen. 2:16 "And the LORD God commanded the man, saying, Of every tree of the garden thou mayest freely eat":

> **LORD God** means self-Existent, Eternal, or breath; and represents the Directive Intelligence which works upon the various levels of consciousness.
> **Commanded** in Hebrew is *tsavah* (tsaw-vaw') which means to constitute, enjoin, appoint, bid, or charge.
> **Man** means ruddy, a human being, an individual, or person. Man is the universal symbol of the spirit-mind in two aspects of a higher and lower nature. It signifies intellect, reason, intelligence, or mental qualities.
> **Tree** in Hebrew is *ets* (ates) which means firmness, wood, stock, or timber. Tree signifies the connecting link between earth and heaven (between body and mind, the formless and the formed).
> **Garden** symbolizes the spiritual body in which man dwells after the creation of spirit-mind and the formation of the soul.
> **Eat** in Hebrew is *akal* (ak-al') which means burn up, consume, or devour.

Metaphysically, this verse might read: **"And Directive Intelligence enjoined the mental qualities, saying, Of every connecting link between the formed and formless of the spiritual body you may freely consume;"**

A tree is a clever comparison to a human being, just as the river was to human life. Trees, metaphysically, represent nerves, and nerves are expressions of thoughts of unity. Trees have their roots in the earth, but grow upward toward the light of the sky, or heavens. The human being is a smaller replica of the Divine Mind in whose image man was made. *As God is a Tree of Life, so man is also.* All things pertaining to a tree correspond to things of man; such as branches, leaves, flowers, fruit and seeds. Branches signify the sensual and natural truths in man, the leaves are his rational truths, flowers are the primitive spiritual truths in the rational mind, fruits are the good of love and charity, and the seeds are the last and first principles of man.

The Directive Intelligence encourages the mental qualities to freely consume of the formed (material) and the formless (spiritual) of the consciousness, and use this experience to discern the good of spiritual life and evolve to the perfect consciousness that the Divine Mind envisioned. Thus, the mental qualities must freely consume of both the Material and Spiritual aspects of life in order to understand that the material realm is simply a vehicle for obtaining knowledge that leads to the Truth of its being. Without the formless (Spirit), the formed would not be capable of discerning the Truth from the illusions of the physical world.

Gen. 2:17 "But of the tree of knowledge of good and evil, thou shalt not eat of it; for in the day that thou eatest thereof thou shalt surely die."

Tree signifies the connecting link between earth and heaven (between body and mind, the formless and the formed).

Knowledge in Hebrew is *daath* (dah'-ath) which means cunning, know, or awareness. Knowledge is knowing that you know.

Good in Hebrew is *towb* (tobe) which means a good thing, beautiful, bountiful, graciously, joyful, or pleasant.

Evil in Hebrew is *ra* (rah) which means bad, adversity, affliction, or distress, and is from the root word *raa* (raw-ah') which means to spoil, good for nothing, or mistake. Evil represents the missing of the spiritual mark.

Eat in Hebrew is *akal* (aw-kal') which means burn up, consume, devour, or dine.

Day in Hebrew is *yowm* (yome) which means to be hot, sunrise to sunset, continually, or chronicles. Day, metaphysically, represents understanding.
Eatest in Hebrew is the same as eat above.
Die in Hebrew is *muwth* (mooth) which means death, destroy, sly, or kill. Metaphysically, to die represents being unconscious to the Truth.

Metaphysically, this verse might read: **"But of the connecting link of the awareness of the beautiful and adverse, you shall not consume of it: for in the understanding that you consume of it you shall surely become unconscious to Truth."**

The literal interpretation of this verse has caused man to be fearful of God, and to impose death upon anyone who breaks one of the Divine Commandments. However, when one looks at the deeper spiritual message, a different perception appears. Death, or dying, is the letting go of the physical in favor of the spiritual. In reality, there is no such thing as death in the spiritual world, because life is eternal. In the unawakened consciousness, death in the physical world is always the result of a failure to recognize God as the source of wisdom and Life. When the soul falls short in this respect, it misses the mark and there is a physical dissolution that is but the outer symbol of mental negation or spiritual inertia. Even the Christ Consciousness, demonstrated by Jesus the Christ, had to transcend the physical world to be born into Spirit.

Once again the analogy of a tree helps to explain this verse. A branch that is separated from its source withers and dies. If man consumes of negative thoughts he will live in the darkened consciousness of his being, and will bring destruction upon himself. The negative thoughts will keep him from partaking of the precious life-giving spiritual fruits.

Note that the Directive Intelligence is not denying man anything, because he is already created perfect. The Directive Intelligence is simply warning that if this commandment is broken there will be a negative effect resulting from this decision (Law of Cause and Effect). That is, he will become unconscious to the spiritual Truth. Thus, the "tree of knowledge of good and evil" represents the discerning capacity of the mind. Man first perceives Truth; then he must discern the relation of ideas before perfect activity is set up within. If the mental quality does not consume negative thoughts, it will evolve to a higher level of consciousness without mental confusion. It is the mental confusion that causes us to become unconscious to the Truth.

Gen. 2:18 "And the LORD God said, It is not good that the man should be alone; I will make him a help meet for him."

LORD God means self-Existent, Eternal, or breath; and represents the Directive Intelligence which works upon the various levels of consciousness.

Good in Hebrew is *towb* (tobe) which means a good thing, beautiful, bountiful, gracious, joyful, or pleasant.

Man means ruddy, a human being, an individual, or person. Man is the universal symbol of mind in two aspects; a higher and a lower nature. It signifies intellect, reason, intelligence, or mental qualities.

Alone in Hebrew is *bad* (bad) which means separation, apart, only, or besides.

Make in Hebrew is *asah* (aw-saw') which means to do, accomplish, advance, appoint, bring forth, or bestow. 'Make', according to Webster's Dictionary, is to bring into being, knead, press, or physically or mentally build.

Help/Meet in Hebrew is *ezer* (ay'-zer') which means help, and comes from the root word *aza*r (aw-zar) which means to surround, protect, aid, or succor (assistance in time of distress, relief). It also represents an equal, mate, companion, or spouse.

Metaphysically, this verse might read: **"And the Directive Intelligence said, It is not a good thing that the mental**

qualities should be separated; I will appoint him an aid to help him."

It is not sufficient that the personal consciousness, or ego, be left alone to unfold to the perfect state of consciousness using only tools of reason and analysis, so the Directive Intelligence brings forth an aide that will provide relief in times of distress. The intellectual portion of the mental qualities need Love, Spirit, and intuition, before the personal consciousness can ascend to Higher consciousness levels. Choices made strictly from the intellect will always fall short of the goal of perfection, because reason and analysis separate information from the whole, and the resulting perceptions are always interpreted. The Christ Consciousness requires both Wisdom and Love, so it would not be gracious of the Directive Intelligence to give the mental qualities only intellect. *It is through Love that the intellect is raised to Spiritual Intelligence.*

Gen. 2:19 "And out of the ground the LORD God formed every beast of the field, and every fowl of the air; and brought them unto Adam to see what he would call them: and whatsoever Adam called every living creature, that was the name thereof."

Ground means soil, country, land, or earth. Ground is a symbol of the lower nature of the soul, which requires "tilling" and "sowing" to produce good "fruit".

LORD God means self-Existent, Eternal, or breath; and represents the Directive Intelligence which works upon the various levels of consciousness.

Formed in Hebrew is *yatsar* (yaw-tsar') which means to mold into a form, to press, fashion, or make. 'Formed', according to Webster's Dictionary, means "the shape or outline of anything; excluding color, texture, and density."

Beast in Hebrew is *clay* (khah'ee) which means alive, living thing, wild, life, or congregation. Beasts are symbolic of desires, passions, and instincts of the lower nature. The desires, passions, and instincts can sometimes feel wild and other times they are tamed or domesticated.

Field in Hebrew is *saday* (saw-dah'ee) which means to spread out, country, ground, land, or soil. Field is a symbol of the lower nature within which the soul's evolution takes place. *It is the field of experience.*

Fowl in Hebrew is *owph* (ofe) which means a bird (as covered with feathers, or rather, as coverings with wings), and is from the root word *uwph* (oof)) which means to cover (with wings, or obscurity). Birds are symbols of aspiration, or aspiring thoughts which soar heavenward in the mind (air). Birds were used by Jesus as illustrations of God's providence. In this connotation, I believe that "fowl of the air" refers to *free thoughts*.

Air in Hebrew is *shameh* (shaw-meh') which means lofty, the sky, the invisible, or heavens, and is a symbol of the mind of humanity. Air is the mid-plane between the lower plane (earth) and the upper plane (heaven). The higher, or spiritual mind, is the teacher of the soul in the lower mind, or physical world. In between are all things relating to perception, thought, and faith. Faith is of the thought according to the perception of understanding.

Adam in Hebrew is *adam* (aw-dawm') which means ruddy, a human being, or man, and is the name of the first man. Adam, metaphysically, represents the first movement of the mind in its contact with life and substance. It signifies the individual-man idea in consciousness.

Creature in Hebrew is *nephesh* (neh'-fesh) which means breathing creature, vitality, accommodated, sense (body and mental), body, or desire. Creatures are the symbol of the outgoing desires, passions, and emotions of the lower nature, which feed on instincts and sensations.

Name is a symbol of a mark, or memorial of individuality, authority, or character.

Metaphysically, this verse might read: **"And out of the lower nature of the soul, the Directive Intelligence molded**

every desire of the field of experience, and every aspiration of the human mind; and brought them to the individual-man idea to see what he would call them: And what the individual-man idea called every living desire, passion and emotion that was the nature thereof."

The Directive Intelligence molds the passions, desires, and emotions from the lower nature of the field of soul experiences, and brings them to the individual-man idea. The individual-man idea, or human being at this point, is the thinking part of the soul, and as such reasons and analyzes everything that it perceives. Through this process, the human being *gives authority to everything that it experiences.* Please note that the separation from God actually begins here in that the consciousness of the individual mind identifies and names everything the Directive Intelligence presents to it. Thus, everything is changed from what is, to what the personal consciousness wants it to be.

The naming process, by its very nature, requires an object to be removed from the whole and analyzed. The analysis process requires that the object be grouped according to unique characteristics (such as color, size, shape, special features, etc.) before giving it a name. In effect, the human being places a box around the object and gives it authority according to what is in the box, and ignores the relationship to everything that is outside the box. *Thus, the object is changed from what it is, to what he wants it to be.* From the very beginning, the personalized consciousness, or ego, receives what the Directive Intelligences gives it, separates it, and changes it to a form that is more acceptable to the personalized consciousness. The Directive Intelligence intended that the desires, passions and emotions be used as experiences that would help the mental qualities unfold in awareness to a higher plane of knowing. Instead, the mental qualities changed the experiences and perceived that *they* were the authority.

Gen. 2:20 "And Adam gave names to all cattle, and to the fowl of the air, and to every beast of the field; but for Adam there was not found a help meet for him."

Adam means ruddy, a human being, or man; and is the name of the first man. Adam, metaphysically, represents the first movement of the mind in its contact with life and substance. It signifies the individual-man idea in con - sciousness.

Name is a symbol of a mark, or memorial of individuality, authority, or character.

Cattle in Hebrew is *behemowth* (behay-mohth') which means to be muted, dumb, beast, or large quadruped animal. Cattle are symbols of emotions of the lower nature which are under the control of the higher nature (which implies domestication).

Fowl means a bird, and is a symbol of aspiration, or aspiring thoughts which soar heavenward in the mind (air).

Air means lofty, the sky, the invisible, or heavens, and is a symbol of the mind of humanity.

Beast means alive, living thing, wild, life, or congregation. Beasts are symbolic of desires, passions, and instincts of the lower nature.

Field means to spread out, country, ground, land, or soil. Field is a symbol of the lower nature within which the soul's evolution takes place. *It is the field of experence.*

Found in Hebrew is *matsa* (maw-tsaw') which means to come forth, appear, or exist.

Help/Meet in Hebrew is *ezer* (ay'-zer') which means help, and comes from the root word *aza*r (aw-zar) which means to surround, protect, aid, or succor (assistance in time of distress, relief)

Metaphysically, this verse might read: **"And the individual-man idea gave authority to all domesticated emotions, and to aspirations of the mind, and to every desire,**

passion and instinct of the field of experience; But for the individual-man idea there did not exist an aid for assistance in time of distress for him."

The mental aspect in its reasoning and analyzing was all alone, and not capable of handling the evolving emotional experiences without some assistance in times of distress. To evolve, the human mind requires more than just **Wisdom**; it must also have **Love,** which is of Spirit. When Wisdom and Love are united, they will produce the Christ. At this point, the human mind is not of the One Mind, but is an individual, personalized mind with a tendency to see things differently than the creator. Without a spiritual helper, the individual-man idea will lose spiritual illumination; because what it has is a second emanation of the creative ideal.

SUMMARY OF THE RULES OF THE SPIRITUAL BODY

The mental qualities consist of two components. The first is the upper mind, or nature, in which the substance of Intelligence and Truth are given from the Divine Mind. The upper nature, being based upon Truth, is unchanging and is real. The second is the lower mind, or nature, and is based on perceptions from the material senses and desires. The material senses and desires are constantly in the process of evolving to the Truth, and as such are always in the process of change. Thus, illusions are not real. The lower nature proceeds from the higher nature, but is a deficient copy of the higher nature. The lower nature cannot understand the higher nature, because it can only reason and analyze and must *evolve* to the state of intelligence. Thus, the intellect is offended by the intelligence of the upper nature, and is stubborn, proud and unable to inherit the things of eternal life. The intellect is the formative power of the mind, and tends to limit its own activity and cannot expand of itself. Therefore, the effort of Spirit from above is needed to assist it.

The Directive Intelligence places the mental qualities in the spiritual body. The spiritual body is a harmonious, productive state of consciousness designed to serve the lower nature, so that it can evolve to the Intelligence of the higher nature of the mental qualities. The Directive Intelligence encourages the mental qualities to freely consume of the material and spiritual components of the consciousness and use this experience to discern the good of spiritual life in order to evolve to the perfect consciousness that the Divine Mind envisioned. However, the Directive Intelligence forbids the mental qualities to consume of the connecting link of the awareness of the attractive and adverse, because once it has consumed of it, the mental qualities will become unconscious of the Truth. Thus, the Directive Intelligence is warning the mental qualities that there is an adverse effect if this commandment is broken. The adverse effect allows negative thoughts to enter the consciousness, which brings great confusion to the mental qualities. To eliminate the confusion, the mental qualities must first perceive the Truth; then must discern the Truth from the illusions, before perfect activity is acquired. Thus, the road of adversity was not imposed by the Directive Intelligence, but was freely chosen by the mental quality, in spite of the warning.

At this stage of development, the mental quality cannot unfold to the perfect stage of consciousness with only the tools of analysis and reason (intellect), so the Directive Intelligence brings forth assistance. Choices made strictly from the intellect will always fall short of the goal of perfection, because the intellect separates and analyzes everything. What it perceives must then be interpreted. So Spiritual qualities must be added in the form of emotions and desires. Eventually, analysis and reason will evolve to Wisdom and emotions and desires will evolve to Love. Thus, it is through Love that the intellect is raised to Spiritual Intelligence. The Directive Intelligence molds the passions, desires and emotions from the lower sensual nature and brings them to the mental quality to experience them and the mental quality gives names to everything that it experiences. In this process of naming, the mental quality changes what is, to what it wants it to be, and gives authority to it.

The mental quality in its reasoning and analyzing is still all alone, and not capable of handling the evolving experience without some assistance in times of distress. To evolve, the human mind requires more than just Wisdom, it must also have Love, which is of Spirit. When Wisdom and Love are united, they produce the Christ. At this point, the human mind, is not of the One Mind, but is an individual or personalized mind with a tendency to see things differently from the creator. Without a spiritual helper, the reasoning and analyzing mind will lose spiritual illumination. This happens because the spiritual helper is the feeling component which is derived from Love. Therefore, it is the feeling consciousness that ties the intellect (the reasoning and analyzing mind) to the principles of the Divine Mind. However, the feeling consciousness must also overcome the illusions of the outer manifestation to grow to Love in the same way that the intellect grows to Wisdom.

CHAPTER 11:

THE MAKING OF A SPIRITUAL HELPER

The mental quality in its reasoning and analyzing was still all alone, and not capable of handling the evolving experience without some assistance in times of distress. To evolve, the human mind requires more than just wisdom, it must also have love which is of Spirit. When Wisdom and Love are united they will produce the Christ. Thus, a spiritual helper must be made for the mental quality. Genesis 2:21 through 2:25 describes the making of this spiritual helper.

Gen. 2:21 "And the LORD God caused a deep sleep to fall upon Adam, and he slept: and he took one of his ribs, and closed up the flesh instead thereof."

LORD God means self-Existent, Eternal, or breath; and represents the Directive Intelligence which works upon the various levels of consciousness.

Deep in Hebrew is *tardemah* (tar-day-maw') which means lethargy, trance, or deep sleep, and is from the root word *radam* (raw-dam') which means stun, stupefy, or sleep.

Sleep in Hebrew is *yashen* (yaw-shane') which means to be slack or languid, to grow old, or remain long. Sleep is a condition of body rest where there is little or no conscious thought, sensation, or movement. This condition resembles death. Therefore, sleep is a symbol of a state of oblivion to spiritual enlightenment, or a state of unconsciousness of external things.

Fall in Hebrew is *naphal* (naw-fal') which means be accepted, cast down, cease, die, or divide. Fall is a symbol of the descent of the evolving soul, or consciousness, from higher to lower planes.

Adam means ruddy, a human being, or man; and is the name of the first man. Adam, metaphysically, represents the first movement of the mind in its contact with life and substance. It signifies the individual-man idea in consciousness.

Ribs in Hebrew is *tsalah* (tsal-aw') which means side, curve of the body, or an object. Ribs are a symbol of the spiritual nature to which the higher mental qualities of the soul are attached. Ribs in man are at right angles to the spinal column, and if the spinal cord is equal to the "tree of life", the rib is at cross purposes with life.

Flesh in Hebrew is *basar* (baw-sawr') which means to be fresh, full body, person, self, or skin. Flesh is a symbol of life in the lower nature in which the Spirit is involved. 'Flesh', according to Webster's Dictionary, means the body as distinguished from the soul. Thus, flesh in this connotation is the separation of the soul from Spirit.

Closed in Hebrew is *cagar* (saw-gar') which means to shut, to surrender, close up, deliver, or give over.

Instead in Hebrew is *tachath* (takh'-ath) which means the bottom, below, or underneath, and is from the root word *towach* (to'-akh) which means to depress, or humble.

Metaphysically, this verse might read: **"And the Directive Intelligence caused a trance, oblivious to spiritual enlightenment, to fall upon the individual-man idea, and he took one of his curved body members, and closed up the self underneath it."**

Please note that nowhere in the Bible does it say that the Directive Intelligence, God, or anyone awakens the individual-man idea in consciousness from this trance oblivious to spiritual enlightenment, which implies that the individual-man idea must awaken himself by experiencing life, discerning the illusions from the Truth, and choosing only things of Spirit. There are a number of passages that allude to man awakening to the Truth of Spirit: for example, "As for me, I will behold thy face in righteousness: I shall be satisfied, when I awake, with thy likeness" (Psalm 17:15). Jacob, in Genesis 28:12 -16, falls asleep and dreams of a ladder set up to reach between the earth and the heavens. Angels of God ascend and descend on this ladder, and at the top the Lord stood above it and spoke to Jacob: "And behold, I am with thee, and will keep thee in all places whither thou goest, and will bring thee again into this land; for I will not leave thee, until I have done that which I have spoken to thee of. And Jacob awakened out of his sleep, and he said, Surely the Lord is in this place; and I knew it not." Please note that Jacob, metaphysically, represents the "idea of Christ" in consciousness. The ladder set up reaching between heaven and earth is describing the collective consciousness that will unfold in degrees of awareness (land) to Spiritual Enlightenment. These verses indicate that the Lord, or Spirit, is with us always, from the most sensual and darkened spiritual state to the highest Spiritually enlightened state. Spirit is always there to help; all we need to do is to ask for assistance, and be willing to accept spiritual guidance. Spiritual enlightenment is there for the asking.

Gen. 2:22 "And the rib, which the LORD God had taken from man, made he a woman, and brought her unto the man".

Rib means side, curve of the body, or an object. Ribs are a symbol of the spiritual nature to which the higher mental qualities of the soul are attached.

LORD God means self-Existent, Eternal, or breath; and represents the Directive Intelligence which works upon the various levels of consciousness.

Man in Hebrew is the same as Adam. Adam, metaphysically, represents the first movement of the mind in its con-

tact with life and substance. Man is the universal symbol of spirit-mind in two aspects, higher mind or lower.
Made means to do, accomplish, bestow, bring forth, or commit. 'Made', according to Webster's Dictionary, is to shape, form, or artificially produced.
Woman in Hebrew is *nashiym* (naw-sheem") which means a female person, wife, or a mortal. Woman is a symbol of the emotional nature of the soul, which is to be transmuted from the astral to the Christ Consciousness.
Brought in Hebrew is *bow* (bo) which means to go or come, apply, besiege, bring forth, call, carry, depart, or employ.

Metaphysically, this verse might read: **"And the Spiritual Nature, which the Directive Intelligence had taken from mind, brought forth the emotional nature of the soul, and departed it unto the spirit-mind."**

The mental plane is the connection between the soul and the physical plane. The mental plane is of a higher state of consciousness (rib) and was specifically selected in accordance with the Divine scheme. It is the abode of the higher soul related to the Christ Consciousness. The Christ Consciousness is the Love in which the emotional-nature (woman) is to evolve. And so, a new factor was brought into relation with the lower mind. Woman, metaphysically, represents the unspiritualized love that is natural to the body. It is the feeling consciousness; the avenue through which the inspiration of Spirit comes.

The Directive Intelligence brings the feeling consciousness into the thinking consciousness of the lower mind. Whenever the illuminated Directive Intelligence centers its attention on the spiritual body there is at once a quickening of intelligence and a reaching out for higher things by the consciousness functioning there. Metaphysically, woman represents the unspiritualized love that is natural in the body. Thus, the soul has two aspects, a thinking component and a feeling component. When used together, they provide the necessary tools for the evolution from thinking to Wisdom, and from feeling to Love. Originally, the mind and emotions were not in conflict, for the desire had not yet entered. The first process within them was the instinctive, automatic fulfilling of their own truth. Unconsciously they acknowledged the Supreme source of their being. The Bible implies that the feminine in us partakes of both the good and evil. However, when the Directive Intelligence assumes mastery over the soul, it brings forth only the good.

Gen. 2:23 "And Adam said, This is now bone of my bones, and flesh of my flesh; she shall be called woman, because she was taken out of man."

Adam means ruddy, a human being, or man; and is the name of the first man. Adam, metaphysically, represents the first movement of the mind in its contact with life and substance. It signifies the individual-man idea in consciousness.

Bone/bones in Hebrew is *etsem* (eh'-tsem) which means strong bone, substance, body, and is from the root word *atsam* (aw-tsam) which means to bind fast, powerful, numerous, or to be increased. Bones are the symbol of the spiritual nature to which the higher and lower qualities of the soul are attached.

Flesh means to be fresh, full body, person, self, or skin. Flesh is the symbol of the desires and passions of the lower nature of spirit that envelopes the soul. 'Flesh', according to Webster's Dictionary, means the body as distinguished from the soul. Thus flesh in this connotation is the separation of the soul from the Spirit.

Woman means a female person, wife, or a mortal. Woman is a symbol of the emotional nature of the soul, which is to be transmuted from the astral to the Christ Consciousness.

Man is the universal symbol of spirit-mind in two aspects, higher mind or lower.

Metaphysically, this verse might read: "**And the individual-man idea in consciousness said, This is now the Spiritual Nature of my substance, and the envelope of my soul: it shall be called feeling consciousness, because it was taken out of spirit mind.**"

The mind acknowledges the better half of itself to be of its own substance, and recognizes in mind-emotion that which is apparently dual within the mind itself. The emotional element in the soul is the first to be implicated through desire; as signified in the story of the Garden of Eden, which will be discussed in detail in Part III of this book. Because the emotion-nature was formed from Adam, it must be subject to the dictates of the reasoning spirit-mind (man); thus, truth, justice, equity, peace and mercy are all suppressed in the soul. The emotion-nature must assert itself in an orderly manner, but it is not its function to teach and lead (I Timothy 2:11-15). The spiritual mind (Adam) at first is not affected by either the motives of the spirit above or the desires below. On the other hand the emotions (Eve) are functionally affected by the Spirit above and the desires below. The salvation of the emotion-nature is affected by it turning to the Holy Spirit, and, through purification (virginity), bringing forth the Christ in the mind, whereby both mind and emotions are freed from desire and the consciousness rises to a higher level.

According to Luke 24:39, Spirit does not have either flesh or bones. Therefore, this verse must be indicating that unspiritualized love (woman) is comprised of a substance that is different from that of Spirit, and yet has a substance similar to the individual-man idea consciousness. The soul is to have a spiritual body that is different from that of Spirit, or intelligence.

Gen. 2:24 "Therefore shall a man leave his father and mother, and shall cleave unto his wife; and they shall be of one flesh".

Man is the universal symbol of mind in two aspects, higher mind or lower. It is the thinking part of the mind.
Leave in Hebrew is *azab* (aw-zab') which means to loosen, relinquish, permit, forsake, fortify, or help.

Father in Hebrew is *ab* (awb) which means patrimony, principal, or chief. Father is the symbol of a prior and inferior condition of the soul which begets a superior. 'Father', according to Webster's Dictionary, is a protector or a male, or a thinking parent.
Mother in Hebrew is *em* (ame) which means bond of family, dam, or mother. Mother is a symbol of the feminine, or receptive aspect of the manifesting Spirit. 'Mother', according to Webster's Dictionary, is a female, feeling parent that gives birth.
Cleave in Hebrew is *dabaq* (daw-bak') which means to impinge, cling, adhere, be joined together, pursue hard, or stick to. 'Cleave', according to Webster's Dictionary, means to adhere, cling, or be faithful to.
Wife in Hebrew is *ishshah* (ish-shaw') which means woman, female, together or companion. Wife is a symbol of the emotion-nature in alliance with the mind.
Flesh means to be fresh, full body, person, self, or skin. Flesh is a symbol of the desires and passions of the lower nature of Spirit that envelopes the soul.

Metaphysically, this verse might read: **"Therefore shall the lower mind forsake his inferior condition of the soul and his receptive aspect of manifesting Spirit, and he shall join together unto his emotion-nature in alliance with the mind; and they shall be as one life in the lower nature."**

The literal interpretation of this verse has been used to justify marriage, in which both the bride and the groom leave their respective father and mother, and embark upon a new life together. At this stage of creation, there is no physical body in which to have sexual intercourse to produce future generations. So, it should be clear that the father and mother of the soul is not of the physical world. Since the individual-man idea was formed from the lower nature of desire and passion, it must leave this inferior condition and evolve to higher spiritual qualities. The mother principle directs the soul's evolution, and eventually, through intuition, the soul will rise to higher states of consciousness. Thus, there must be an alliance between the lower mind (man) and the emotion-nature (woman), and they must be as one soul to transform the life of the lower mind. The feminine aspect of the One shines forth and is the means of awakening the faint beginnings of true life in the soul. Emotion is the highest symbol of which any concept can be framed in the mind. Therefore, I believe that the father and mother mentioned in this verse are describing the elements of creation, which are both spiritual in nature. Thus, the thought and its feeling manifestation will become one soul.

Gen. 2:25 "And they were both naked, the man and his wife, and were not ashamed".

Naked in Hebrew is *arom* (aw-rome') which means nude, and is from the root word *aram* (aw-ram') which means to make bare. To be naked is to be unclothed, meaning the soul is exposed, and without spiritual covering or protection. However, nakedness is a symbol of purity, and is free from limitations and opinions (garments of the lower nature).

Man is the universal symbol of mind in two aspects, higher mind or lower. It is the thinking part of the mind.

Wife means woman, female, together or companion. Wife is a symbol of the emotion-nature in alliance with the mind.

Ashamed in Hebrew is *buwsh* (boosh) which means to pale, to be disappointed, cause, delayed, or shame.

Metaphysically, this verse might read: **"And they were both pure, the lower mind and his emotion-nature in alliance with the mind, and were not disappointed."**

Nakedness in this connotation is not referring to the soul as being exposed and without spiritual protection. The soul at this point is still residing in the Garden of Eden, is in complete harmony with the Divine ideals, and is thus protected by Spirit. So the soul is not disappointed with its new state, because the exalted emotions have cast away all limitation and restriction, and revealed the Truth within. This verse implies that the reasoning and analytical part of the mind are equal and balanced with the emotion-nature. Only when the desires of the lower nature take command is there a need for protective clothing, because the soul's purity is now masked by desire, and purity is replaced by shame.

SUMMARY OF THE MAKING OF A SPIRITUAL HELPER

From the very beginning, the Divine Mind envisioned a spiritual being that would experience the passions and desires of the lower mind, would overcome the attraction and adversity of this lower nature, and would become the master over it and grow into higher spiritual concepts. As the involution of Spirit progresses, the created personalized spirit becomes less like the Divine Mind. The created spiritual mind was formed into an "imperfect" individual-man idea, which could only reason and analyze, by design, what it experienced. Since this individual-man idea was not affected by motives of either the higher or lower minds, it was not capable of evolution within itself. Thinking begets thinking, and cannot evolve from an intellectual state to that of Spiritual Intelligence without the help of Spirit. So the Directive Intelligence placed the individualized-man idea into a trance oblivious to spiritual enlightenment, and made a helper for it. Both the individual-man idea and its helper were formed or made, and the True concepts of Spirit contaminated by these artificial creations. Thus, a trance was required to protect the original created spiritual mind. Since the individual-man idea was formed of the desires and passions of the lower nature, the helper must also be made from the same substance in order to maintain a perfect balance. Thus, the helper brings spiritual qualities to the individual-man idea. However, the helper is given only feelings and emotions, which are the lowest form of love, in order that it could also evolve.

The alliance of the individual-man idea and the emotion-nature becomes one living soul, and now the *evolutionary* process can begin. Thus, the soul, or spiritual mind, consists of a thinking and a feeling component. Because the thinking component came first, the soul is subject to the intellect first. Without the intellect, truth, justice, peace and mercy would be suppressed in the soul. The emotional component of the soul must assert itself in an orderly manner, but its function is not to teach or lead. Many religious bodies have misinterpreted this information as authority that women are inferior to men. This is clearly an error, as each one of us has both male and female characteristics in our being. The feminine aspect of the One shines forth and is the means of awakening the spiritual life in the soul. It is the female within us that directs the soul's evolution, and eventually, through intuition, the soul will transform life in the lower mind and evolve to the Christ Consciousness. Both intellect and emotions are required to evolve to the perfect Christ Consciousness that the Divine Mind envisioned. A problem exists only when the priority of the soul creates an imbalance where one has power over the other. The exalted emotions cast away all limitation and restriction, and reveal the Truth within, which indicates there is a state of balance, or equilibrium, between the two components. As long as there is balance between the two components of the soul, the spiritual mind will evolve to a higher understanding of Spiritual Truths.

PART III

THE GARDEN OF EDEN

CHAPTER 12:

THE TEMPTATION AND FALL

The soul in its first contact with life and substance, begins the process of evolution in the Garden of Eden. In the process of unfolding the consciousness to the higher awareness of Spirit, the soul encounters the temptations of the desires and passions of the lower nature of life. Thus, Genesis 3:1-7 describes the story of what happens to the soul in its first contact with substance.

Gen. 3:1 "Now the serpent was more subtle than any beast of the field which the LORD God had made, And he said unto the woman, Yea hath God said, Ye shall not eat of every tree in the garden?"

Serpent in Hebrew is *nachash* (naw-khawsh') which means a snake and is from the root word *nachash* (naw-khash') which means to hiss, whisper, a magic spell, enchantment, or learn by experience. Metaphysically, the serpent represents the spell of sense consciousness.

Subtle or subtil in Hebrew is *aruwm* (aw-room') which means cunning, crafty, or prudent.

Beast means alive, living thing, wild, or life; and is a symbol of the desires, passions, and instincts of the lower nature.

Field means spread out, country, ground, land, or soil; and is a symbol of the lower nature in which the soul's evolution takes place; the field of experience.

LORD God means the Self-existent, Eternal, and is the Directive Intelligence which works upon the various levels of consciousness.
Made means to do, accomplish, bring forth, or commit. 'Made', according to Webster's Dictionary, is to shape, form or artificially produce.
Woman means a female person, wife or a mortal; and is a symbol of the emotional-nature of the soul.
God is the general term for the Divine Mind.
Eat means to burn up, consume or devour.
Tree represents the connecting link between earth and heaven (body and mind, formed and formless).
Garden symbolizes the spiritual body in which man dwells in complete harmony with Divine Mind after the creation of the spirit and the formation of the soul.

Metaphysically, this verse might read: **"Now the sense consciousness was more cunning than any desire or passion of the lower nature of the field of experiences which the Directive Intelligence had artificially produced. And the sense consciousness said unto the emotional-nature of the soul, Did Divine Mind say, You shall not consume of every connecting link between body and mind of the spiritual body?"**

A serpent is often used in the Bible to describe Satan (Angel of Light in 2 Corinthians 11:14 and Satan in Revelations 12:9, 12:14, 12:15, and 20:2). Many varieties of serpents are beautiful and very graceful. Without conditioning the conscious mind to believe that serpents are undesirable, bad, hurtful or evil; the serpent would appear to be a thing of beauty and very attractive to the feeling consciousness. The serpent is often called desire, sensation, or the activity of life in an external expression apart from the Source of life. When the serpent is lifted to the realization that it is Spirit, it becomes healing. This is illustrated by Moses when he lifts up the serpent in the wilderness, and is the reason that the medical profession uses the serpent in its logo.

Now the Sense Consciousness was more cunning and precise than the other desires, passions, and instincts of the lower mind and asks the emotional-nature, "Did the Directive Intelligence say that you could not consume of every connecting link between the body and the mind of the spiritual body?" This is a logical question to the Sense Consciousness, because everything in the spiritual body that is beautiful and desirable is to be enjoyed or consumed.

Gen. 3:2 "And the woman said unto the serpent, We may eat of the fruit of the trees of the garden:"

Woman means a female person, wife, or a mortal; and is a symbol of the emotional-nature of the soul.

Serpent means a snake and, metaphysically, represents the spell of the sense consciousness.

Eat means to burn up, consume, or devour.

Fruit in Hebrew is *periy* (per-ee') which means reward, and is from the root word *parah* (paw-raw) which means to bear fruit, bring forth, fruitful, grow or increase. Fruit, metaphysically, represents the reward of consciousness of spiritual life directly from the Source.

Tree represents the connecting link between earth and heaven (body and mind, formed and formless).

Garden symbolizes the spiritual body in which man dwells in complete harmony with the Divine Mind after the creation of the spirit and the formation of the soul.

Metaphysically, this verse might read: "**And the emotional-nature of the soul said unto the sense consciousness, We may consume of the consciousness of spiritual life of the connecting link between body and mind of the spiritual body:**"

When one consumes of the spiritual consciousness directly from the Source, the resulting experience of the connecting link between the mental and the emotional parts of the soul will lead to spiritual understanding and knowing. There is no confusion of the soul, in spite of the desires, passions and instincts of the lower mind, because the Effect of the experience comes directly from the Cause (Divine Mind). Therefore, there is no need to interpret the experience. Without mind confusion, Truth is received as Truth.

Gen. 3:3 "But of the fruit of the tree which is in the midst of the garden, God hath said, Ye shall not eat of it, neither shall ye touch it, lest ye die."

Fruit means reward, bring forth, fruitful, grow or increase. 'Fruit', metaphysically, represents the consciousness' reward of spiritual life directly from the Source.

Tree represents the connecting link between earth and heaven (body and mind, formed and formless).

Midst in Hebrew is *tavek* (taw'-vek) which means center, among, between, half, or middle.

Garden symbolizes the spiritual body in which man dwells in complete harmony with the Divine Mind after the creation of the spirit and the formation of the soul.

God is the general term for the Divine Mind.

Eat means to burn up, consume, or devour.

Touch in Hebrew is *naga* (naw-gah') which means lay the hand upon, draw near, or join.

Lest in Hebrew is *pen* (pane) which means removal, and is from the root word *panah* (paw-naw') meaning to turn, look, or behold. According to Webster's Dictionary, 'lest' means, "for fear that".

Die in Hebrew is *muwth* (mooth) which means to die, to kill, or to destroy; and represents being unconscious of Truth. Death, or dying, is that state of negation in man's consciousness where he no longer can retain possession of his body.

Metaphysically, this verse might read: **"But of the spiritual life of the connecting link between the body and mind which is in the middle of the spiritual body, Divine Mind has said, You shall not consume of it, neither shall you draw near it, for fear that you become unconscious of Truth."**

The connecting link between earth and heaven is the *human mind.* It is the mind that discerns information between Spirit and the spiritual body, and as such acts as an interpreter. The Divine Mind needs no interpretation. Therefore, the use of this connecting link will *distort* the Truth and the Reality of being, which is detrimental to the soul's spiritual development. Man is not being denied anything, because he is already created perfect. Divine Mind knew that man was not prepared to handle both good and negative thoughts (good and evil), without losing his spiritual identity. Thus, the commandment was intended to save the soul from itself.

Note that a distinction is being made in this verse; *God,* rather than the *LORD God* (Jehovah), instructed both the man and the woman not to eat of the fruit. This commandment, then, comes directly from the Source.

Gen. 3:4 "And the serpent said unto the woman, Ye shall not surely die:"

> **Serpent** means a snake and, metaphysically, represents the spell of the sense consciousness.
> **Woman** means a female person, wife, or a mortal; and is a symbol of the emotional-nature of the soul.
> **Die** means to kill, or to destroy; and represents being unconscious of Truth. Death, or dying, is that state of negation in man's consciousness wherein he no longer can retain possession of his body.

Metaphysically, this verse might read: **"And the sense consciousness said unto the emotional-nature of the soul, You shall not surely lose consciousness of Truth;"**

From the sense consciousness' perspective, eating of the forbidden fruit would not cause the emotional-nature of the soul to die, because life is eternal. The sense consciousness always interprets everything it experiences according to how it perceives it. The Sense Consciousness' interpretation is always of the lower mind, and thus, beguiles us away from True Spiritual values.

In the unawakened consciousness, death in the physical world is always the result of a failure to recognize God as the source of wisdom and Life. When the soul falls short in this respect, it misses the mark, or sins, and there is a physical dissolution of the outer symbol of mental negation or spiritual inertia. Since life is eternal, death then implies that the human consciousness rises to a higher level after leaving the physical body. Since the personal consciousness is mortal, it disappears and unites with the immortal Individuality at the end of the cycle. "For since by man came death, by man came also the resurrection of the dead. For as in Adam all die, so also in Christ shall all be made alive". (1 Corinthians 15:21 & 22).

Gen. 3:5 "For God doth know that in the day ye eat thereof, then your eyes shall be opened, and ye shall be as God, knowing good and evil".

God is the general term for the Divine Mind.

Know/knowing in Hebrew is *yada* (yaw-dah") which means knowledge, observation, recognize, acknowledge, or being aware.

Day in Hebrew is *yowm* (yome) which means to be hot, one sunrise to sunset, or full life. Metaphysically, day means understanding.

Eat means to burn up, consume, or devour.

Eyes in Hebrew is *ayin* (ah'-yin) which means eye, affliction, outward appearance, look, or sight; and is the symbol of mental perception.

Opened in Hebrew is *paqach* (paw-kakh') which means to be observant, or open the senses.

Good in Hebrew is *towb* (tobe) which means beautiful, cheerful, or pleasant; and is a symbol of perfection.

Evil in Hebrew is *ra* (rah) which means bad, adversity, affliction, or calamity; and is from the root word *raa* (raw-ah') which means to spoil.

Metaphysically, this verse might read: **"For Divine Mind does know that in the understanding you consume of**

it, then your mental perception shall be observant, and you shall be as Divine Mind, knowing perfection and adversity."

The sense consciousness, being more precise, interprets what God said. The sense consciousness did not tell an untruth, it simply left out the most important information. That is, there is an adverse consequence associated with the choice. The Divine Mind knew that once the forbidden fruit was tasted, mental perceptions would be experienced, the consciousness would merge with the non-spiritual and spoil the pure intent of the lower mind. The mental perceptions of desire, passion and instincts contaminate the consciousness, resulting in mental confusion. Thus, the sense consciousness beguiles the emotional-nature of the soul.

Gen. 3:6 "And when the woman saw that the tree was good for food, and that it was pleasant to the eyes, and a tree to be desired to make one wise, she took of the fruit thereof, and did eat, and gave unto her husband with her; and he did eat."

Woman means a female person, wife or a mortal; and is a symbol of the emotional-nature of the soul.

Tree represents the connecting link between earth and heaven (body and mind, formed and formless). In this case the connecting link is the mind, or mental-nature.

Good means beautiful, cheerful or pleasant; and is a symbol of perfection.

Food in Hebrew is *maakal* (mah-ak-awl') which means eatable, and is from the root word *akak* (aw-kal') meaning to eat, devour or consume. Food is the symbol of Truth, or the Real, which gradually takes the place of illusions, or the unreal. This is where the phrase, "food for thought" comes from.

Pleasant in Hebrew is *taavah* (tah-av-aw') which means longing, delight, satisfaction or desire.

Eyes means eyes, affliction, outward appearance, look or sight; and is the symbol of mental perceptions.

Desired in Hebrew is *chamad* (khaw-mad') which means delight in, beauty, greatly beloved, delectable thing, desire or lust.
Make in Hebrew is *asah* (aw-saw') which means to do, accomplish, advance, bestow or become.
Wise in Hebrew is *sakal* (saw-kal') which means intelligent, has good success, to teach or to understand.
Fruit means reward, bring forth, fruitful, grow or increase. 'Fruit', metaphysically, represents the consciousness' reward of spiritual life directly from the Source.
Eat means to burn up, consume or devour.
Husband in Hebrew is *iyah* (eesh) which means a man as an individual or a male person, a companion or a servant; and is the symbol of the mental-nature united with the soul.

Metaphysically, this verse might read: "**And when the emotional-nature of the soul saw that the mind was perfect for Truth, and that it was delightful to the mental perception, and a connecting link to be desired to advance the intelligence, it took of the spiritual life directly from the Source, and did consume, and gave to the mental-nature of the soul with it; and it did consume.**"

To the emotional-nature the forbidden fruit is something to be desired because it enlarges the consciousness to the Truth. Knowledge reflects truth, and truth permeates knowledge. However, the imperfect knowledge of the lower mind is based on mental perceptions, which no longer represent the Truth; and what is Real is inverted by the desires, passions and emotions of the lower nature. Once Truth has been inverted to an illusion, or something unreal, the soul consumes the unreal and replaces that which is True. Now the soul must transmute the illusion to what is Real through experience, and choose what is Real in order to return to the Truth again. Truth is from all eternity, and is the supporter and healer of all qualities which are deficient of itself. Therefore, it is through the growth of the emotions and the regulation and mastery of the burning desires of the lower nature that the healing truth is obtained. The phrase "pleasant to the eyes" indicates the eyes are looking through the sensual feeling capacity of the consciousness, as opposed to spiritual vision.

The phrase "to make one wise" is indicating that the intellect (mental-nature) is also affected by the desires of the sense consciousness. The intellect is of man, and intelligence is of God. Thus, the joined soul desired to *be* God, and not just to serve HIM.

Gen. 3:7 "And the eyes of them both were opened, and they knew that they were naked; and they sewed fig leaves together, and made themselves aprons."

Eyes means eyes, affliction, outward appearance, look and sight; and is the symbol of mental perceptions.

Both in Hebrew is *shenayim* (shen-ah'-yim) which means twofold or couple. In this case "both" represents the joined emotional and mental nature of the soul.

Opened means to be observant or to open the senses.

Knew means to know, recognition, observe, recognize or understanding.

Naked means nude or bare. To be naked is to be unclothed, meaning the soul is exposed and without spiritual covering or protection.

Sewed in Hebrew is *taphar* (taw-far') which means sew together.

Fig Leaves are from a fig tree which is the symbol of Divine Life, and represent the spiritual growth unobserved by the lower nature.

Aprons in Hebrew is *chagorah* (khag-o-raw') which means a belt, and is from the root word *chagar* (khaw-gar') meaning girded with, to put on, to be afraid or to restrain. 'Apron', according to Webster's Dictionary, is a garment worn over the front part of the body, which implies hiding of the sexual organs.

Metaphysically, this verse might read: "**And the mental perceptions of both of them were observant, and they recognized that they were bare, and they sewed together a belt of Divine Life.**"

The mental perception observes that the soul is without clothing, and experiencing the effect of the lower nature, as opposed to the truth. Now, both the emotional-nature and the mental-nature of the soul perceive their utter ignorance and the loss of Truth as the protective covering. Then the emotional-nature and the mind cover themselves with secrecy, and conceal the inward growth of the Spirit. Thus, they feel guilty about their bodies and try to hide them. Nudity is associated with sensual thoughts, and must be hidden. It is not being nude that misses the mark, but the perception of passion that is associated with nudity that causes the problem. So they try to repress, or hide their desires and passions in order to maintain their innocence.

SUMMARY OF THE TEMPTATION AND FALL

The soul is created from the substance of the lower nature of the mind as well as from the spiritual ideals of the higher mind. The soul is then placed in a spiritual body that is in complete harmony with the Divine Mind. It was always the intent of the Divine Mind that the soul would evolve from the lower level of desire, passion and instinct to the higher spiritual level based on Truth. This evolution is accomplished in the field of experience according to the original Divine Ideals envisioned for the soul. That is, the soul evolves in an environment where only Truth exists. To accomplish the desired goal, the Directive Intelligence commands the soul not to eat of the tree of good and evil, because if the soul consumes of Truth and error thoughts, the mind is forced to choose between them. To choose correctly is to be as God, and discern between that which supports positive growth and that which hinders spiritual growth. The soul was not created with spiritual discernment, and so, it is not capable of separating Truth from illusions. Thus, the mind becomes confused, and the soul loses spiritual consciousness.

The Sense Consciousness, or serpent, asks the emotional-nature of the soul whether the emotional-nature could eat of every fruit of the garden. The emotional-nature indicates that the soul can consume of all rewards (fruit) of the connecting link between Spirit and desire, except of the tree of good and evil in the middle of the garden, for if they consumed of this fruit they will die. The connecting link between Spirit and desire, in the spiritual body, is the **mind**; which was not designed to have spiritual discernment; so the result is mental confusion. As long as the Truth flows directly from the higher mind to the lower mind, the communication remains pure, but if the communication is interpreted by the human mind, confusion will always be the result.

The serpent, and other animals of the garden, did not apparently have this restriction, and so the serpent tells the emotional-nature of the soul that "she will not surely die", because life is eternal, and if she consumes of the forbidden fruit her eyes will be opened to the Spiritual Truth and she will know perfection and adversity. What the serpent did not say, is that with this action comes a negative Effect, and adversity is the result. Instead of evolving to perfection in complete harmony with the Divine Mind, the soul will now experience adversity, pain and sorrow, and will struggle with the desires and passions of life, in order to become perfect. The end goal is the same, but the journey is completely different.

Both the emotional and mental components of the soul are beguiled by the Sense Consciousness, and they consume of the forbidden fruit in order to become as God and have intelligence. Intellect is of the evolving soul, and intelligence is of God. In other words, the soul is not willing to *evolve* to spiritual intelligence, but rather wants it now. The soul is not content to be what it is, and attempts to change the situation to what it wants it to be.

The result of this action brings into play mental perceptions, which change perceptions to something that is not based on the Truth. Now the soul is exposed to the illusions of ignorance and loses the protective covering of Truth. The emotions and mind cover themselves with secrecy and conceal the inward growth of the spirit.

CHAPTER 13:

EGO DYNAMICS

With the consuming of both good and evil thoughts, the discerning mind becomes confused, and a new dominating force attempts to take over the evolutionary process from the Directive Intelligence. This new directive force is called the self will, the personal consciousness, or the ego. Thus, Genesis 3:8 through 3:13 describes the dynamics of this new directive force.

Gen. 3:8 "And they heard the voice of the LORD God walking in the garden in the cool of the day: and Adam and his wife hid themselves from the presence of the LORD God among the trees of the garden".

Heard in Hebrew is *shama* (shaw-mah) which means to hear intelligently, attention, discern, give ear or perceive.

Voice in Hebrew is *qol* (kole) which means to call aloud, sound, cry, lightness or proclamation.

LORD God means the Self-existent, Eternal, and is the Directive Intelligence which works upon the various levels of consciousness.

Walking in Hebrew is *halak* (haw-lak') which means along, continually, be conversant or enter.

Garden represents the spiritual body that is in complete harmony with the Divine Mind.

Cool in Hebrew is *ruwach* (roo-akh') which means wind, breath, spirit or rational being; and is from the root word *ruvach* (roo'-vakh) meaning to blow, breath or make of quick understanding.

Day, metaphysically, means understanding.
Adam represents the first movement of the mind in its contact with life and substance. Adam also epitomizes the individual-will idea in consciousness.
Wife represents woman, female, together or companion. Wife is a symbol of the emotional-nature in alliance with the mind.
Hid in Hebrew is *chaba* (khaw-baw') which means secrecy, to hide the self, conceal or do secretly.
Presence in Hebrew is *paneh* (paw-neh') which means the face, heaviness, form or prospect.
Tree represents the connecting link between earth and heaven (body and mind, formed and formless).

Metaphysically, this verse might read: "**And they perceived the proclamation of the Directive Intelligence entering into the spiritual body in the wind of understanding, and the individual-man idea and his emotional-nature concealed themselves from the prospect of the Directive Intelligence among the mental qualities (the connecting links between the body and mind) of the spiritual body.**"

Symbols such as heard, voice, walking, and cool are words of the physical world, and as such appear to be out of place in describing a spiritual body. These words, I believe, were used to highlight the concept of mental perception, as opposed to *knowing* the presence of the Directive Intelligence. Once the soul's eyes are opened to mental perception and the desires and passions of the lower nature are consumed, the soul feels ashamed, and tries to hide its action from the Directive Intelligence. The phrase "hid themselves" is the first indication of the Effect of their action, which is *Guilt*. Guilt is a feeling associated with doing something wrong. This feeling replaces the feeling of Love in the Garden of Eden. Guilt is always disruptive, because being unreal, it is an attack on the Directive Intelligence. As long as we believe that guilt is justified in any way, we will not look within for guidance, and separation will result. Thus, guilt replaces love through the mind's perception. Nothing has really changed, except how we perceive the situation! We now perceive that we have sinned against our creator, and we try to hide from Him among the mental qualities of the spiritual body.

Gen. 3:9 "And the LORD God called unto Adam, and said unto him, Where art thou?"

LORD God means the Self-existent, Eternal, and is the Directive Intelligence which works upon the various levels of consciousness.

Called in Hebrew is *qara* (kaw-raw') which means to call out, address, proclaim, or pronounce.

Adam represents the first movement of the mind in its contact with life and substance. Adam also epitomizes the individual-will idea in consciousness.

Metaphysically, this verse might read: **"And the Directive Intelligence calls out to the individual-will idea, and said to it, 'Where are you?'"**

This verse implies that the soul is lost to the spiritual body, thus the Directive Intelligence must inquire where the individual-man idea in consciousness has placed itself. Hiding in the mental qualities of the mind separates the soul from Spirit.

Gen. 3:10 "And he said, I heard thy voice in the garden, and I was afraid, because I was naked; and I hid myself."

Heard means to hear intelligently, attention, discern, give ear, or perceive.

Voice means to call aloud, sound, cry, lightness, or proclamation.

Garden represents the spiritual body that is in complete harmony with the Divine Mind.

Afraid in Hebrew is *yare* (yaw-ray') which means to fear, to frighten, dread, or revere.

Naked means nude or make bare. Naked is to be unclothed, meaning the soul is exposed and without spiritual covering or protection.

Hid means secrecy, hide the self, conceal or do secretly.

Metaphysically, this verse might read: "**And the individual-man idea said, I perceived your proclamation in the spiritual body, and I was frightened, because I was without spiritual protection; and I concealed myself.**"

The second effect of the decision to consume of the forbidden fruit is *Fear*. Fear is brought about by the guilt associated with the misperception of usurping the power of the Divine Mind. Of course, in reality the individual-man idea does not have the ability to usurp this power, but the perception of the mind *believes* that it can. To usurp the power of the Directive Intelligence must be a "sin", according to the reasoning mind, and it becomes afraid that the Directive Intelligence will punish it for this action. *Guilt always demands punishment*. Rather than accepting the responsibility for the error, the individual-man idea invents the perception of SIN. Sin is always done in secret and must be concealed, so the individual-man idea conceals himself from the Directive Intelligence. Sin is the failure to obey, which is the cornerstone of the concept of separation. Separation produces guilt, and guilt creates fear of being punished by the Directive Intelligence. This is a very complex way to justify being disobedient, and can be perceived only by an ignorant mind in denial of the Truth. Sin is simply an error that needs correcting. I like to think of SIN as an acronym for <u>S</u>elf <u>I</u>mposed <u>N</u>onsense.

Gen. 3:11 "And he said, Who told thee that thou wast naked? Hast thou eaten of the tree, whereof I commanded thee that thou shouldest not eat?"

Naked is to be unclothed, meaning the soul is exposed, and without spiritual covering or protection.

Eaten/eat means to burn up, consume, or devour.

Tree represents the connecting link between earth and heaven (body and mind, formed and formless). In this case "tree" represents the perceptive mind.
Commanded in Hebrew is *tsavah* (tsaw-vaw') which means to constitute, enjoin, appoint, charge, or send a messenger.

Metaphysically, this verse might read: **"And Directive Intelligence said, Who told you that you were without spiritual protection? Have you consumed of the perceptive mind, that I commanded you that you should not consume?"**

Only in the perceptive mind does the individual-man idea think that he does not have spiritual protection. The Directive Intelligence knows that this is an illusion, and knows immediately that the individual-man idea has consumed of the tree of good and evil (the perceptive mind). Only the desires and passions resulting from the misperception of nudity would perceive it as bad. The purity of innocence never perceives a naked body as anything other than natural. After all, this is the condition in which we enter into this world; and children are symbols of innocence.

Gen. 3:12 "And the man said, the woman whom thou gavest to be with me, she gave me of the tree, and I did eat."

Man means ruddy, a human being, an individual, or person; and, metaphysically, is the universal symbol of mind in two aspects; a higher and lower nature. It signifies intellect, reason, intelligence, or mental qualities.
Woman means a female person, wife, or a mortal; and is a symbol of the emotional-nature of the soul.
Gavest in Hebrew is *nathan* (naw-than') which means add, apply, appoint, ascribe, or assign.
Tree represents the connecting link between earth and heaven (body and mind, formed and formless). In this case, "tree" represents the perceptive mind.

Eat means to burn up, consume, or devour.

Metaphysically, this verse might read: **"And the mental qualities said, the emotional-nature that you assigned to me, she gave me of the perceptive mind, and I did consume."**

When confronted, the mental quality shifts the responsibility from itself, by projecting the *blame,* to the emotional-nature of the soul. The mental quality attacks the emotional-nature, because it believes the emotional-nature has deprived it of the spiritual body. By feeling deprived, and projecting its own rejection, the mental quality believes that the emotional-nature is trying to take the spiritual body away from it. The best way to protect one's innocence, according to the mental quality, is to project the guilt and blame onto someone else. This may work for a short period of time, but sooner or later the attack results in more guilt, because at some level the mind knows it is not taking responsibility; and the guilt process is repeated again and again. Thus, the attack equates the mental quality with the desires of the lower mind, or body, and denies that it is of Spirit.

Gen. 3:13 "And the LORD God said unto the woman, What is this that thou hast done? And the woman said, The serpent beguiled me, and I did eat."

LORD God means the Self-existent, Eternal, and is the Directive Intelligence which works upon the various levels of consciousness.

Woman means a female person, wife, or a mortal; and is a symbol of the emotional-nature of the soul.

Serpent means snake, and represents the sense consciousness.

Beguiled in Hebrew is *nasha* (naw-shaw') which means to lead astray, mentally delude, seduce, or deceive.

Metaphysically, this verse might read: **"And the Directive Intelligence said to the emotional-nature, 'What is this**

that you have done?' And the emotional-nature said, 'The sense consciousness deceived me, and I did consume.'"

The emotional-nature of the soul also refuses to take responsibility for its action and blames the sense consciousness. The mental and emotional qualities, under the dominion of the desires and passions of the lower mind, do not see the situation as an opportunity for the soul to spiritually grow. Instead, both the mental and emotional natures of the soul blame someone, or something else, for their perception of sin. Projection is part of the mind quality that does not believe it is responsible for itself, and being without the assistance of the Directive Intelligence, the self-will, or ego, is incapable of trust. It projects its insane belief that someone else has been treacherous to the Creator, and is trying to take the Directive Intelligence from it. Projection always sees its wish in others. Thus, the total consciousness has fallen under the spell of the sense consciousness and the soul becomes separated from the Directive Intelligence.

SUMMARY OF THE EGO DYNAMICS

Genesis 3:8 through 3:13 describes the formation of the mental self-will, or ego, and its mode of operation. The ego is the questioning aspect of the post-separation self, and is capable of asking questions, but not of perceiving meaningful answers. This is because answers involve knowledge, which cannot be perceived. The mind is, therefore, confused, and in conflict because it is out of accord with itself. Thus, the ego is nothing more than a part of its belief about itself, and is part of the mind that believes in separation. The ego has an authority problem based on the concept of usurping the Divine Mind's power. The ego believes that the soul has usurped the power of the Divine Mind and the soul perceives itself as guilty. Whenever the soul responds to the ego it will experience guilt and fear punishment. The ego is quite literally a fearful thought. Since the ego believes in separation, and is of the mental plane that the Directive Intelligence forbids the soul to consume, it is extremely important that we understand its dynamics. Understanding the dynamics of the ego will result in knowledge. Knowledge will set us free of the egos ridiculous beliefs in separation.

Figure 9 illustrates the Ego Dynamics Model. Because the ego is counter productive, the information is presented in a counterclockwise flow. However, time is also of the ego, and time flows in a clockwise direction. Therefore, the flow could be in either direction. What is important is the sequence of the model and not the direction of the flow.

The whole cornerstone of the ego dynamics is the belief that we have separated from the Divine Mind, or God. *Sin* is the symbol of separation, and is based on the firm conviction that minds can attack, and, thus, the mind is guilty, and will remain so until a mind not a part of it can give it absolution. ***"Sin is not an error, for sin entails an arrogance which the idea of error lacks. To sin would be to violate reality, and to succeed! This is the arrogance of the ego, because it beieves that attack is real and guilt is justified."*** (ACIM Text Book 374 to 375) The reality is, sin is but a mistake in judgment that needs correction. As a mistake, it can be brought to truth. When the soul accepts the ego's premise, it senses the loss of peace and harmony, perceives that it is lacking and in conflict with every thing around it, and fears for its safety.

Feelings of scarcity, conflict, and suffering bring the soul to accept that it is guilty. *Guilt* establishes sin's reality because the soul believes that it has attacked the Divine Mind. Thus, guilt is always disruptive to the spiritual process of evolution. ***"For guilt establishes that you will be punished for what you have done, and thus depends on one-dimensional time, proceeding from the past to future. Guilt, then, is a way of holding past and future in your mind to en- sure the ego's continuity is guaranteed."*** (ACIM Text Book 222) As long as the soul believes that guilt is justified, it will not look within to discover the spiritual truth. Guilt has no useful function at all, and its attraction is found in sin, and not error. As long as the guilt remains, the mind will suffer.

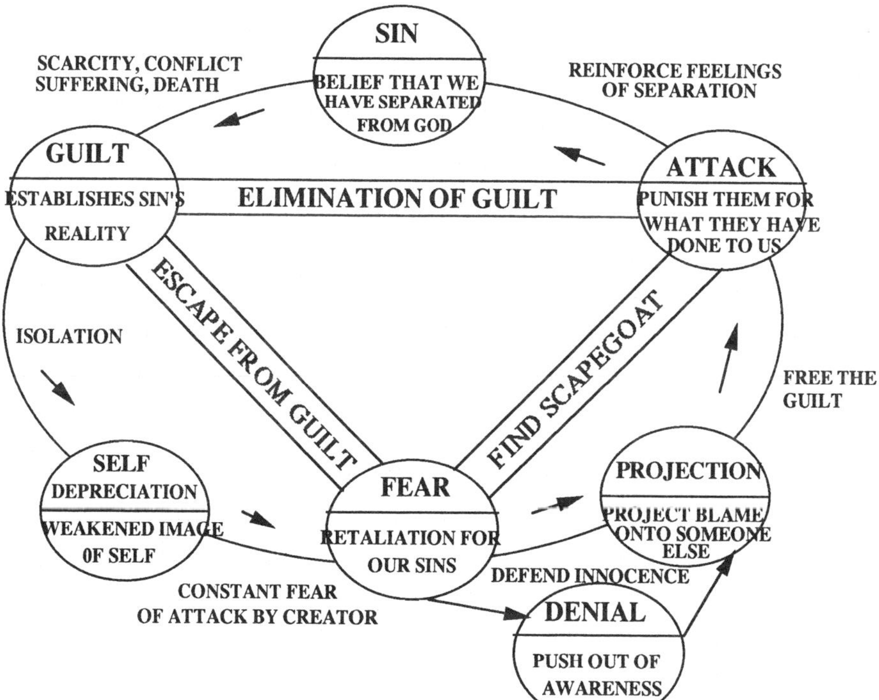

FIGURE 9 - EGO DYNAMICS MODEL

With the acceptance of guilt, the soul is isolated from the truth, and there begins the weakening of the image of the individualized-man idea. The denial of Self results in illusions, while correction of the error brings a release from it. ***"...the ego... always evaluates itself in relation to other egos. It is, therefore, continually preoccupied with the belief in scarcity that gave rise to it. Its whole perception of other egos as real is only an attempt to convince itself that it is real. "Self-esteem" is always vulnerable to stress, a term which refers to any perceived threat to the ego's existence."*** (ACIM Text Book 52) The ego always attempts to gain spirit's acknowledgement and, thus, establish its own existence, but Spirit in its knowledge is unaware of the ego. While the ego is equally unaware of spirit; it does perceive itself as being rejected by something greater than itself. This is why self-esteem in ego terms must be delusional. When the soul excludes any part of the Spirit, it is no longer whole. A split mind cannot perceive its fullness and needs the miracle of wholeness to dawn upon it and heal it. In its separated mind, it is in constant fear that the Directive Intelligence will punish it for its imaginary sins.

Fear is ultimately the misperception that the soul can usurp the the power of the Divine Mind, and the Directive Intelligence will retaliate against the soul and punish it. Major crimes are always punishable by death. Of course, the soul does not have the ability to usurp the power of the Divine mind. But the unawakened mind believes it has done just that, and is in total terror. ***"Only after the deep sleep fell upon Adam could he experience nightmares. If a light is suddenly turned on while someone is dreaming a fearful dream, he may initially interpret the light itself as part of his dream and be afraid of it. However, when he awakens, the light is correctly perceived as the release from the dream, which is then no longer accorded reality."*** (ACIM Text Book 15) The correction of fear is the acceptance that the error never really occurred. Fear is a symptom of a deep sense of loss in the past. Therefore, the escape from fear is to bring it to the truth of the present, because Spirit only resides in the present and fear does not exist there. Fear is only possible in the past and the future. This is why the ego attempts to bypass the present by building a bridge from the past to the future. This is a bridge that leads nowhere.

In the unawakened mind, there are two ways to escape fear. The first is *Denial*. Denial is the attempt to defend our innocence by pushing the concept of sin from the mind and denying that it exists. This may work for a short time, but there is a part of the mind that knows what we have done, so eventually the guilt will return. The second technique is to *project* the blame onto someone else. What the ego projects, it attempts to disown (the guilt that it feels), while at the same time it tries to protect its innocence. In order for the mind to project, it must also judge as guilty that which is being attacked. The projection and future attack reinforce separation, because it strengthens the belief in the illusion of the split mind. The ego imagines it is safe, because it has projected the guilt out of its mind. What is out of mind is out of sight. Projection and attack always go together, because projection is always a means of justifying the attack. Anger without projection is impossible. Projection is simply the denial of taking responsibility for its actions, by blaming someone, or something else.

Thus, the mind reasons that freedom from guilt is obtained by *attacking,* in order to punish the "thing" for what the mind imagines that it has done to us. The attack is justified, because the mind perceives it as a means of depriving the "thing" of something it values and wants. In reality, this only enforces the feeling of scarcity, which keeps us locked into the ego dynamics. As if this were not enough, fear is also reinforced because the mind believes that someone is attacking it to tear heaven from it. When attack enters the mind, it is equating the soul with the body, and this concept reinforces the belief in separation. Thus, the errors of the mind strengthen the illusion and reinforce the concept of separation, and the soul becomes confused. Therefore, we lose the innocence, purity, and harmony associated with the Divine Mind. What an insidious concept. Now, it should be clear why the Directive Intelligence forbid the soul to partake of these fruits. Once the error was made, it continues in an endless cycle, until knowledge and Truth enter the mind to set it free.

Eventually, the Ego Dynamics is shortened to the unholy trinity, where fear is the escape from guilt, and attack is the scapegoat and means of protecting innocence. The mind believes that the attack eliminates the guilt; however, the soul knows that the attack was unjustified, and eventually the guilt returns to start the process all over again. Without the help of the Holy Spirit there is, indeed, no hope, but the Holy Spirit knows both Spirit and the physical world and acts as an interpreter (see Figure 9 - Vital Life Principals). As long as the Ego Dynamics is allowed to operate unchecked, the unholy trinity will always keep the mind centered in the lower mind of sense and passions, and keep us separated from Spirit. The cycle can be broken by Spiritual knowledge and Truth. In order to accomplish this, the mind must be willing to listen and follow the Holy Spirit's direction.

CHAPTER 14:

EFFECTS OF THE MENTAL PLANE

The mind is now in a state of constant confusion, and the peace and harmony of the Garden of Eden has been violated. These are the effects that result from breaking the Divine Law. Please note that the Directive Intelligence is not punishing us for our actions. The negative result is simply the by-product of misusing the Law. It is similar to climbing a tree in our youth, losing our footing, falling from the tree to the ground, and breaking an arm. The broken arm is the result of the action of the natural law of gravity. The law of gravity is simply carrying out its natural function by drawing us to the ground; the force of the impact with the ground breaks the arm. The climbing of the tree, in all probability, was breaking one of "Mom's" laws in the first place. All natural laws have a useful purpose, and suffering the consequences is the result if the law is violated. Thus, Genesis 3:14 through 3:19 describes the consequences of the mental, emotional, and sense consciousness' action of violating the warning not to eat of the fruits of the mental plane.

GEN. 3:14 "And the LORD God said unto the serpent, Because thou hast done this, thou art cursed above all cattle, and above every beast of the field; upon thy belly shalt thou go, and dust shall thou go, and dust shall thou eat all the days of thy life."

LORD God means the Self-existent, Eternal, and is the Directive Intelligence which works upon the various levels of consciousness.

Serpent means snake, and represents the sense consciousness.
Cursed in Hebrew is *arar* (aw-rar') which means execrate, or bitterly curse. Curse is the judgment of the sense consciousness by the Directive Intelligence. It represents the limitation of activity of the lower nature through Divine Law and conditions imposed upon matter.
Cattle means muted, dumb, beast, or large quadruped animal. Cattle are symbols of emotions of the lower nature which are under the control of the higher nature (implies domesticated emotions).
Beast means alive, loving thing, wild, life, or congregation. Beast is symbolic of desires, passions, and instincts of the lower nature.
Field means to spread out, country, ground, land, or soil. Field is a symbol of the lower nature within which the soul's evolution takes place. It is the field of experience.
Belly in Hebrew is *gachown* (gaw-khone') which means external abdomen, and is from the word *giychown* (ghee-khone') meaning stream. Gichon (Gihon) is a river in paradise. Gihon is the symbol of the lower mental nature as a current of life on the lower planes.
Dust means powdered or gray; hence clay, earth, mud, ashes, ground, or mortar. "Dust" is defined as "fine pulverized particles of earth." "Dust" also means confusion or disintegrating thought, according to Webster's Dictionary.
Eat means to burn up, consume, or devour.
Day, metaphysically, means understanding.
Life in Hebrew is *chay* (khah'ee) which means alive, which is from the root word *chayah* (khaw-yaw') meaning to live, to revive, to nourish, preserve, or save. Life in this context means physical life, because dust comes from the ground, which is a physical term.

Metaphysically, this verse might read: **"And Directive Intelligence said unto the sense consciousness, Because**

you have done this, you are limited in activity above all emotions, and above every desire, passion, and instinct of the lower nature; upon your lower mental nature shall you go, and confusion and turmoil shall you consume all the understandings of your physical existence."

Please note that Directive Intelligence is not punishing the Sense Consciousness for its action, but is describing the effect and the limitation of activity through Divine Law and conditions imposed upon matter. The law is neutral and treats all equally. Confusion and turmoil are the natural result of not having the Directive Intelligence guide us by the understanding of Truth.

The Sense Consciousness is the most limited, restricted, and lowest level of all the consciousness levels. Even the emotions, desires, passions, and instincts have higher mental positions than that of the Sense Consciousness. The Sense Consciousness locks us into the illusions of the physical world, and we believe that we are our bodies. Being the furthest from Spirit, the Sense Consciousness, lacks understanding and knowledge. In its ignorance it makes decisions that cause pain and suffering. It can learn to evolve to a higher state of consciousness to escape the consequences of this ignorance. Thus, the Sense Consciousness suffers confusion and turmoil as long as it consumes of the lower mental nature as its current of life on the lower planes.

Gen. 3:15 "And I will put enmity between thee and the woman, and between thy seed and her seed; it shall bruise thy head, and thou shalt bruise his heel."

Enmity in Hebrew is *eybah* (ay-baw') which means hostility, antagonism, or hatred, and is from the root word *ayab* (aw-yab') meaning to hate, be hostile, or be an enemy.

Woman means a female person, wife, or a mortal; and is a symbol of the emotional-nature of the soul.

Seed in Hebrew is *zera* (zeh-rah') which means fruit, plant, posterity, or sowing time, and is from the root word

zara (zaw-rah') meaning to sow, disseminate, fruity,or conceive seeds. Seed is the symbol of the manifesting Divine Mind, which is the source of all things.
Bruise in Hebrew is *shuwph* (shoof) which means to snap, to overwhelm, break, or cover.
Head in Hebrew is *rosh* (roshe) which means easily shaken, forefront, principal, captain, ruler, or top. Head is the symbol of the mind or intellect.
Heel in Hebrew is *iqqebah* (ik-keb-aw") which means track, rear, hoof, last, or liar in wait; and is from the root word *aqab* (aw-kab') meaning to swell out or up, to seize by the heel, to circumvent, or restrain. Heel is the symbol of the lower nature of the human soul.

Metaphysically, this verse might read: "**And Directive Intelligence put hostility between the sense consciousness and the emotional-nature, and between sense manifestation and emotion manifestation; hostility shall overwhelm the sense mind, and emotions shall overwhelm the sense-nature of the human soul.**"

An ethical distinction is being drawn between the sense-nature with its appetites and delights, and the higher emotional-nature; and through this distinction shall the struggle within the soul proceed. From this conflict, the lower mental-will, or intellect (head), will be crushed out by the Divine Love (Christ) within the soul, and it will lead to the dissipation of the lower part of the soul (heel).

The soul must become aware of the dual nature within it, a divine one and an earthly one. But the soul pays a heavy price for this self-knowledge. Thus, the soul is at war with itself, the Divine Mind and the Sense Consciousness all fighting for mastery.

Without spiritual guidance, the Sense Consciousness and the emotional-nature will be at odds with each other's productive thoughts, which bruise the intellect and understanding of the soul. It is this bruising of the intellect that causes the disharmony, and is the real reason why the soul must leave the garden of Eden.

Gen. 3:16 "Unto the woman he said, I will greatly multiply thy sorrow and thy conception; in sorrow thou shalt bring forth children; and thy desire shall be to thy husband, and he shall rule over thee."

Woman means a female person, wife or a mortal; and is a symbol of the emotional-nature of the soul.

Multiply in Hebrew is *rabah* (raw-baw") which means to increase or abundance.

Sorrow in Hebrew is *itstsabown* (its-tsaw-bone') which means worrisome, labor, pain or toil. Sorrow is the symbol of deprivation of the higher qualities when it descends into the lower nature; that is, mental suffering caused by loss.

Conception in Hebrew is *herayown* (hay-raw-yone') which means pregnancy; and is from the root word *harah* (haw-raw') meaning conceive, be with child or progenitor. Conception is symbolic of new mental forms begotten of mind and emotion (opinions, ideas and impressions formed by the lower mind).

Children in Hebrew is *ben* (bane) which means son, nation, quality or condition; and is from the root word *banah* (baw-naw') meaning to build, make or set up.

Desire in Hebrew is *teshuwqah* (tesh-oo-kaw') which means a sense of stretching out after or longing; and is from the root word *shuwq* (shook) meaning to run after, or overflow.

Husband means a man as an individual or a male person, companion or servant; and is the symbol of the mental-nature united in the soul.

Rule in Hebrew is *memshalah* (mem-shaw-law') which means a realm or ruler, domination or power. Rule is a symbol of authority.

Metaphysically, this verse might read: **"Unto the emotional-nature of the soul Directive Intelligence said, 'I will**

greatly increase your toil and your formation in the mind of new ideas produced by thought and emotion; in pain you shall bring forth opinions, ideas, and impressions; and your longing shall be to your mental-nature, and it shall dominate over you."

At first glance, the literal interpretation of this verse is extremely negative and punitive. It is the source of sexual discrimination, in that it indicates that the male is to dominate over the female. It also indicates that the Directive Intelligence is punishing woman with the pain and sorrow of giving birth to children. However, when decoded, the thinking consciousness will always rule over the feeling consciousness, because feelings are illogical to the reasoning and analytical mind. Thus, the mental and emotional natures of the soul will be at odds with each other until the treasures of Spirit provide the Truth and Wisdom; and both are united in One Consciousness. When the soul is deprived of the higher mental qualities, it descends into the lower nature; and mental suffering is the result because of the loss of spiritual direction.

The emotional-nature of the soul at this point has difficulty and distress associated with the formation of fresh ideas, and the realization of Divine Wisdom. As long as the emotional-nature is under the dominance of the lower mind, evolutions of the soul shall be through sorrow; and the ideas begotten of experience through the functioning of the mind, shall be realized with pain. The emotional-nature is subservient to knowledge; and the intellect dominates the love-principal, or emotional-nature.

Gen. 3:17 "And unto Adam he said, Because thou hast hearkened unto the voice of thy wife, and hast eaten of the tree, of which I commanded thee, saying, Thou shalt not eat of it: cursed is the ground for thy sake; in sorrow shalt thou eat of it all the days of thy life;"

Adam represents the first movement of the mind in its contact with life and substance. Adam also epitomizes an individual-will idea in consciousness.

Hearkened in Hebrew is *shama* (shaw-mah') which means to hear intelligently, attention, obedience, diligently, discern, give ear, listen, or obey.
Voice means to call aloud, sound, cry, lightness, or proclamation.
Wife means woman, female, together, or companion. Wife is a symbol of the emotional-nature in alliance with the mind.
Eaten/eat means to burn up, consume, or devour.
Tree represents the connecting link between earth and heaven (body and mind, formed and formless). Tree in this case is the symbol of the human mental qualities.
Commanded means to constitute, enjoin, appoint, charge, or send a messenger.
Cursed means execrate, or bitterly curse. Curse is the judgment of the sense consciousness by the Directive Intelligence. It represents the limitation of acitivity of the lower nature through Divine Law and conditions imposed upon matter.
Ground means soil, country, land, or earth. Ground is the symbol of the lower nature of the soul.
Sake in Hebrew is *abur* (aw-boor') which means cross over, transition, beyond, or fall.
Sorrow in Hebrew is *itstsabown* (its-tsaw-bone') which means worrisome, labor, pain, or toil. Sorrow is the symbol of deprivation of thehigher qualities when it descends into the lower nature; that is, mental suffering caused by loss.
Day, metaphysically, means understanding.
Life means alive, to live, to revive, to nourish, preserve, or save. Life in this context means physical life, because dust comes from the ground which is a physical term.

Metaphysically, this verse might read: "**And unto the individual-will idea Directive Intelligence said, Because you have listened to the proclamation of your emotion-nature, and have consumed of the human mental**

qualities, of which I charged you, saying you shall not consume of them; limitation of ethical standards is the lower nature for your transition; in mental suffering shall you consume of it all the understandings of your physical life;"

The individual-will idea consumed of the forbidden fruit of the human mental qualities and, thus, disobeyed the Directive Intelligence. Spirit is the connecting link between the upper and lower minds; however, when the human mental qualities are consumed, all experiences are interpreted by the individual mind, and Truth becomes distorted. The Divine Mind is constantly giving us Truth and Wisdom, but now the human mind interprets all events and becomes confused. Confusion is the result of two conflicting input sources, and the mind becomes split. Now the ethical standards that the Divine Mind set for the soul become diluted, and limitation of activity of the soul through Divine Law and conditions are the result. Thus, because of the choices that the soul made, the higher qualities are masked, and suffering is the result.

Mental suffering is caused by the soul being out of harmony with the Divine Mind. As long as the soul is ruled by the desires and passions of sense thoughts, there will be suffering due to the loss of spiritual direction. It is interesting to note that suffering is only temporary, and as we transition from the lower Sense Consciousness to the Christ Consciousness, the suffering subsides in direct proportion to the degree that we allow Spirit to direct us. God is not punishing man for his SIN, but telling him how life will be without spiritual guidance.

Gen. 3:18 "Thorns and thistles shall it bring forth to thee; and thou shalt eat the herbs of the field;"

Thorns in Hebrew is *qots* (kotse) which means a sense of pricking and is from the root word *quwts* (koots) meaning to harvest. 'Thorns', according to Webster's Dictionary, means a sharp point, irritation, or annoyance.

Thistles in Hebrew is *dardar* (dar-dar') which means a thorn. 'Thistles', according to Webster's Dictionary, means sharp pointed.
Eat means to burn up, consume, or devour.
Herbs means to glisten, grass, or tender shoot. Herbs are the symbols of the primitive desires and afflictions which are aroused by the activities of the senses. Herbs were used at the Passover, were symbols of suffering (Exodus 12:8 and Number 9:11), and could be used as a modest meal.
Field means to spread out, country, ground, land, or soil. Field is a symbol of the lower nature within which the soul's evolution takes place. It is the field of experience.

Metaphysically, this verse might read: **"Irritations and annoyances shall the Sense Consciousness bring forth to you; and you shall consume of the primitive desires and afflictions of the field of experience;"**

Thorns and thistles are symbols of evil, suffering, and sorrow; which are the result of thoughts associated with the Sense Consciousness. Although the Sense Consciousness is attractive, it will always bring irritation and annoyances and leave a bitter taste in our mouths. This is because this negative thinking is not of Divine Mind, and is, therefore, unnatural. Sin and suffering proceed from the lower primitive nature, and the mental qualities subsist through the products of the sensation-nature and afflictions. Thus, the Sense Consciousness produces non-spiritual experiences. Therefore, *evil* is simply the spoiling of the peaceful and harmonious state of Divine Mind, and *sin* is the missing of the spiritual goal, or mark.

Gen. 3:19 "In the sweat of thy face shalt thou eat bread, till thou return unto the ground; for out of it wast thou taken: for dust thou art, and unto dust shalt thou return."

Sweat in Hebrew is *zeah* (zay-aw') which means perspiration, and is from the root word *yeza* (yeh'-zah) meaning to ooze. Sweat is the symbol of falsity and illusion, or the inverted reflection of truth.

Face in Hebrew is *aph* (af) which means the nose or nostril, or suffering; and is from the root word *anaph* (aw-naf') meaning to breathe hard, to be enraged, or angry. Face is a symbol of the mental aspect of being; knowledge acquired either through the senses or intuition.

Eat means to burn up, consume, or devour.

Bread in Hebrew is *lechem* (lekh'-em) which means food or grain; and is from the root word *lacham* (law-kham') meaning to feed, to consume, devour, or eat. Bread is a symbol of the spiritual food of the soul, namely the truth, the substance of goodness, which is the staff of higher life.

Return in Hebrew is *shuwb* (shoob) which means to turn back, return to the starting point, or to retreat. Return is a symbol of the Wisdom-nature evolving in the soul after its period of obscurity or latency.

Ground means soil, country, land, or earth. Ground is the symbol of the lower nature of the soul.

Dust means powdered or gray; hence clay, earth, mud, ashes, ground, or mortar. 'Dust' is defined as "fine pulverized particles of earth." This implies that it can easily be blown by the winds of turmoil, which suggest that it is temporary. 'Dust' also means confusion or disintegrating thought, according to Webster's Dictionary; and is a symbol of the lower mind.

Metaphysically, this verse might read: "**In the falsity and illusion of your mental aspects of being shall you consume spiritual food of the soul, until you turn back to the lower nature; for out of it were you taken: for confused you are, and to the lower mind shall you retreat.**"

The soul was formed from confusion (dust) of the lower nature, until Spirit breathed the breath of Truth (Life) into it. Once the Truth of Spirit was introduced to the soul, it became balanced and in harmony with the Divine Mind. The unspiritual thoughts of sense desires and passions have again led us back to a state of confusion and disintegrating thoughts. Thus, the lower mind is unstable and subject to every wind of doctrine and opinion that obscures the Truth. So long as the personal consciousness is hidden in the activities of the lower mind, it is unable to apprehend the higher qualities of Love and Wisdom. Thus, the soul is separated and falls from Spiritual Grace. Since the fall of the personal consciousness into the lower nature, the Christ Consciousness (Wisdom and Love) has been hidden from the human soul. This spiritual quality returns when the soul is perfected at the end of the cycle, and the "Treasures of Heaven" are revealed. Thus the mental qualities of the lower mind are the culminating product of the lower evolution. It is the dust (body) which passes away, and does not ascend. However, the soul is eternal.

SUMMARY OF THE EFFECTS OF THE MENTAL PLANE

When the soul consumes of the human mental qualities that the Directive Intelligence instructed it not to eat, the soul and the Sense Consciousness become affected by the limitations of the material world, and they lose consciousness of the Spiritual Truth.

The Sense Consciousness is henceforth restricted by the limitation of activity through the Divine Law and conditions imposed on matter. The material world is based on confusion and turmoil, and is unconscious of Spiritual understanding. The Sense Consciousness is the lowest level of knowledge and is based only on what it perceives. What it perceives, it thinks is real. Even the desires, passions, and instincts of the lower nature have higher mental positions. Because it beguiles the emotional-nature of the soul, the Sense Consciousness is locked into the illusions of the physical world. Lack of understanding and knowledge it needs to make decisions cause it pain and suffering. Thus, it suffers confusion and turmoil as long as it consumes of the lower mental currents of life. Furthermore, there is a division between the appetites and delights of the Sense Consciousness and the higher emotional-nature of the soul. Through this distinction the struggle within the soul proceeds. Eventually, the intellect gives way to the Christ Consciousness (Intelligence) within us, and the Truth disperses the material aspects of the soul. The soul becomes aware of the dual nature of its being; that it is comprised of the Divine as well as the earthly; and both act as one in harmony with the Divine Mind. Thus the soul is fighting for mastery with itself, the Divine Mind, and the Sense Consciousness (serpent) until it seeks spiritual guidance. Without guidance from the spiritual realm, the Sense Consciousness and the emotional-nature will be at odds with each other.

As for the emotional-nature of the soul, the mental-nature of the soul dominates it because feelings are illogical to a reasoning mind. Thus, the emotional and mental nature of the soul are at odds with each other until Wisdom and Love unite them into one consciousness. Thus, the intellect evolves to Wisdom and the emotions evolve to Love; and together they produce the Christ Consciousness. The emotional-nature of the soul has difficulty with opinions, ideas, and impressions formed by the lower mind; and the realization of Divine Wisdom. The evolution from emotion to Love is through the ideas begotten through experience.

Because the individual-will idea listened to the emotional-nature of the soul, and consumed of the human mental qualities, all experiences of the lower mind are interpreted by the individual mind, and the Truth is distorted. Since both the Spiritual Truth and the interpreted truth are presented to the individual mind, it becomes confused and split. With the confusion, the ethical standards set by the Divine Mind are diluted. Thus, because of the choices that the soul has made the higher qualities are masked and suffering is the result. As long as the soul is ruled by the desires and passions of the lower mind, there will be suffering due to the loss of spiritual guidance. This loss is only temporary, because the Divine Plan is for the soul to evolve from the lowest imitated nature to higher Christ Consciousness. Any pain and suffering experienced is directly proportional to the amount of confusion in the individual mind.

CHAPTER 15:

EXPULSION FROM THE GARDEN OF EDEN

Once the soul has sampled the fruits of the mental plane, it can no longer reside in the spiritual body that is in compete harmony with the Divine Mind. The soul must leave the spiritual body because the mind has become confused, and is no longer of the "image and likeness" of the Divine Mind. When errors replace Spiritual Truths, the mind must now rediscover the Truth through experience. Thus, the mind will always be in a state of constant change, which is foreign to the non-changing Divine Mind. Genesis 3:20 through 3:24 describes the preparation of the soul for its journey in the lower nature without Truth, Wisdom and Intelligence (Treasures of Spirit).

GEN. 3:20 "And Adam called his wife's name Eve, because she was the mother of all living."

Adam represents the first movement of the mind in its contact with life and substance. Adam also epitomizes an individual-will idea in consciousness.

Wife means woman, female, together, or companion. Wife is a symbol of the emotional-nature in alliance with the mind.

Name in Hebrew is *shem* (shame) which means mark, honor, character, nature, or authority. Name is the symbol of difference, whereby one quality is distinguished from another.

Eve in Hebrew is *chadashah* (khad-aw-shaw') which means to be new, or cause to be rebuilt. Eve represents the love, or feeling in the individual consciousness. It is very closely identified with the struggle of elementary life. **Mother** in Hebrew is *em* (ame) which means bond of the family, dam, or parting. Mother is the receptive aspect of the manifesting Spirit, and directs the human evolution. **Living** in Hebrew is *chay* (khah'ee) which means alive, flesh, strong, or life; and is from the root word *chayh* (khaw) meaning to live. Living is the symbol of the Christ ideal qualities, which become dualized and inverted in the flesh.

Metaphysically, this verse might read: **"And the individual-will idea called his emotional-nature alliance natural love, because she was the receptive aspect of manifesting Spirit of all Christ ideals in flesh."**

The mind recognizes the life principle within the soul to be the emotional-nature, for it is the originator of all qualities that have in them the spark of higher life. The feeling nature, or love, is the receptive aspect of the manifesting Spirit, which brings forth from within the qualities of Spirit, and directs the human evolution, through intuition, to the Christ Consciousness. A mother's devotion is the sign of that complete and unfeigned love which is willing to expand itself in the interest of all. The Higher Self is allied with the female energy and it is from the Christ Consciousness in the soul that the prototypes of all things are reflected to the lower mind. Love, or the feeling in consciousness, is of Spirit. The mind puts feeling into what it thinks, and so "Eve" (feeling) becomes the "Mother of all living." Eve is very closely identified with the struggle of elementary life; that is, the struggle of the soul to regain its perfect state of existence.

Gen. 3:21 "Unto Adam also and to his wife did the LORD God make coats of skins, and clothed them."

Adam represents the first movement of the mind in its contact with life and substance. Adam also epitomizes the individual-will idea in consciousness.

Wife means woman, female, together, or companion. Wife is a symbol of the emotional-nature in alliance with the mind.

LORD God means the Self-existent, Eternal, and is the Directive Intelligence which works upon the various levels of consciousness.

Make means to do, accomplish, bring forth, advance, or appoint. 'Make', according to Webster's Dictionary, means to bring a form into being mentally or physically.

Coats in Hebrew is *kuttoneth* (koot-to'-neth) which means to cover, garment, or robe. Coat is the symbol of mental coverings, or forms, of truth and error.

Skin in Hebrew is *owr* (ore) which means hide or leather, and is from the root word *uwr* (oor) meaning to be bare, or made naked. Skin is a symbol of the outer envelope of the soul.

Clothed in Hebrew is *labesh* (law-bash') which means to wrap around, to put on a garment, apparel, or wear.

Metaphysically, this verse might read: **"To the individual-will idea and to his emotional-nature alliance did the Directive Intelligence bring forth mental coverings of the outer envelope of the soul and wrapped around them."**

The soul is now without spiritual protection and the Directive Intelligence makes them "coats of skins to cover them." The making of "coats of skin" is the making of the physical body that is visible to the human eye. Under the Divine Law, this corresponds to the quality of thoughts, which have degraded to that of an animal. Prior to this point, man had dominion over animals, because he had a more highly developed spiritual consciousness. The loss of the spiritual consciousness reduces man to the level of an animal. When spiritual thoughts become supreme in consciousness, the coats of skin will give way to the manifestation of the spiritual body, which is the immortal body. The transformation that Jesus made after the crucifixion is from the physical body to the immortal body.

The New Testament provides additional information on coats and cloaks: ***"And if any man will sue thee at the law, and take away thy coat, let him have thy cloke also. And whosoever shall compel thee to go a mile, go with him twain."*** (Matthew 5:40 & 41). These verses indicated that if any reasoning or functioning mind (man) should prove (law) to you the truth of something and, so take away your error (coat), let the reasoning mind also take away opinions, prejudices, conventions, and mental disguises (cloaks). And if intelligence (man) compels you to a course of action, then fully carry it out. In other words, it is Truth that transforms the physical body to the immortal body, and it is well worth the effort to seek out the Truth. To me these verses also confirm the Course In Miracles concept that we are all teachers, as well as students.

Gen. 3:22 "And the LORD God said, Behold, the man is become as one of us, to know good and evil; and now, lest he put forth his hand, and take also of the tree of life, and eat, and live forever;"

> **LORD God** means the Self-existent, Eternal, and is the Directive Intelligence which works upon the various levels of consciousness.
>
> **Man** means ruddy, a human being, an individual, or person; and, metaphysically, is the universal symbol of mind in two aspect; a higher and lower nature. It signifies intellect, reason, intelligence, or mental qualities.
>
> **Know good and evil** represents the discerning capacity of mind. Good is the reality that evil is but an apparent and transitory opposite; that is, to know true and foolish thoughts.
>
> **Lest** means removal, to appear, look, cast out, or empty. According to Webster's Dictionary, 'lest' means "for fear that".
>
> **Hand** in Hebrew is *yad* (yawd) which means power, or direction (open hand). Hand is the symbol of the directive principle of activity either outgoing (right) or incoming

(left), and represents the positive and negative aspects of Divine action in the soul.

Tree of life represents the absolute life principle established in man's consciousness by Divine Mind. It is the current of the Divine life flowing downward through the Christ Consciousness.

Live means to receive, or save life, and represents continuously embodying the spirit of good, wholeness and perfection.

Metaphysically, this verse might read: "**And the Directive Intelligence said, 'Behold, the human being has become as one of us, to discern true and foolish thoughts: and now, for fear that he put forth his directive principle (mind), and take also of the absolute life principle, and consume, and receive the good of Spirit forever;'**"

The human mind is now placed in a position where it must choose between positive and negative thoughts, just as the Christ Consciousness does. The major difference is that the Christ Consciousness has spiritual direction and discerns only the good. Because man no longer takes direction from the Directive Intelligence, the soul experiences both positive and negative thoughts, and lives with the material manifestation of the Effects of each choice.

The phrase "put forth his hand" is very symbolic, in that, an outstretched hand is open to receiving, while a closed hand hangs on to what it cherishes and is a symbol of anger. An open hand releases whatever it has been holding, in order to receive something new. It is generally acknowledged that one receives through the left hand and releases through the right hand.

Good and evil is simply the ramification of experiences on the lower plane which bear fruit, and symbolize the evolving moral nature of the soul. It is through the attraction of the Sense Consciousness that the growth of the soul begins. This serves to gratify its awakened cravings. It is from the center of the spiritual body (garden), or Christ Consciousness, that the ray of

Divine Mind extends downward (the tree of life), and through this process the moral nature of knowing good and evil is obtained. To receive only the good, the soul must consume of the Absolute Life Principle, because this is where the Truth is to be found.

Therefore, man first perceives Truth; then he discerns the relation of Spiritual ideas before perfect activity is set up within him.

Gen. 3:23 "Therefore the LORD God sent him forth from the garden of Eden, to till the ground from where he was taken."

LORD God means the Self-existent, Eternal, and is the Directive Intelligence which works upon the various levels of consciousness.

Sent in Hebrew is *shalach* (shaw-lakh') which means to send away, send out, cast out, let depart, leave, or push away.

Garden means to hedge about, protect, or defend; and represents the spiritual body that is in complete harmony with the Divine Mind.

Eden means pleasure, delight, time, or season; and represents a pleasant, harmonious, productive state of consciousness in which are all possibilities of growth.

Till in Hebrew is *abad* (aw-bad') which means to work, serve, keep in bondage, bring to pass, or transgress. 'Till' is a symbol of the Higher Self, as the Divine Cultivator, Tiller, or Sower of the lower nature.

Ground means soil, country, land, or earth. Ground is a symbol of the lower nature of the soul, which requires "tilling" and "sowing" to produce good "fruit".

Taken in Hebrew is *laqach* (law-kakh') which means to take, bring, drawn, fetch, receive, or send for.

Metaphysically, this verse might read: **"Therefore the Directive Intelligence let depart the mental qualities from the spiritual body of the pleasant, productive, and**

harmonious state of consciousness, to work the lower nature from where he was drawn."

Sense thoughts cannot live in harmony with the Spiritual ideals. Thus, the human mind lost consciousness of its divine nature in Spirit. It must leave the spiritual body and begin again to lay hold of the potential ideas in substance; "Till the ground from whence he was taken." This implies that the two aspects of man, the Higher Self and Lower Self, are both of Divine Life. However, the Lower Self is in the process of manifesting itself, and struggles upward through the lower planes of sense and desire. The Higher Self is never revealed to the human consciousness in its fullness, for the unmanifested cannot be apprehended in its true nature. The Lower Self, in manifesting, is always limited and falls short of itself, but as it develops its qualities, it gradually approaches completion. When complete and perfect it unites with its counterpart on the upper planes.

The soul now has complete freedom and must choose the course of action, as opposed to being led by Spirit, or the Higher Self. The soul must choose under all kinds of circumstances, all kinds of feelings, under the stress and forces of all kinds of motives, and experience the result of each choice. Through the process of evolution, the soul develops character and demonstrates strength and mastery over the Lower Self. Worded slightly differently, the weaker personal-will yields to the nobler Divine Will; as the physical world yields to the Spiritual Realm. The purpose of the Higher Self is to make the Lower Self perfect, and unite with it. This is done through the process of Involution.

Gen. 3:24 "So he drove out the man; and he placed at the east of the garden of Eden cherubims, and a flaming sword which turned every way, to guard the way of the tree of life."

Drove in Hebrew is *garash* (gaw-rash') which means to drive out from a possession, expatriate or divorce, cast out, drive away, or expel.

Man means ruddy, a human being, an individual, or person; and is the universal symbol of mind in two aspects; a higher and lower nature. It signifies intellect, reason, intelligence, or mental qualities.
East in Hebrew is *qedmah* (kayd'-maw) which means the front, fore part, or time (antiquity); and is from the root word *qadam* (kaw-dam') meaning to project oneself, or precede. East, metaphysically, means within.
Garden means to hedge about, protect or defend; and represents the spiritual body that is in complete harmony with the Divine Mind.
Eden means pleasure, delight, time, or season; and represents a pleasant, harmonious, productive state of consciousness in which are all possibilities of growth.
Cherubim in Hebrew is *keruwb* (ker-oob') which means a cherub or imaginary figure. Cherubim is a symbol of transcendental keepers of the Divine Law applicable only to the higher planes; and represents protection of the sacred life.
Flaming in Hebrew is *lahat* (lah'-hat) which means a blaze, magic, or enchantment; and is from the root word *lahat* (law-hat') meaning to lick, blaze, burn, set on fire, or kindle. Flaming is a symbol of the burning Truth, or Word of God.
Sword in Hebrew is *chereb* (kheh'-reb) which means drought, a cutting instrument, a knife, or dagger; and is from the root word *chareb* (khaw-rabe') meaning to parch, destroy, kill, dry up, or lay waste. Sword is a symbol of outgoing positive energy, either of the higher mind or the lower mind, and indicates conflict between the true and the false.
Keep means to hedge, protect, attend, look narrowly, or observe.
Way in Hebrew is *derek* (deh-'rek) which means a road, a course of life or mode of action, or journey; and is from the root word *darak* (daw-rak') meaning to tread. bend, guide, or walk.

> **Tree of life** represents the Divine Life which spreads through the universe and soul, and produces all forms and activities on the planes of manifestation.

Metaphysically, this verse might read: **"So Directive Intelligence cast out the human being; and he placed at the forefront of the spiritual body of a harmonious state of consciousness keepers of the Divine Law, and an enchanting Truth of conflict between true and false which rotates every way, to protect the journey of the Divine Life."**

Because of the downward attraction of desire, the mind is now driven out from its conditions of primeval innocence. The Higher Self becomes as a watcher (Cherubim) to bar the direct way to heaven, which is now only to be obtained by experience and struggle. The lower mind is, thus, cut off from the higher mind. The flame of a "sword" is a symbol of the spiritual strength which it is necessary to possess in order to gain the secret of Life eternal. The burning Truth, or word of the Divine Mind, will generate a positive, outgoing energy to protect and guide all forms and activities of manifestation. Thus, the higher, or inner, spiritual life is protected from the coarser, outer consciousness. The connecting link unites the Lower Self with the Higher Self through spiritual thought, meditation, and prayer.

It is interesting to note that we often find in the ancient eastern cultures, figures of strange beings, half-human and half-animal, placed at the doors of palaces and temples. To me, it is clear that they represent guardian spirits. According to the description in Ezekiel 1:5-10, and from other hints in the Bible, they were known by the name of cherubs.

When man deviated from the Spiritual Law, he drove himself from the spiritual body, which is in complete harmony with the Divine Mind. It was the confused mind of the human being that created a disharmonious state of consciousness; and disharmony is incompatible with the Spiritual life. Therefore, the human being had to leave the spiritual body until harmony is restored through the process of evolution. But the loss of spiritual harmony is not final and irreparable, since the Directive Intelligence (Jehovah) placed the Cherubim (angel) in the spiritual body, as well as a burning desire for Truth that rotates every which way. No matter which direction the soul might take, the "flaming sword" is there to light the path of the human consciousness with positive, outgoing energy to return the soul to the Divine Life.

SUMMARY OF EXPULSION FROM THE GARDEN

The reasoning and analyzing part of the soul recognizes that the emotional-nature is the life principle within the soul. It is the feelings that provide the qualities for the spark of higher life. The primitive feeling nature of the soul is the receptive channel to receive love and direction, which brings forth the qualities of Spirit in the manifestation of all forms in the lower nature of the mind. The Higher Self is allied with the female energy, and it is from the Christ Consciousness in the the soul that the prototypes of all things are reflected to the lower mind. The mind puts feelings into what it thinks, and the emotional-nature becomes the "Mother of all living things."

Because the mental qualities are firmly entrenched in the desires of the lower mind and become confused between Truth and desires, the soul is no longer in a state of harmony and must leave the productive state of spiritual consciousness. Without spiritual protection, the soul is reduced to the consciousness of an animal. And, like the animal, the soul requires an outer covering to protect it. Thus, the Directive Intelligence makes them "coats of skin" to cover them. Now the soul is self contained and must choose which part of the mind it will follow, and experience the results of each choice. Through experience, the soul reasons whether the experience is good or detrimental to its desire to return to the natural place of peace and harmony. The Spiritual Truth constantly surrounds the soul and all that is required is to extend the open hand and receive the good of Spiritual Life.

Thus, the good and evil of the outer manifestation are simply the ramification of experiences in the lower mind, which manifest fruit directly proportional to the thoughts. When the thoughts are generated from the Higher Self, good is always the result; but thoughts generated from sense desires generate pain and suffering. In either case, the soul learns to discern Truth from illusions and evolves to its moral nature. It is through the attraction of the Sense Consciousness that the soul begins to grow as it gratifies its awakening cravings. This would be cruel punishment indeed, if it were not for the Christ Consciousness (tree of life) in the middle of the spiritual body which extends the Truth of the higher mind downward to the soul. To receive only the good, the soul must consume of the Absolute Life Principle, because this is where the Truth is to be found. Therefore, the soul must first perceive Truth; then it must discern the relation of Spiritual ideas before perfect activity is set up within the soul.

The Higher Self and the Lower Self are both of the Divine life. However, the Lower Self is in the process of manifesting itself, and must struggle upwards through the lower planes of sense and desires. The Higher Self is never revealed to the human consciousness in its fullness, because the unmanifested cannot be apprehended in its true nature. The Lower Self in its manifesting is always limited and falls short of itself, but as it develops higher qualities, it gradually approaches perfection, and when it is perfect it is united with the Higher Self.

Truth must always be separated and protected from non-truths, because the non-truths will contaminate the Spiritual Truth. Without Spiritual Truths there would be no hope of escaping the passions and desires of the Sense Consciousness. Thus, the Higher Self becomes the watcher to bar the direct way to heaven. The lower mind is cut off from the higher mind, and must obtain the Truth through struggles with the temptations of the lower mind. However, the burning desire for Truth and the spiritual strength of the Divine Mind, will generate positive outgoing energy to protect all forms of manifestation. Thus, the higher, or inner, spiritual life is protected from the coarser outer manifestations. The lower mind reaches the higher mind through prayer, meditation and spiritual thoughts.

Because the human being deviated from the Spiritual Law, it could no longer remain in the spiritual body in complete harmony with the Divine Mind. The soul must now correct the confusion and disharmony of the mind through the process of evolution. However, the soul is not alone in this journey, because the burning Truth rotates every which way to light the way for it, no matter which direction the soul might choose to go. It was the soul's choice to consume of the fruit of the forbidden mental plane, and now it must freely choose Spiritual Direction, discern Truth from the illusions, and overcome the passions and desires of the outer manifestation.

PART IV

PATHWAY TO CHRIST

CHAPTER 16:

SPIRITUAL EVOLUTION OF MAN

Who wrote the Bible? Jewish and Christian history tells us that Moses is the author of the first five books (Genesis, Exodus, Leviticus, Numbers, and Deuteronomy). These books are known as the Pentateuch, which in Greek means "five scrolls". Moses is the major figure through most of these books. However, inconsistancies indicate that at least four authors were responsible for writing this one continuous history. Understanding the various sources helps to explain many of the discrepancies with the literal interpretation of the Bible. According to Biblical scholars, sources referring to the deity as "Yahweah or Jehovah" are referred to as source "J". Those referring to the deity as "God or Elohim" are referred to as source "E". Sources that concentrate on legal matters and have to do with the priesthood are referred to as source "P". And finally, the book of Deuteronomy is unique within itself, and is coded as source "D". The various authors are reflecting a story from their point of view, which explains the apparent differences.

From the literal interpretation, the second chapter of Genesis retells the story of creation told in the first chapter. However, as we have seen in Parts I & II of this book, the spiritual interpretation of these stories reflects a different purpose and intent. From the Biblical scholar's point of view, the first chapter of Genesis was written by the "E source" while the second chapter of Genesis was written by the "J source." Only in the outer, or physical, interpretation does an apparent conflict exist. In the first story the inner spiritual message reveals the **creation** of a Spiritual Realm. In the second, a spiritual mind was **made** in the "image and likeness" of the Divine Mind. These stories describe how the spiritual mind manifests at lower mental levels, and experiences the effects of the outer manifestation. Then man, or spiritual mind, can evolve to the Christ Consciousness that the Divine Mind envisioned.

According to the Bible, as a person's nature or authority changed, their name also changed; Abram to Abraham (Gen. 17:5), Sarai to Sarah (Gen. 17:15), Jacob to Israel (Gen. 32:28), Eliakim to Jehoriakim (2 Kings 23:34), Mattaniah to Aerekiah (2 Kings 34:17), and Daniel to Belteshazzar (Dan 1:6&7). Even the name of God was changed to Lord God in the second story of creation because a different aspect of the Creator was being described. In the New Testament, according to Mark 3:16, Jesus changed Simon's name to Peter (which is Greek for *rock-like*). Therefore, a name is much more than a proper noun to identify a specific person in the Bible. It is also an indication of the character of the individual and a clue to the mysteries in the evolution of the Collective Consciousness.

The Bible is the main source for the proper names of the ancient tribes of Israel. As you know, a name is a proper noun by which people and places are identified. So, names represent a perception of difference, whereby one quality is distinguished from another. "Whatsoever Adam called every living creature, that was the name thereof," (Gen. 2:19). This verse indicates that the primitive lower mind (Adam) began to perceive and reflect upon the sensations and desires that the lower emotions (Eve) presented to the consciousness. Knowledge commences in the perception of the differences; by experiencing the differences between things of spirit and matter we obtain knowledge. This is the Law of Natural Growth. Thus, the proper names presented in the Bible indicate the individual nature, or personal consciousness, as it proceeds through evolution from the material to the desired spiritual nature of the Christ Consciousness. We will look at each name presented as a symbol, or key, that can help unlock the hidden messages of the Bible.

Genesis is unique, in that of all the genealogy presented throughout the Bible, Genesis is the only book where a time frame is given. Of what value is it historically, or spiritually, to know when an individual was "begat" and when he died? It must be very important because in Genesis forty-four (44) chapters are devoted to revealing this information. I investigated numerology in hopes that it would assist in my understanding. It did not help, perhaps because of my inexperience with the technique. So, because of my engineering background, I decided to accumulate and plot the data presented. To my utter amazement, there was a gold mine of information. The rest of this chapter will present the analysis of this data.

The first twenty-four names in the genealogy of man and the associated references were obtained from Genesis 5:3 through 47:28.

		FATHER'S			YEARS		
NO.	NAME	REF.	AGE	YEARS*	REF.	LIVED	YEARS*
1.	GOD						
2.	ADAM		0		G5:5	930	930
3.	SETH	G5:3	130	130	G5:8	912	1042
4.	ENOSH	G5:6	105	235	G5:11	905	1140
5.	CAINAN	G5:9	90	325	G5:14	910	1235
6.	MAHALALEAL	G5:12	70	395	G5:17	895	1290
7.	JARED	G5:15	65	460	G5:20	962	1422
8.	ENOCH	G5:18	162	622	G5:23	365	987
9.	METHUSELAH	G5:21	65	687	G5:27	969	1656
10.	LAMECH	G5:25	187	874	G5:31	777	1651
11.	NOAH	G5:28	182	1056	G9:29	950	2006
12.	SHEM	G5:32	500	1566	G11:11	600	2166
13.	APAPHAXAR	G11:10	100	1656	G11:13	438	2094
14.	CAINAN**						
15.	SHALAH	G11:12	35	1691	G11:15	433	2124
16.	EBER	G11:14	30	1721	G11:16	464	2185
17.	PELEG	G11:16	34	1755	G11:19	239	1994
18.	ARAN	G11:18	30	1785	G11:21	239	2024
19.	SERUG	G11:20	32	1817	G11:23	230	2047

		FATHER'S				YEARS	
NO. NAME	REF.	AGE	YEARS*	REF.	LIVED	YEARS*
20. NAHOR	G11:22	30	1847	G11:25	148	1995
21. TERAH	G11:24	29	1876	G11:32	205	2081
22. ABRAHAM	G11:26	75	1951	G25:7	175	2126
23. ISAAC	G21:5	100	2051	G35:28	180	2231
24. JACOB	G25:26	60	2111	G47:28	147	2258

* Normalized years from creation

** Note that no data is provided for the second Cainan

This table was generated by accumulating the father's age when the son was born, and the number of years that each person lived. All data pertaining to life has been normalized from the formation of Adam, as this is the starting reference. By normalizing, we mean the age of the father at the birth of his son is added to the previous creation time line. For example, the age from creation of Enosh's birth was 130 (Adam's age when Seth was born) plus 105 (age of Seth when Enosh was born) equals 235 years from the formation of Adam. The number of years lived from creation is obtained by adding the year from creation to the number of years lived. For example, take Cainan. He was born 325 years from the formation of Adam and lived to be 910 years old. Thus Cainan died 1235 years from the formation of Adam. Please note that the Bible uses the term "begat", which could mean either conception or birth. It is highly unlikely that the reproductive cycle of gestation was even known at that time, so I personally believe it refers to the event of birth. In any event, the data has a maximum error of nine (9) months which is several magnitudes better than anything that science has been able to correlate with events of the Bible.

GENESIS' GENEALOGY OF MAN

What does the "begatitudes" of Genesis mean, and why is the data presented? To answer this question, I decided to plot the birth date from creation and the death date from creation of each name provided. When this is accomplished, something interesting happens. Figure 10 illustrates the plot of the Genesis Genealogy of Man. The first thing that struck me was that the plotted information resembles a pathway, with a major change at Arphaxad. Genesis 11:10 tells us that Arphaxad, or Arpachsad (Arpak'-shad), was born two years after the flood. Therefore, the flood can be pinpointed to the year 1654 from creation. Note that the sum of the digits for the number 1654 equals 16, and the sum of 16 equals 7. Since seven represents physical completion, it is possible that the flood is a symbol of the completion of the physical and the beginning of a spiritual state of mind. Arpachashad, in Hebrew, means "realm of astrology" and, metaphysically, represents a belief that good depends wholly upon something outside of oneself; that is, ruling stars, fate, or providence. Thus, this is the point in time in which man begins to think of something greater than himself. It is interesting to note that in the flood, the rain represents the down pouring of Truth to the lower mind. This results in the enlargement of the field of consciousness. Thus, Truth is the purification that allows the consciousness to begin to perceive Reality as opposed to the illusions of ignorance.

The second major change occurs with the name Peleg. Peleg, in Hebrew, means "moral distinction" and, metaphysically, represents the germination of the spiritual in man's consciousness. This is the first realization of the differences between the apparent physical body and the inner spiritual ideals. The Genesis information concludes with the name Jacob. Jacob, in Hebrew, means "leaving behind" and, metaphysically, represents the idea of the I AM, or Christ Consciousness. His name was later changed to Israel, which means "contending for God" and, metaphysically, represents a great light of understanding. This understanding leads the struggling soul when it discovers that there is a Divine-Natural body.

Finally, the leading edge of the plot resembles an "S curve", but what was the key to obtaining the vertical axis? The metaphysical meaning of each name that I had looked at so far, seemed to provide a deeper understanding of the individual nature of that person, so I decided to investigate further. Indeed, the metaphysical meaning of each name did provide a pattern of movement.

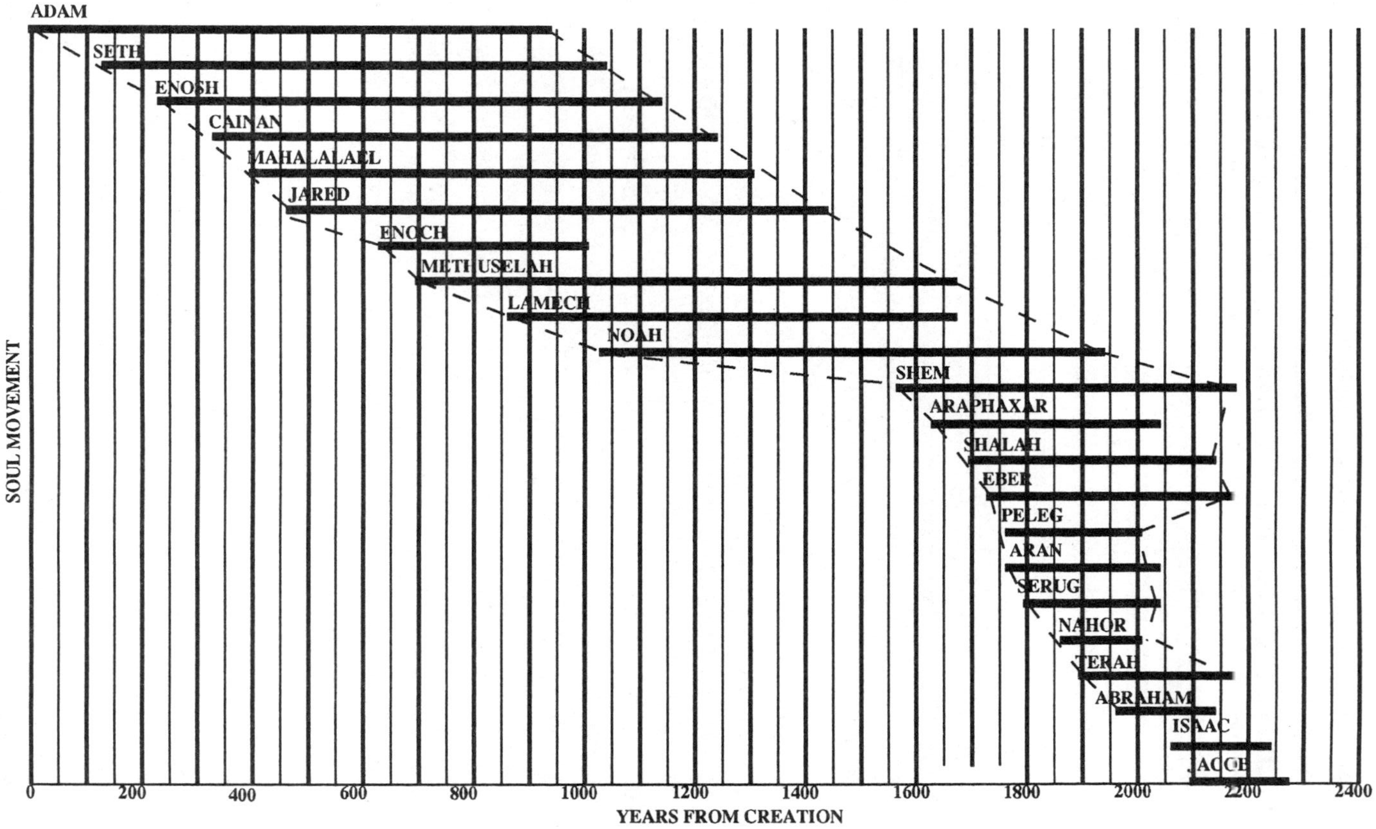

FIGURE 10 - GENESIS GENEALOGY OF MAN

By movement, I mean the Hebrew and metaphysical meaning of each name indicated a mental movement describing the decline of spiritual values, a change from the previous pattern, or an uplifting of spiritual values. Please note that the same twenty-four names presented in Genesis are also delineated in Luke's Genealogy of Jesus (Luke 3:23-38), which will be explored in detail later in Part IV of this book.

In addition to a movement from the previous name, there was a unique pattern that began to develop. Every twelfth name, except the first and the last, was a name indicating something Spiritual; such as, "Law of Reaction" (Noah), "joy of a new birth" (Isaac), "love individualized" (David), "God exalted" (Joram), "intellectual perception" (John), and "humbling the little self" (Jannai). Secondly, the first name of each new cycle of twelve also had a spiritual theme, such as "righteous thought" (Shem), "bring to an end" (Jacob), "reaching out to spirit" (Nathan), "God is help" (Eliezer), "celebration of God" (Judah), and "divine will ruling" (Melchi). Metaphysically, twelve always refers to spiritual fulfillment. The number twelve is found extensively in the Bible; the twelve sons of Jacob, the twelve running springs in Helim, the twelve stones in Aaron's breast plate, the twelve loaves of bread, and the twelve disciples, to name just a few. Thus, twelve signifies spiritual perfection and completion.

Finally, there was a definite Spiritual change in the meaning of each seventh name of a twelve name set; such as, "new state of thought" (Enoch), "leading to new pastures" (Reu), "Prophet or seer" (Nahshon), "God adds to" (Joseph), "will ruling" (Melchi), and "errors dissolve" (Elsi). Seven is a perfect number and, metaphysically, signifies physical completion. Seven follows six, which stands for the completeness of a process (six days of creation). Applied chronologically, seven indicates the beginning and the ending of a cycle, that is, the "alpha and omega".

It is clear to me that the Genesis time information and Luke's genealogy of Jesus present the soul movement, or pathway, from the first human being (Adam) to the perfect man, Jesus. This will become very clear in future chapters where the details of the Hebrew and the metaphysical meanings of each name will be presented. However, we do have enough information now to generate a plot of the Genesis time information against the meaning of each name. If one assumes the horizontal axis to be a Time Line from Creation, as well as a "God line" from which everything evolves, and the vertical axis is the Soul Movement, we are ready to start our plot. Adam was formed in the "likeness and image" of the Creator, so he is plotted on the so-called "God line". From Adam to Jared, there is a clear falling away from the original spiritual values, so they are plotted in a downward direction.

Starting with Enoch, there is a profound change that occurs. His name means "new state of thought" which implies a more spiritual thought. In fact, Enoch walked with God and God took him (Genesis 5:22 - 24). All the names from Enoch to Reu indicate a spiritual movement upwards. Reu in Hebrew means "leading to pasture." Metaphysically, Reu represents the unfolding of personal consciousness to a sense of loving and taking responsibility for the welfare of others. From Serug to Jacob, the movement is again toward Spirit. Figure 11 represents the plotting of the Genesis time information against the soul's movement.

What does Figure 11 tell us? First, there are two phases, a negative and a positive amplitude, that describe a complete cycle approximately every 2,000 years. Secondly, the beginning and ending points of each phase are clustered around the horizontal, or "God line", and have the spiritual qualities of rest, peace, joy, etc. Thirdly, man goes from one extreme to another, yet Reu is no better off than is Jared because both are on the outer edge of physical consciousness. Therefore, the desired path to obtain maximum Spiritual good is about the "God Line". "Oh how narrow is the door and how difficult is the road which leads to life. And few are those who are found on it," (Matthew 7:14 and Luke 5:48). Finally, this curve describes the Law of Cause and Effect. It is the spiritual thinking that centers us. "For as he thinketh in his heart, so is he" (Proverbs:7). Therefore, the Law of Cause and Effect states that an effect is directly proportional to the cause (thought).

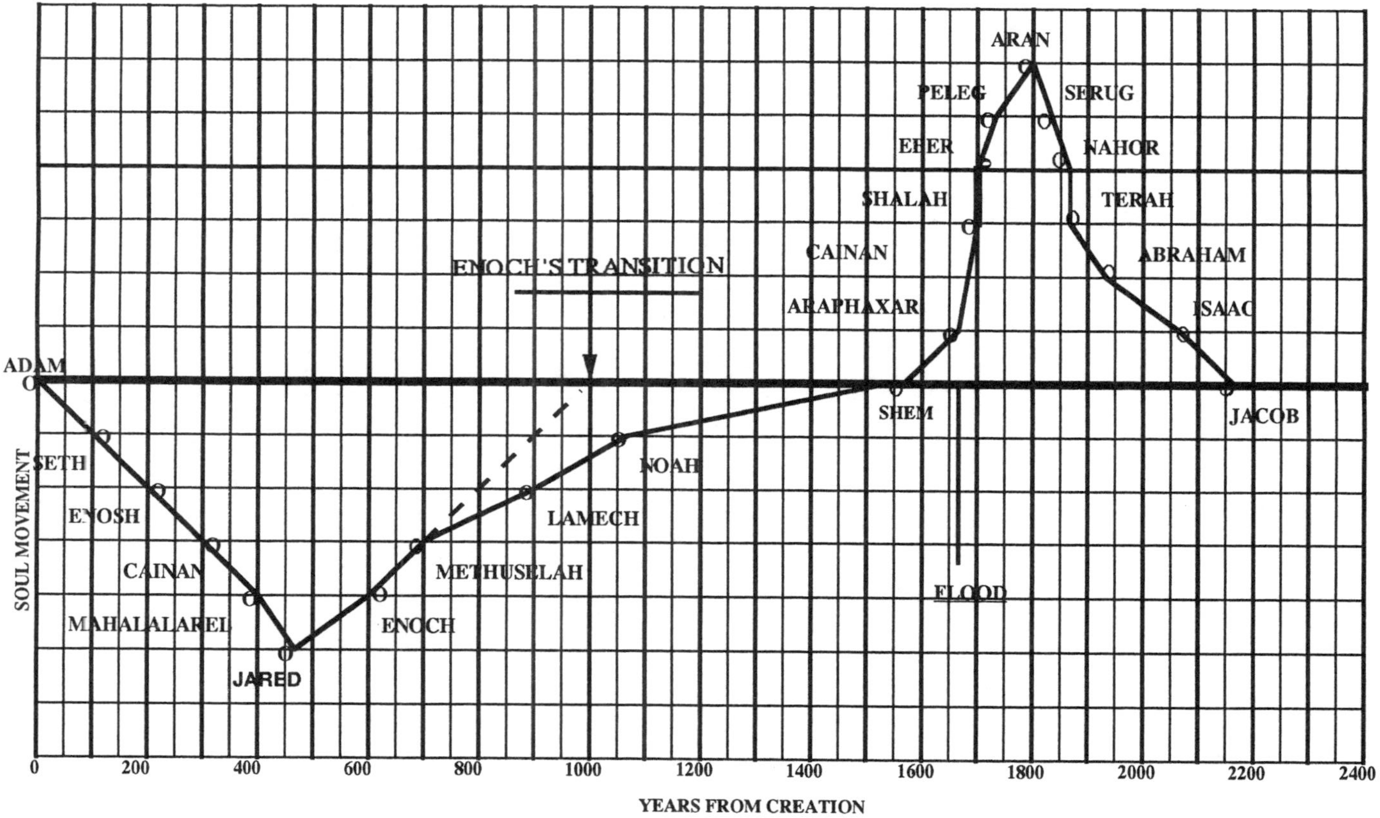

FIGURE 11 - GENESIS TIME VERSUS SOUL'S MOVEMENT

This curve also helps to explain the Duality Force that affects our lives. The law of electricity demonstrates how the "S"curve, law of sines, or the Law of Cause and Effect works. An electron that is exposed to a two pole system of opposite magnetic attraction will create a motion similar to a sine wave. As the electron loses energy, it is attracted by the negative polarity, until it begins to take on the properties of the negative pole and is repelled (minimum energy). As it is being repelled, it is at the same time being attracted by the positive pole, which causes the electron to increase its speed. It continues to gain speed until it again takes on the properties of the positive pole and is again repelled (maximum energy). This pattern continues indefinitely, as long as the electron is influenced by two opposing magnetic attractions.

This sine wave helps to explain the physical universe. First, the earth rotates about its axis every 24 hours, creating approximately 12 hours of darkness (minimum energy at midnight) and 12 hours of sunlight (maximum energy at noon). Secondly, the earth rotates around the sun, creating four seasons (winter, spring, summer and fall). In the Northern Hemisphere the minimum energy occurs in late December, and the maximum energy in July. Thirdly, the earth is tilted approximately 23 degrees, such that the north pole points to a different constellation approximately every 2,000 years. This constellation appears to have a definite effect upon everything we do; from what we eat to what we believe.

Please note that the above examples of the Duality Force are from a physical perception. Without the concept of time, the curve would be a circle, and if the curve were to continue it would form the infinity sign. Since there is no time or space in the Spiritual Realm, there is also a Spiritual explanation for the Duality Force. However, we must once again revert back to a physical example. Visualize the turbulent forces of a hurricane. A hurricane is defined as winds greater than 74 miles per hour. The turbulent force of the hurricane can create much damage, but at the eye of the hurricane there is peace and calm. The further we transgress from the eye, or center, the greater the degree of turbulence that we will experience. The same is true of a bicycle tire that is rotated at a high speed. If an object is placed on the outer rim of the tire, the centrifugal force will throw the object off the tire. Yet, if the same object is placed at the center, it will not move regardless of the speed of the rotation of the tire. I believe that this is also a good description of the Spiritual process. The further we transgress from our spiritual center, the greater the degree of discomfort and pain that we will experience. If it were not for the Holy Spirit, who helps to bring us back, we would destroy ourselves by transgressing further and further from our spiritual center, like the object that is thrown off the rotating bicycle tire.

Thus, it seems to me that the purpose of life is to experience it. We can learn from our errors, eliminate all of our negative and limited thoughts, and choose the higher formed thoughts of Spirit. This is exactly the message of Figure 11. Extrapolating Figure 11, with the information of Luke's Genealogy of Jesus, we find that there are seven (7) phases, or levels, representing three major components of man (body, mind, and spirit). Figure 11 is a pictorial view of the body phase of the soul's development. If the seven continuous phases are rotated to a vertical position, it represents the outer dimensions of a spiral staircase, with the supporting beam being God. Thus, the purpose of life is to move from the lower Sense Consciousness toward the Christ Consciousness. This journey is one of unfolding awareness. It is the Pathway to Christ.

The levels of Collective Consciousness were first presented in Genesis 1:26 in Part I of this book, and are illustrated by Figure 12. With the Genealogy of Jesus we can develop a very detailed model for the steps necessary to "Become perfect, just as your father in heaven is perfect," (Matthew 5:48). The Pathway to Christ will be presented in detail in the next seven chapters. However, since the Pathway to Christ is introduced in this chapter, it is fitting that the seven levels be identified here as well. The Pathway to Christ Model consists of three major phases as follows:

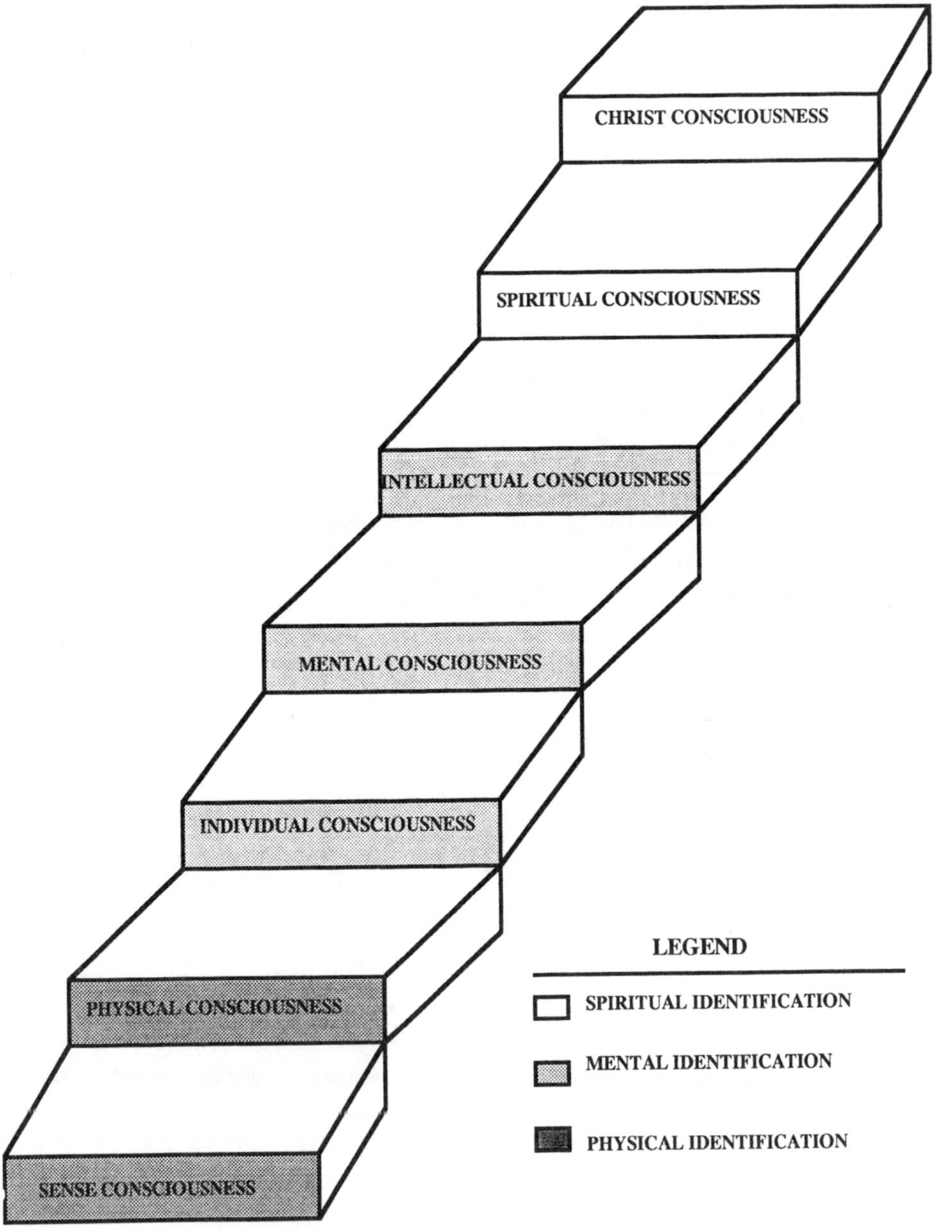

FIGURE 12 - COLLECTIVE CONSCIOUSNESS

PHYSICAL IDENTIFICATION

LEVEL 1 - Sense Consciousness (Adam to Noah) - 10 names. At this level of unfoldment, man is consciously unaware of the source of his being, or who he is. He thinks that he is what his senses tell him, that he is a body. To awaken the consciousness requires that he know and understand that his body and the physical world were created by non-spiritual thoughts.

LEVEL 2 - Physical Consciousness (Shem to Isaac) - 12 names. At this stage of unfoldment, man must be watchful of all his thoughts, and separate the physical from the spiritual. Only the spiritual in him creates the good, and the good comes from within. However, at this stage he is likely to place his good in things like astrology and psychics, and believe that his soul is connected with the earth and heavenly bodies.

MENTAL IDENTIFICATION

LEVEL 3 - Individual Consciousness (Jacob to David) - 12 names. At this stage of unfoldment, active spiritual thoughts, as opposed to physical thoughts, begin to give power to the Divine Mind. Spiritual thoughts are introduced by the use of praise which expresses approval for what the Divine Mind has given. Through praise the intellect becomes exalted. However, this understanding is based on magic and is still not truly spiritual.

LEVEL 4 - Mental Consciousness (Nathan to Joram) - 12 names. At this level of unfoldment, man perceives the meaning and implication of an invisible world. Spiritual understanding is a mental quality, or state, that is able to discern and comprehend spiritual knowledge. Understanding is the power to think and learn, which creates intelligence.

LEVEL 5 - Intellectual Consciousness (Eliezer to John) 12 names. At this level of unfoldment, Truth begins to translate the useless to the useful. It is spiritual thoughts that bring light and understanding to the illusions of the physical world and expose them for what they are, nothing. Thus, the Truth begins to free man from the bondage of the physical world.

SPIRITUAL IDENTIFICATION

LEVEL 6 - Spiritual Consciousness (Judah to Jannai) 12 names. At this level of unfoldment, man receives an active understanding of the grace of God. He becomes humble, the personal will decreases, and the I AM is exalted. When obedient to the Divine Law, the Collective Consciousness is polished by removing error thoughts.

LEVEL 7 - Christ Consciousness (Melchi to Jesus) - 6 names. At this level of unfoldment, Love is the uniting force behind the grace of God. It is the Divine Will, and not the little personal will, that is ruling man. Jesus the Christ is the greatest teacher of this level of consciousness. He served humanity, demonstrated the way to eternal life, and opened the way for humanity to return to its original condition of perfection. "Be perfect as the Father in heaven is perfect". From perfection to perfection. Figure 12 illustrates the Collective Consciousness that leads man to the Christ.

Before we conclude the Genesis Genealogy of Man, we need to bring the physical and spiritual material together. The Bible is both a spiritual and a physical history of man. Much of the physical history is scientifically correlatable through archeology and other scientific techniques. Yet, science has not been able to use any of its tools to correlate the historical data from Adam to Abraham. The Genesis Genealogy of Man data indicates that there are 1951 years between the birth of Adam and the birth of Aram (Abraham). The events around Abraham have been correlated to a time frame somewhere between 2,000 and 1,500 B.C. This means that the events of the Bible cover 4,000 years. We are in the process of completing 6,000 years of evolution since the beginning of Biblical times. Through carbon dating techniques, scientists think there is evidence to support the existence of man for millions of years, which is not compatible with the 6,000 year figure represented in the Bible, archeology, and other scientific evidence relating to Christianity. I believe the Bible is indicating that man was not given the power of choice until 6,000 years ago. Prior to that time he had a consciousness similar to that of an animal, and lived his life according to instinct, as opposed to the intellect. It is the quality of choice that separates us from the lower forms of life. Thus, the remainder of this book will examine the evolution of the spiritual man, in a physical body, as the personal consciousness progresses from the lowest outer sensation to the highest spiritual level represented by Jesus the Christ.

SUMMARY OF THE SPIRITUAL EVOLUTION OF MAN

The Bible provides information for both an historical and spiritual evolution of man. The historical accounts are reflected in the literal interpretation of the Bible, and the spiritual accounts are obtained by decoding the literal information. The key to obtaining the spiritual information is through metaphysics, which means "beyond the physical". By the use of metaphysics, additional information is provided that would otherwise be invisible. The major key to understanding the Spiritual Evolution of man is through understanding the nature, character, or authority of each name provided in the Bible. As a person's nature, character, or authority changes, his name is also changed.

Genesis identifies the same twenty-four names as Luke's Genealogy of Jesus; however, Genesis provides a timeline not found anywhere else in the Bible. This in itself is very interesting, in that the Bible frequently presents important information more than once. Often, when information is repeated there is a conflict of words which can be confusing. Genesis devotes forty-four (44) chapters to telling individual stories that are repeated elsewhere in the Bible; yet the timing information is not repeated. The timing information is not easily obtained, however, as it must be carefully extracted and plotted before the secrets are unlocked. The plot of the twenty-four names resembles a pathway. When this data is merged with the meaning of each name, a sine wave is revealed that covers 2111 years.

This information by itself tells only a partial story; the rest is provided by the Gospel of Luke. Even though the Gospel of Luke does not provide timing information, the same pattern developed in Genesis continues. That is, there are twelve names in each subcycle, except for the first and last subcycle, and the beginning and ending name of each subcycle has a spiritual meaning. Secondly, there is a major shift with every seventh name of a subcycle. Seven is a symbol of physical completeness and twelve, a symbol of spiritual fulfillment.

The first subcycle, Adam to Noah, was terminated by the flood, because the earth was corrupt. This is a very important event in the Spiritual Evolution of Man. Therefore, a summary of the metaphysical interpretation of Genesis 6:11 to 8:4 will be provided to assist the reader in understanding this great event. The whole man, (Noah, his wife, and his three sons and their wives), enters the spiritual part of itself (the ark) as a means of preserving the individual qualities of the soul, while the lower conditions of the consciousness are swept away (by the flood). Thus, equilibrium (Noah), Spiritual Thoughts (Shem), physical thoughts (Ham), mental thoughts (Jatheth) and their joined feeling components (wives) enter into the spiritual part of man (ark). Thus, man (ark) takes into the spiritual part of himself all the thoughts inherent in Being represented by beasts, cattle, creeping things and birds. The positive and the negative desires and passions, male and female, (two and two of all flesh) never separate. The flood illustrates a purification of negative thoughts, or a baptism of the Soul. It poured Truth for forty days (a complete process) and the mental (water) lifted up the spiritual part of man (ark). The Truth in the mental potential (water) prevailed and increased greatly in the unfolding consciousness (land), and the spiritual part of man (ark) was raised above the surface of errors and illusions of the mental possibilities of the lower mind. All desires and passions (flesh) in the lower mind, and all the thoughts inherent in Being (cattle, beasts, creeping things), and every spirit (man) died. Even the ideas that seemed to contain the "breath of life" are lost in the fuller realization of Spirit as the only presence and power. The spiritual part of man rested in the fullness of the Divine Law of perfection, upon the aspirations of the soul to a higher plane of consciousness (mountain) of a holy place (Ararat represents a sacred land unknown to the spiritually unwakened man).

A transition is made from the physical errors of limited thinking to higher mental possibilities. The lower mind, or subconscious mind, acts automatically on the desires and passions presented to it and, thus, it needs help in making this transition. Without the assistance of Spirit, man would be stuck in the lower planes of Being and the Spiritual Evolution could not proceed. Thus, the spiritual understanding of these passages unlocks a story of how the Divine Mind helps man to evolve to the next level. Man is Not being punished for his sins as the literal interpretation might suggest.

The Gospel of Luke indicates that there are seven subcycles, representing the three components of man (body, mind, and spirit). To return to a state of perfection, one must understand the Spiritual Evolution of Man. Therefore, the remainder of this book will address in detail Luke's Genealogy of Jesus.

CHAPTER 17:

LEVEL 1: SENSE CONSCIOUSNESS

The Book of Genesis reveals the creation of two states of mind. One state reflects the spiritual qualities, while the second reflects material qualities. The two opposite states of mind provide a mental condition where choice is possible. All types of thoughts and emotions are available to assist in the unfoldment of Spiritual Knowledge. In order not to contaminate this Collective Mind, the Divine Mind separated the intelligence of Spirit from the illusions of the physical realm. In between these two states of mind, the Divine Mind placed the mental potential, which obtains information from both the upper and lower minds.

The mental potential unfolds in degrees of understanding. It translates from the lower state of mind to the higher Spiritual state. Truth and Wisdom completely surround the Collective Consciousness to protect it from the untruths of the subconscious, or lower mind. As seen in chapter 6 the mental potential unfolds in seven separate levels: Sensual, Physical, Individual, Mental, Intellectual, Spiritual, and Christ Consciousness.

The Divine Mind then formed a spirit in its own likeness and image, and instructed it not to consume of the mental potential in the middle of the spiritual body. The mental and emotional components of the formed spirit (soul) are beguiled by the Sense Consciousness and partake of the mental potential. Since they consumed of the forbidden fruit, the formed spirit and its partner become confused by conflicting information, lose their innocence, and are forced to leave the spiritual body. Having lost its perfection, the soul must now experience life and choose between the Truths of the upper mind and the illusions of the lower mind. The Truth and Wisdom of Spirit no longer protect the Collective Consciousness from the illusions of the lower mind, and the soul must now decide which thoughts bring it the good. Thoughts that do not result in only good can be corrected and the soul can earn its way back to a state of perfection. The Pathway to Christ gives us a detailed road map of the soul's journey to perfection, and we can learn from the examples given.

Before we start this journey, we need to understand the significance of the Biblical verse, ***"....visiting the iniquity of the fathers upon the children, and upon the children, unto the third and to the fourth generation,"*** (Exodus 34:7). In this verse, the LORD God is talking to Moses, which indicates that the LORD God has refrained from punishing man and has forgiven him for his weaknesses in breaking moral principles. But, this does not clear the guilt, and this guilt will revisit to the third and fourth generations. In other words, God's action does not eliminate the effects of man's actions. Only man can do this.

Sin is simply the result of not living spiritual principles. Once the error has been committed, it is passed down to the children for three or four generations. Psychology has confirmed this principle, for example, in that a child who has been abused becomes an abuser, and the cycle continues until it is consciously broken.

In studying the Genealogy of Jesus, the nature of each new individual must be looked at in relationship to the previous three or four names to understand the true meaning of that step.

The Genealogy of Jesus in Luke 3:23 through 3:38 indicates seven cycles from the fall of Adam to the perfect man Jesus. Except for the first and the last, each of the seven levels consist of twelve steps. Twelve, as you remember, metaphysically represents spiritual fulfillment. The physical plane is a manifestation of realities. The seventh step of each level indicates a physical fulfillment or completion of all that has preceded it. This Collective

Consciousness Model can guide us to our original perfect state of consciousness.

The journey of the Pathway to Christ is from the outer material to the inner spiritual realm. The outermost level of the Collective Consciousness Model is the Sense Consciousness. Figure 13 illustrates the ten (10) steps associated with the Sense Consciousness Level. The Sense Consciousness is the lowest level of the physical realm.

STEP 0 - ONENESS WITH THE LIFE PRINCIPAL (GOD)
God is the Principal of Life, Truth, and Love. Originally, man was created as spiritual illumination. Spirit breathed into him the necessary inspiration and knowledge to have superior understanding. In this state of consciousness there is oneness with God in thought and action. Only Wisdom and Truth exist at this level. However, man beguiled by the sense consciousness, consumed negative thoughts, and had to leave the Garden of Eden. Man must now obtain spiritual knowledge and, through experience, return to the spiritual life of perfection. Thus, man must evolve to spiritual perfection by experiencing the Law of Cause and Effect in order to eliminate non-spiritual thoughts.

STEP I - BELIEF IN FORMS (ADAM).
At this stage, the human consciousness comes in contact with life and substance, and sees only forms, as opposed to the vision of Spirit. Adam, in Hebrew, means "red, ruddy, or firm", which indicates a consciousness in contact with the illusions of the physical world as opposed to the Truth of Spirit. Please note that Genesis makes a distinction between two different Adams. In the first chapter of Genesis, Adam is the ideal man, while the second chapter describes him as being formed from the dust of

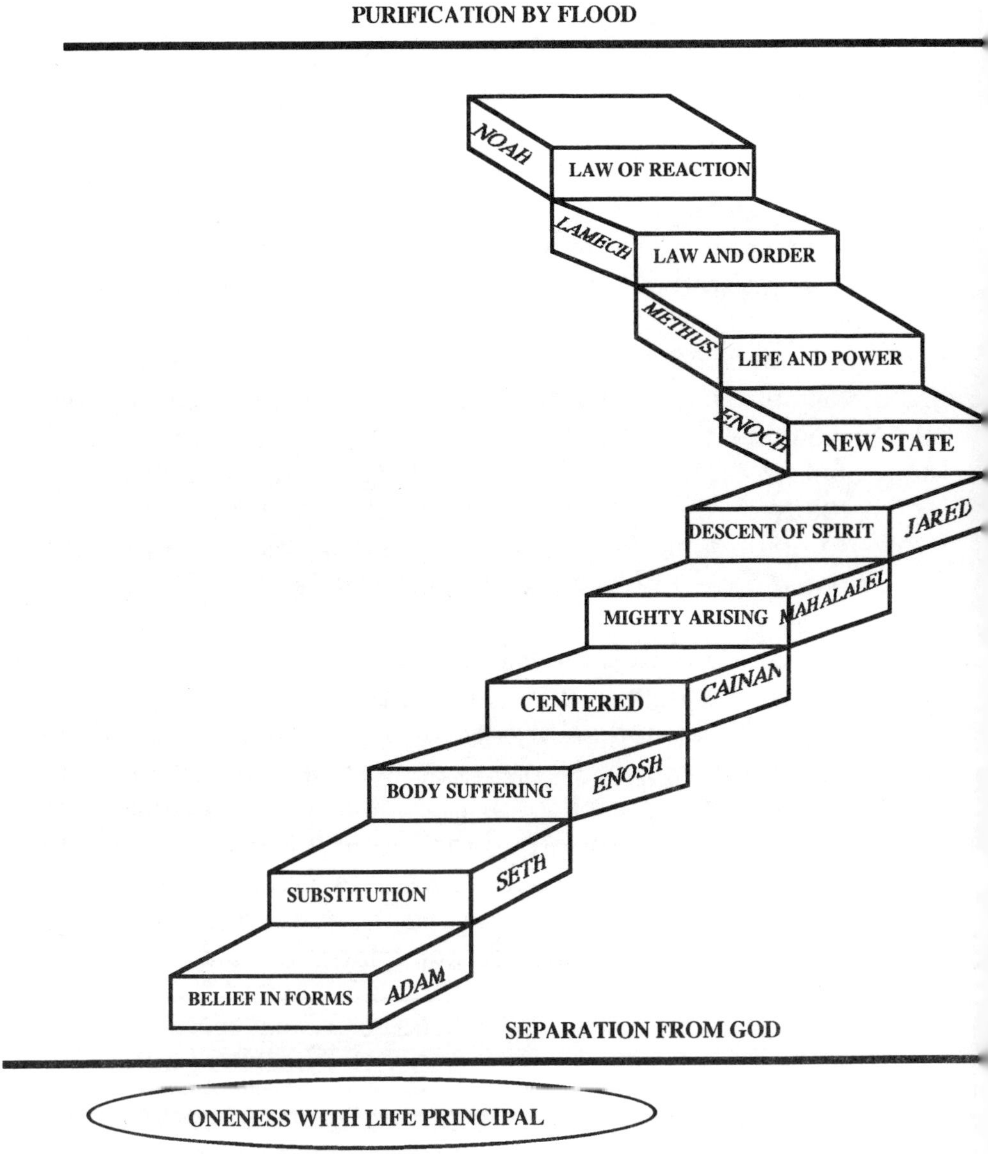

FIGURE 13 - LEVEL 1, SENSE CONSCIOUSNESS

the earth. Therefore, Adam is a symbol of the Divine nature of humanity as well as a symbol of the lower mind energized by desires. Thus, Adam is a symbol of the union in the soul of both the physical and Spiritual principles. Adam originally was of the Divine Ideal, but fell to the temptations of the desires of the physical world. The fall was caused by the serpent (Sense Consciousness) that beguiles the soul to consume of a two power concept. That is, God and not God (good and evil). As a result of eating the forbidden fruit, man becomes confused and begins to consume negative ideas that are not in alignment with Divine Ideals. The human mind then becomes split, and falls away from the spiritual life and all that it involves.

The choice for the material realm is a choice for separation, which creates mental disharmony that opposes the spiritually pleasant, harmonious, productive states of consciousness (Garden of Eden). Now the subconscious mind is being led by the desires and passions of the Sense Consciousness, as opposed to Wisdom and Truth. The personalized consciousness, now begins to believe that *it is a body.* It becomes confused, and must now leave the peace and harmony of the One Mind, and choose a personal, or individualized mind to replace the One Mind. The personalized consciousness is forced to choose between the two opposite ideas, and experience the effects of each choice.

STEP 2 - SUBSTITUTION OF GOOD (SETH).

At this stage there is a balancing power from the animal forces and a substitution of good. Seth, in Hebrew, means "settled, determined, substituted, or compensated", which indicates an alternative consciousness is being created. The Bible tells us that Adam and Eve had two sons before the birth of Seth. Cain killed his younger brother Abel in Genesis 4:25. Cain represents the physical consciousness and Abel represents the mental realm that controls the animal functions, or physical. This story indicates that the physical is always manifested first, followed by the mental. However, the mental always controls the animal functions. We are told that Able was a sheep raiser. The mental is more closely related to spiritual consciousness than the physical, and its offerings are more acceptable to Spirit than those of the physical. Thus, the physical consciousness comes first in consciousness and must eliminate the mental consciousness if it is to survive (killing of Abel). This action brings pain and suffering to man; without the mental, man wanders to his extreme physical limits, a great reaction sets in, and he is led back to the mental.

There must be a balancing power for good or man would self destruct. Thus, Seth is a symbol of hope, or mental desire for immortality. "And Adam knew his wife again; And she bare a son, and called his name Seth; for God, said she, hath appointed me another seed instead of Abel, whom Cain slew." (Gen. 4:25). The lower emotional-nature (Eve) expands and realizes that it may be receptive of that which cannot be taken away, because hope is a promise of eternal life. Seth becomes a balancing power for good, which cannot be obtained until man realizes the futility of relying on his human/physical efforts and recognizes that his good comes from a higher source. There must be a surrounding sympathetic movement that envelops the soul and defines it's limits. The Law of Destiny is a substitution for the mental control of the animal functions because growth is accelerated by knowledge; "the Truth shall set you free" (John 8:32).

STEP 3 - BODY SUFFERING (ENOSH)

At this stage, the Sense Consciousness in its limited, material, corruptible form causes physical suffering. Enosh (E'-nos) in Hebrew means "mutable being, mortal man, suffering man, or miserable man". A belief in material forms, that the human consciousness is controlled by animal functions, will always result in suffering. Suffering is a clear indicator that man has strayed too far from the spiritual principals, and a correction must be made. The body may suffer until the soul gives up material ways, and returns to the peace and rest of Spirit. This is the hope symbolized by Seth. God did not create the suffering; man violated the natural law, and suffering will continue until the thoughts are corrected. THE DIVINE LAW IS NEUTRAL. It does not play favorites.

STEP 4 - ESTABLISHES CENTER (CAINAN)

At this stage, the higher and more spiritual thought, found in Seth, begins its work in the human consciousness. Cainan (ca'-nun), in Hebrew, means "possessor, centralizer, or one who fixes and establishes his center." The belief in physical forms, the human consciousness controlled by animal functions, and the suffering of the body, forces the human consciousness to reestablish its center. Since Spirit is all there is, the body is, in essence, spiritual also. Because it carries out the work of the mind; the mind is also Spirit. The body is never the cause of anything. It is neutral.

At this stage, the human consciousness has not yet made the connection to its spiritual nature. However, because of the balancing power of good (Seth), the human consciousness undergoes a change after recognizing the futility of its efforts, and begins to accept that its good comes from a higher source. Thus, the human consciousness begins to establish its center on more spiritual ideals.

STEP 5 - MIGHTY ARISING (MAHALALEL)

At this stage, man expresses his innate tendency to praise God. Mahalalel (ma-hal'-a-le-el), in Hebrew, means "mighty arising, glory of brightness, praise of God, or splender of God." With the human consciousness being controlled by animal functions, suffering of the body experienced, and the establishment of a more spiritual center, there is a mighty arising in the human consciousness. It is the suffering of the physical form, that forces the human consciousness to return to a belief in a power greater than itself. This is the mighty arising in the human consciousness which begins to seek guidance, through prayer, for its problems. To exalt God uplifts the human consciousness. Prayer is the first step in returning the soul to its Spiritual nature.

STEP 6 - DESCENT OF SPIRIT (JARED)

At this stage, there is the descent of Spirit to the human consciousness, through praise and acknowledgment of God. Jared (ja'-red), in Hebrew, means "descent, low country, or declining." A human consciousness, being controlled by animal forces yet willing to acknowledge Divine Mind through praise, can bring about thoughts that will allow spirit to descend into human consciousness. However, because of the animal forces, the human consciousness continues to slide away from spiritual ideals. Spirit cannot help the human consciousness until it first asks for guidance, and acknowledges Divine Mind as the source of all good. The human consciousness must first change its belief system from the outer physical thoughts to the inner spiritual ideals. Thus, descent of Spirit through praise, acknowledgment, and a strong belief in Divine Mind lifts the human consciousness to a higher state. Descent of Spirit is the source of Light and Life and is the author of the individual Self.

STEP 7 - INITIATOR OF NEW STATE (ENOCH).

At this stage, there is an entrance and instruction in a new state of thought and understanding. Enoch (e'nosh), in Hebrew, means "founder, centralizer, teacher, or initiator." With a fixed center, and the descent of Spirit into the human consciousness, there is a new state of thought brought forth into the human consciousness. Enoch is the seventh name in the genealogy of Jesus; seven in this case represents the completion of the Sense Consciousness. Enoch walked with God, so the new state of thought indicates that the soul has survived the desires and passions of the physical and is immortal. We are told that Enoch translated to heaven and did not experience death (Hebrew 11:5). Thus, the Spiritual seed of Jared germinates in Enoch and he translates from the physical plane to the spiritual realm.

STEP 8 - LIFE AND POWER (METHUSELAH).

At this stage, there is the quick piercing thought of life, power, and oneness with God in the human consciousness. Methuselah (me-thu'-se-lah) in Hebrew means "man of the sword, swift hurled dart of death, sending forth of death, or sting of death." The Sense Consciousness yields to the praise of God, which allows Spirit to descend to a new State of Thought, and the sting of death is put off. However, while this thought causes a renewal of consciousness and serves to lengthen life in the body, it is not strong enough to eliminate lack of understanding. Methuselah lived the longest of anyone in the Bible (969 years per Gen. 5:21-27). Human consciousness, at this stage of unfoldment, has not as yet accepted spiritual ideals and must be cleansed by Truth (the great flood).

STEP 9 - LAW AND ORDER (LAMECH)

At this stage there is the strength of youth in human consciousness, that vitality in us that overcomes thoughts and tendencies that destroy and separate. Lamech (la'-mek), in Hebrew, means "overthrown, leveler, principle of law and order, strength, and power." With a new state of thought, there is a renewal of youth, limited sensual thoughts are being over-thrown, and law and order begins to establish peace and calm in the human consciousness. There begins the building of a new body and re-entrance into a higher consciousness. However, thoughts of ignorance and lack of understanding have not as yet been enlightened by Spirit. Only by overcoming thoughts of separation, evil and sin is it possible to bring forth spiritual activity that will bring it peace and rest.

STEP 10 - LAW OF REACTION (NOAH)

At this stage, the human consciousness idealizes the material and attaches its spiritual enthusiasm to things of sense. Noah (no'-ah), in Hebrew, means "rest, calm, peace or equilibrium." With the initiation of a new state of thought; quick piercing thoughts of life, power and strength; and with the principles of law and order established, the Law of Reaction sets in. "And Noah was a just man perfect in his generations, and Noah walked with God" (Genesis 6:9). Noah represents the obedience through which the spiritual seed of consciousness is saved. Please note that Noah was perfect, which indicates a spiritual fulfillment of the first subcycle. Because of non-spiritual thoughts in the human consciousness, the Law of Reaction sets in and the wicked thoughts of materialism are swepted away and drowned (Noah and the flood). For this stage of evolution, Noah is perfect and walks with God, which means he has balanced the effects of the Spiritual and the material worlds. Thus, Noah, his three sons and their wives are spared from the purification of the flood.

The flood becomes necessary because the mind has been used in wrong relation to Truth, and all lesser ideas die or disappear through the process of transmutation (change from one thing to another). Water (flood) represents the mental potential that brings forth Truth, intelligence and purification; which in turn bring forth Spirit. The flood is a symbol of the downpouring of Truth into the lower mind, which enlarges the field of consciousness in the illusion of the lower life. Thus, truth is reflected in the awakening of mind to a more spiritual quality. A new state of consciousness is brought forth.

This new state of consciousness consists of the spiritual (Shem), the physical (Ham), and the intellectual or reasoning (Japheth). This is the trinity of man. The law of spiritual equilibrium is now working itself out in rest.

Thus, the flood completes the Spiritual development of the Sense Consciousness level of our Collective Consciousness model.

SUMMARY OF THE SENSE CONSCIOUSNESS

The first level (Adam to Noah) represents the Sense Consciousness or the first level of our Collective Consciousness model. At this level of unfoldment, man consciously has lost sight of who he is and the source of his being. Beguiled by Sense Consciousness, man identifies with the physical world and denies his natural spiritual state. He believes that he is a body, and the physical world is real. The world that he perceives is a fearful, lonely, and frightening place in which to live because he has allowed the "sea monsters" of the lower mind to rule his human consciousness. The sea monsters are the illusions created by non-spiritual thoughts. Without these negative thoughts, the human consciousness is protected by Spiritual Truth and Wisdom. The illusions, represented by the sea monsters, are exposed for what they are; NOTHING. The awakened human consciousness requires that we know and understand that our bodies and the physical world are created by non-spiritual thoughts. A consciousness fixed in the physical world receives information only from the five physical sensors; and perceives only desires and passions; like hunger, fear, warmth, and sexual needs. These perceptions are limited and deny the qualities of Spirit. Therefore, these perceptions must be eliminated, purified, and flooded by Truth before the next level of consciousness can be revealed. This new state of consciousness consists of three components, 1) spiritual (Shem), 2) physical (Ham), and 3) mental (Japheth).

CHAPTER 18:

PHYSICAL CONSCIOUSNESS

The original created idea of man was contaminated with negative thoughts resulting in undesirable moral character that led to violence. Violence resulted because the mind was used in the wrong relationship to Truth, and certain destructive processes set in. The man-made realm of thought was in a state of corruption. Here the Law of Reaction begins to regulate the human consciousness. Noah, his wife and his three sons and their wives enter the spiritual part of themselves (ark) as a means of preserving the individual qualities of the soul, while the Sense Consciousness is purified by the flood of Spiritual Truth. All the desires and passion of the flesh held in the subconscious (or lower mind), all the thoughts inherent in being and every mental thought died. Even the ideas that seemed to contain the "breath of life" are lost sight of in the fuller realization of Spirit as the only presence and power. "And the ark rested in the seventh month, on the seventeenth day of the month, upon the mountains of Ararat" (Genesis 8:4). The metaphysical interpretation of this verse might read, "And the spiritual part of man rested in the fullness of the Divine law of perfection, upon the aspirations of the soul to a higher plane of consciousness of a holy place". Ararat represents a sacred land unknown to the spiritually unwakened man. Thus, the second level of the Collective Consciousness Model begins to unfold. Figure 14 illustrates the Physical Consciousness level of the Collective Consciousness model.

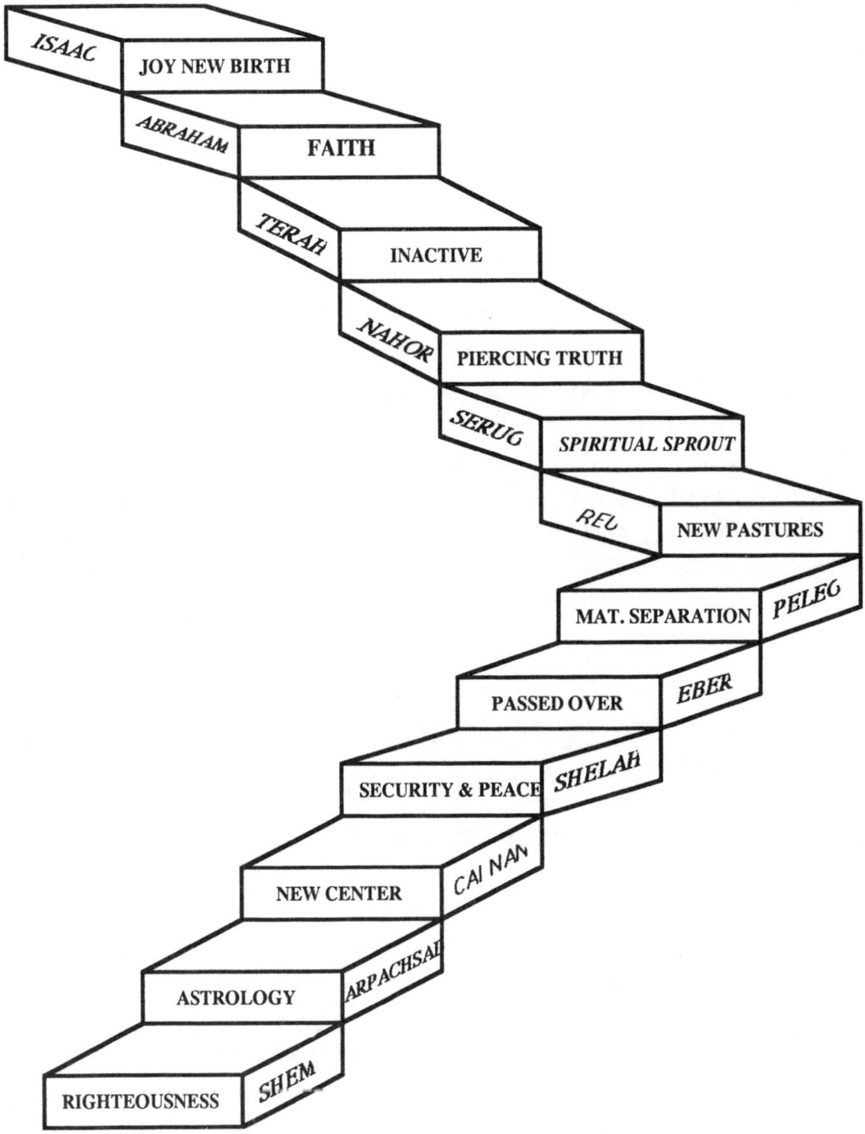

FIGURE 14 - PHYSICAL CONSCIOUSNESS, LEVEL 2

STEP 1 - RIGHTEOUS THOUGHT (SHEM)

At this stage of consciousness, the source of all manifestation is in the mind. Shem, in Hebrew, means "upright, righteous, brilliant, splender, or dignity"; and represents the spiritual in the human consciousness. The new state of thought of Enoch, brought into equilibrium (Noah), is cleansed of all negative thoughts, and becomes manifested at a higher Physical Consciousness. The Physical Consciousness begins to understand and know that there is one intelligence of the universe. Therefore, God, Spirit and Mind are words describing the same creative source. An idea arises in human consciousness of something it wants to do. This idea is the Son. It manifests exactly like the Father; and is the Father in degree. Thus, Shem begins to understand the spiritual ideals. However, since the human consciousness is still focused on the outer physical realm, the idea of spirit has not yet germinated.

STEP 2 - REALM OF ASTROLOGY (ARPACHSHAD).

At this stage, the human consciousness believes that good depends wholly upon something outside itself. Arpachshad (ar-pak'-shad), in Hebrew, means "providential regeneration or realm of astrology." He is called Arphaxad (ar-fax'-ad) in Luke 3:36. When the thoughts of separation and sin have been overthrown, and mental potential has been purified, human consciousness begins to understand that there is a greater intelligence. However, thoughts in human consciousness are still being dominated by the senses and, in its confusion, the Physical Consciousness still thinks that good comes from something, or someone, outside of itself. The Physical Consciousness is just beginning to understand spiritual concepts, and assumes the good is from the realm of astrology. There a belief in the ruling power of the stars, or providence, instead of its own inner power. Although these psychic thoughts are of higher quality than the physical thoughts, they are not spiritual, but shine from borrowed light, or understanding.

STEP 3 - ACQUISITION OF NEW CENTER (CAINAN). At this stage, Spiritual concepts begin to be understood as man shifts his thoughts from himself to something greater than himself. Cainan (ca'-nun), in Hebrew, means "possessor, centralizer, one who fixes and establishes his center, or acquisition." The human consciousness *begins* to understands that the source of all manifestation is in the mind, but there is still a *belief* that its good comes from outside itself, and the human consciousness establishes a new center on Spiritual concepts. However, righteous thoughts in the human consciousness are being dominated by a belief in providence that brings about the change. This change is the result of psychic thoughts, which are of higher quality than those of the physical thoughts. Thus, at this point the human consciousness believes that its good comes from the heavenly stars. Stars, metaphysically, represent revelations of Truths that are as yet remote, and are lights of reason on the subconscious mind. However, the resulting understanding is from a reflected truth, similar to the moon obtaining its light from the sun. The moon of itself does not generate light. Thus, the understanding is truth that has been interpreted by the human consciousness, and is not Truth direct from the Source. At this point in human consciousness, it cannot conceive of the wonders and immensity of the universe of stars and heaven that is available to it.

Please note that the Bible does not give any data of when this Cainan was born, or when he died. He is the only one of the first twenty-four names where this data is missing. I believe that this Cainan is only a place marker to make the model complete (see chapter 16).

STEP 4 - SECURITY AND PEACE (SHELAH). At this stage, there begins to be established an inner connection with a concept of God. Shelah (she'-lah) is Hebrew, and the name means, " tranquility, security, and peace," that comes about through prayer. When the human consciousness *begins* to understands that the source of all manifestation is in the mind, but still thinks its good comes from the outside, and a new center is acquired, then there is a sense of peace and tranquility that comes about through the use of prayer. Prayer is the communication between the human consciousness and the Divine Mind. We can affirm the words of Truth and meditate on them, then be still and wait in the silence of Divine Mind to make them real to us. "What things soever ye desire, when ye pray, believe that ye receive them, and ye shall have them," (Mark 11:24). Why do we need to ask when we are told, "Your father knoweth what things ye have need of before ye ask him," (Mark 6:8)? Asking is an indication of our willingness to own it, knowing that Divine Mind is a greater reservoir that can be tapped by man's individualized mind. In other words, the individual mind can choose the Truth of Spirit over the illusions of the lower mind. If the human consciousness is clogged with doubt and fear, the answers will be blocked. These limitations can be overcome by faithful knocking and asking, which opens the door to spiritual understanding.

STEP 5 - PASSED OVER (EBER).

At this stage, a new perception of truth begins germinating in the human consciousness. Eber (e'-bur), in Hebrew, means "passed over, overcome, beyond the world, or shoot." Thinking that good comes from outside itself and having established a new center and a sense of security and peace results in the germination of the spiritual phase of its being. "Beyond" indicates that the individual, at this stage of unfoldment, has not yet come to full growth spiritually. It is through prayer that the Spirit germinates, and the human consciousness is lifted to a higher level. Note that a change in consciousness always occurs in the next level after an individual whose name means peace, rest, etc... (Shelah). So, we would expect that Eber would represent the germination of the spiritual phase of being. However, Eber indicates the human consciousness has passed over its old concept of mortality, and has entered into a new perception of truth, and the possibility of limitless attainment. All thoughts of separation, lack, doubt, and fear must be removed before Spirit can move into, and wholly reside, in the human consciousness. Thus, the spiritual phase of being and the separation of the spiritual from the material is not accomplished until Peleg.

STEP 6 - MATERIAL SEPARATION (PELEG).
At this stage, the human consciousness begins to realize the difference between earthly concepts and its higher ideals. Peleg (pe'-leg), in Hebrew, means "moral distinction, separation through grace, or distinction of principle." The acquisition of a new center, the inner connection with the concept of spirit, and the passing over of the material concepts yields material separation. Thus, the spiritual in the human consciousness begins to germinate from the seeds of Shem, in Peleg, as opposed to Eber. This is the stage where the human consciousness first realizes the difference and begins to separate between the material organism and its inner spiritual ideals. Spiritual knowledge comes to the human consciousness through grace. Before this time, the human consciousness only knew the sensual and material thoughts. At this point, the Physical Consciousness begins to break up, and Spirit clears a path for a new level of consciousness.

STEP 7 - LEADING TO PASTURE (REU).
At this stage, there is a new perception of Truth, and there begins the joining of material thoughts with spiritual concepts. Reu (re'-u), in Hebrew, means "leading to pasture, feeding a flock or shepherd." The inner connection with the Divine Mind, the passing over of purely material ideas, and the separation of the material from the spiritual brings the human consciousness to cooperative feelings of fellowship and active concern for others. This is the feeding of the flock and leading it to greener pastures that Reu's name implies. Thus, a new level of understanding is being brought to the human consciousness. Note that this is the seventh name mentioned in this level, and indicates that the body awareness of the material consciousness has been completed and a higher (mental) consciousness begins. At this higher level human consciousness, the human consciousness

begins to have cooperative feelings of fellowship, and takes an active responsibility for the welfare of others. There is a sense of loving, and Love is always of Spirit. This is the first indication of man's willingness to join, or unite with others. Joining is always of God, and is the facility of love in the human consciousness.

STEP 8 - SPIRITUAL SHOOT (SERUG).

At this stage, there is the budding of a spiritual seed in the human consciousness. Serug (se'-rug), in Hebrew, means, "woven together, interwoven, branch, or shoot." When Truth begins to germinate, and the differences between physical and spiritual ideals are recognized, there is a joining of the individualized and spiritual minds, and the budding of a spiritual seed takes place in the human consciousness. It is the budding, sprouting, growing and developing of the spiritual seed, or Truth ideas, down deep in the human consciousness that is preparatory to extending spiritual life to the body. This work is done mostly in secret, because there is only a small ray of light, or understanding, of the spiritual idea. The human consciousness, whether it conceives of itself as individual or universal, "for the two are one", receives images of thoughts as they are created. Therefore, the human consciousness, at this point, is God's intelligence operating upon patterns of thought, without reflective, or self-conscious knowing. Thus, the spiritual work is done in secret without the conscious mind being aware of its presence.

STEP 9 - PIERCING TRUTH (NAHOR).

At this stage, there begins the actual breaking up, or slaying, of the Physical Consciousness. Nahor (na'-hor), in Hebrew, means "angry, passionate, or piercing." When one realizes that there is a difference between physical and spiritual ideals, the joining of these ideals causes the budding of the spiritual seed. The Truth, then, pierces the Physical Consciousness and it begins to break up. However, this process is more subconscious than conscious. This new action creates an inner excitement with the breaking up of the lesser ideal, because so much of the outer, limited, personal and emotional self enters into it. This is the first time that Truth has been able to penetrate the Physical Consciousness, and a new line of thought action can be brought forth.

STEP 10 - INACTIVE SPIRITUALITY (TERAH).
Prior to this stage, man's spirituality has been inactive. Terah (te'-rah), in Hebrew, means "lagging behind, delaying, or waiting in place," which confirms that the human consciousness has been spiritually inactive. With cooperative feelings of fellowship and the spiritual seed beginning to grow in the subconscious, there is a piercing of Truth, and the higher spiritual forces press forth to religious activity. The movement in Physical Consciousness has been delayed by the sense consciousness to the extent that an individual lives in and is guided by the five physical senses. However, the spiritual inner impulse virtually says, "Get thee out of thy country, and from thy kindred, and from thy father's house, unto the land that I will show thee," (Gen. 12:1). As it breaks away from the sense-conscious thoughts, and the associated illusions that are housed in the Physical Consciousness, and moves into the unfolding conscious awareness of the inner spiritual forces, the lofty ideals begin to possess the conscious mind.

STEP 11 - FAITH, THE FIRST STEP (ABRAHAM).
At this stage, the higher desire of spirituality pierces the darkness of materiality and aids in bringing about a new line of thought in the Physical Consciousness. Abraham (a'-bra-ham), in Hebrew, means "father, source, or founder of a multitude." With the spiritual seed budding in the subconscious and the higher spiritual forces bringing forth religious activity, Truth pierces the darkness of materiality and man intuitively knows that God is the living source of all existence. This new thought is the power of the mind to reproduce its ideas in unlimited expression. It is a sense of that which is superior to knowledge, and is the intui-

tion of Truth. The ability of the mind to make substance out of ideals is called faith. Faith is the highest power of reasoning activity, asserting itself and vindicating itself against the lower nature. Faith is the conscious ideal demonstrated by Abraham. When faith is concentrated upon the one God, a God Consciousness is established and man intuitively knows that he is in communication with the ever-living source of all existence.

Jehovah told Abraham that he was to be the "father of a multitude", which means the human consciousness is to express faith by bringing the faith of God into the multitude of manifested thoughts and acts. "If ye have faith as a grain of mustard seed, ye shall say unto this mountain, Remove hence to yonder place; and it shall remove; and nothing shall be impossible unto you," (Matthew 17:20). This is saying that through faith anything is possible. Thus, the first step in spiritual development is the awakening of faith in the invisible.

STEP 12 - JOY OF NEW BIRTH (ISAAC).
At this stage, there is joy of new birth as man begins a new relationship with God. Isaac (i'-za-ak), in Hebrew, means "laughter, joy, or singing," which signifies the joys of the new birth and a new life in relationship to God the Father. When Truth breaks up the subconscious, a new thought action is brought forth, religious activity comes to the forefront, man intuitively knows the source of his being, and there is the joy of a new birth. The concept of faith is born of Spirit, thus, a new relationship with God is established. According to the Bible, Isaac was born after Sarah was past the age of bearing children (90 years old per Genesis 17:17). She had been barren, and there was no possibility that Isaac's conception was of natural causes. He was born of Spirit and not of the flesh. This is similar to the virgin birth of Jesus. Is it possible that Jesus's birth is a symbol of a virgin consciousness that has not been contaminated by either the physical or mental thoughts of the world, and has nothing to do with sexual activity? The physical man has no power to bring forth the "new man" in Jesus the Christ. This new consciousness is not yet spiritual, because it is still of the outer body consciousness, but there is a sense of serenity, peace and joy when man accepts spiritual

things as real and lives, "as seeing him who is invisible." Isaac is the twelfth name in this level, and signifies the completion of the Physical Consciousness.

SUMMARY OF THE PHYSICAL CONSCIOUSNESS

The second level (Shem to Isaac), represents Physical consciousness, which begins to separate the spiritual from the physical thoughts. The human consciousness begins to be watchful of its thoughts, and separates that which is true from the illusions that it perceives. The human consciousness begins to realize that its good comes from Spirit, and not from something outside itself. The realization of the existence of Spirit is the first step in separating from the physical realm. As the human consciousness separates from the physical senses, it has cooperative feelings, it grows in spirit, the senses begin to break up, and it experiences the joy of a new thought system. However, at this stage, the human consciousness still identifies with the physical, and gives power to those outside forces in the realm of astrology, or psychic thoughts that connect the individual with the energies of the Physical Consciousness, the earth and the heavenly bodies. This is not spiritual, but shines by a borrowed light. An example of this consciousness would be to totally rely on a horoscope for guidance. Spiritual knowledge, born of experience, brings the lower nature into harmonious relation with the higher. It is comparable to a small seed capable of developing into a great tree. It can overcome great difficulties with sufficient knowledge to effect the desired results. To the indwelling, spirit nothing is impossible.

CHAPTER 19:

INDIVIDUAL CONSCIOUSNESS

With Isaac, man began a spiritual relationship with God. This new consciousness is begotten by the Divine Seed and fulfills the admonition, "Let Christ be formed in You." This new consciousness is not yet spiritual, because it is still of the body consciousness, but there is a sense of peace and joy when spiritual things are accepted as real by the human consciousness. This new state of consciousness moves out of the purely physical to the intellect and imagination. This mental identification involves choice between uniting with, or rejecting, concepts of different perceptions that are presented to it. This choosing faculty introduces *will*, which makes man (individuality) as God. It is the function of the intellect to disclose differences and perceive similarities but, unaided by intuition, it can never reveal the perfect Truth because it unites with that which it perceives. It, therefore, requires an expanding influence, and this it finds in uniting with the emotions, which strive against limitations. Intellect that accepts the good and true is instinctively drawn towards the Divine ideals, and the personal consciousness evolves toward perfection, into intelligence through knowledge and understanding of the Divine ideals. The intellect at first is unaware of the existence of a higher source of Truth, for it cannot conceive of that which is not self-derived; it can only imagine that knowledge which is obtained through the physical senses. The mental phase of our journey to perfection will be discussed in the next three chapters. Figure 15 illustrates the Individual Consciousness, which is the first level in the mental identification, and the third level in our Collective Consciousness Model.

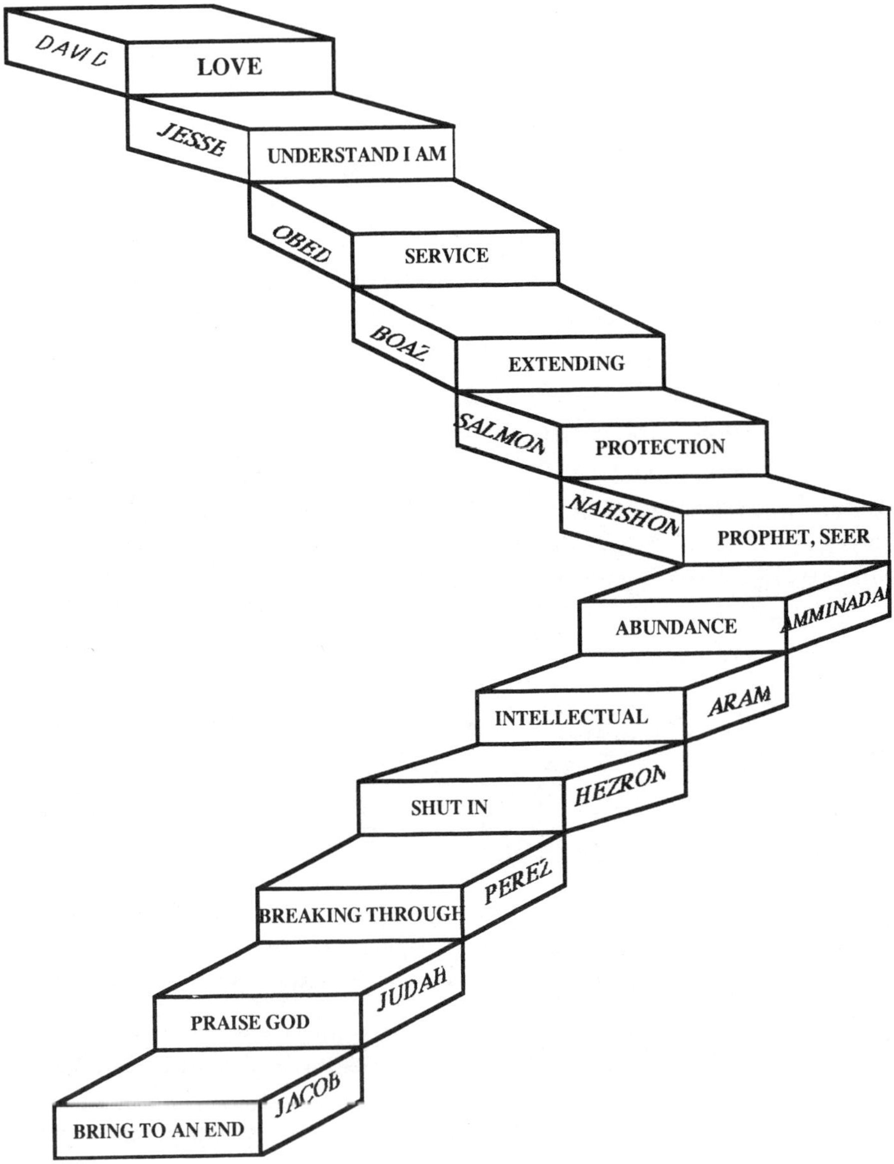

FIGURE 15 - INDIVIDUAL CONSCIOUSNESS, LEVEL 3

STEP 1 - BRING TO AN END (JACOB).
At this stage, the individual gives power to the mind as opposed to the physical. Jacob (ja'-cub), in Hebrew, means "heel catcher, supplanter, leaving behind, or bringing to an end." When the Spirit becomes active and Faith pierces the darkness of the Physical Consciousness, there begins a new relationship with God, which brings about an Individual Consciousness. This Individual Consciousness supplants, or overrides the animal nature, and is not reached without conflict. We are told that Esau was the first-born of Isaac, and not Jacob. This means that the animal consciousness (Esau) comes first into expression until it is supplanted by a higher mental consciousness (Jacob). Jacob and Rebekah trick Isaac into giving his blessings to Jacob instead of Esau, the first-born. This can hardly be considered a spiritual act until it is seen in the light of spiritual understanding. In this story we see the subtle working of the soul in spiritual evolution, which is under the guidance of the Divine Mind. The soul is progressive, and must always go forward and upward. In this evolution, the soul meets and overcomes its limitation. The mental is more closely aligned with Spirit than the material consciousness of Esau. Thus, the mental gains supremacy and the physical loses power. To do this, Jacob and Rebekah persuade Isaac to acknowledge the importance of mind as first in consciousness. Then, the spiritualized thoughts of the mind become the seeds that bless all the world. Thus, Jacob's ladder represents a step-by-step realization of the Truth.

In Genesis 33:1-15, we are told of the reunion of Jacob and Esau (the mental preparing to unite with the physical expression). At first the mind is willing to share its expansion, but the body (Esau) cannot receive the gift until it is uplifted. Verses 10 and 11 indicate that the body and mind are reconciled and adjusted, and share alike the gifts of Spirit. However, the mind must always come before the body, because the mind is of Spirit. Verse 13 indicates that this new idea is being established in human consciousness. Verses 14 and 15 indicate no hostility between the mind and the body. Differences exist only at different stages of conscious awareness. When the body becomes an obedient servant to the mind, both are united in Divine Mind.

STEP 2 - PRAISE GOD (JUDAH).
At this stage, there is an increase in the mental through prayer and praise. Judah (ju'-dah), in Hebrew, means, "praise Jehovah, celebration of Jehovah, or laud Jehovah." When the higher desires of spirituality pierce the darkness of materiality, a new concept of a spiritual relationship with God is born, the physical conscious desires are brought to and end, and the mental is increased through prayer and praise. Prayer quickens the mind and causes it to attract, like a magnet, the realm of causes which fulfill the desires. Prayer is an expression of the spiritual consciousness. Prayer is accumulative, and accumulates spiritual substance, life, intelligence and everything else necessary to man's highest expression. When prayer is done with spiritual understanding, the highest realm of mind comes in touch with the universal and impersonal Mind, and the mind of man is joined to the very mind of God. Thus, God answers our prayers in ideas, thoughts and words, which are translated into the outer realm of form, in due time. "For everyone that asketh receiveth; and he that seeketh findeth; and to him that knocketh it shall be opened," (Luke 11:10). To me, this verse says that every spiritual appeal from the lower self meets with a response from the Higher. Prayer is the desire to rise above the limitations of our imperfect nature, and enter into communion with that larger life of which we are only dimly conscious. To seek God is to seek goodness, which brings the human consciousness into the current of God's purposes. It is the means whereby the human consciousness ascends to higher knowledge.

STEP 3 - BREAKING THROUGH (PEREZ).
At this stage, there is victory through praise, and making a way out of limitation and error. Perez (pe'-res), in Hebrew, means "broken through, breached, torn asunder, or demolished." When power is given to the mind, as opposed to the things of desire and sense, physical thoughts are brought to an end, the mental is increased and there is a break through from limitation and error thinking. Progress is now being made toward working out

apparent limitations and errors, and rising above them by means of prayer and praise. Praise and thanksgiving multiply and increase everything that human consciousness centers its attention on. Jesus gave thanks before He raised Lazarus from the dead, and before He multiplied the loaves and the fishes. Praise keeps the soul fresh, pure and beautiful; it is the power that opens the inner portals of the soul to the full and free inflow of spiritual light and aspiration. Both the higher and lower natures of the soul conform to the Divine laws of evolution and progress.

STEP 4 - SHUT IN THOUGHTS (HEZRON).

At this stage, there are thoughts that belong to seeing, praise and prayer in the mind. Hezron (hez'-ron), in Hebrew, means "enclosed, shut in, or green pastures." When the Physical Consciousness is broken up and brought to an end, there is a breakthrough of the Individual Consciousness to thoughts related to "seeing". Since man already has physical eyes for seeing, I believe "seeing" in this case pertains to spiritual seeing, or vision: a perception of understanding and truth. However, these thoughts are not yet free in their expression in the Individual Consciousness and the seeing is clouded by the imperfect Individual Consciousness thinking. They are enclosed, shut in by limiting error beliefs. A belief is the union of the mind with a percept, or concept, that is presented to it. The human mind unites with any idea, if there is no opposing idea that is already accepted. Truth reveals itself in symbols; beliefs reveal themselves in forms. When beliefs become hardened and inflexible they resist growth, and thus limit the soul's evolution. "For as he thinketh in his heart, so is he...." (Proverbs 23:7). However, at this stage, these limiting beliefs are being thrown off and the truth is expressing itself more and more freely and fully.

STEP 5 - INTELLECTUAL THOUGHTS (ARAM).

At this stage, the intellect has its foundation in Spirit, but in unawakened man, one who is still limited to physical consciousness, it has linked itself entirely with the outer material realm. Aram (a'-ram), in Hebrew, means, "highlands, high, or exalted," and is referring to the intellect. When the mental is increased and the errors and limitations of the human consciousness are broken up and removed, then truth is expressed as intelligence. However, the Individual Consciousness reasons from the base of sense instead of acknowledging Divine Mind as the source of intelligence. The intellect is very necessary to man, and it becomes truly high and exalted when it is illuminated by Spirit. In fact, this is intelligence. The Individual Consciousness, in its confusion, exalts the intellect even above the wisdom of Spirit. Such exaltation cannot last, because intellectual understanding gives way, at some point, to spiritual knowing. The intellect cannot of itself inherit the things of Spirit, but when united with intuition it produces love and truth.

STEP 6 - ABUNDANCE (AMMINADAB).
At this stage, there is the broad-mindedness and generosity of true spiritual thoughts in the individual. Amminadab (am-min'-a-dab), in Hebrew, means, "people of liberty, people of willing generosity, or my people in abundance," which indicates generosity of Spiritual thoughts. Breaking through from its errors and limitations opens the soul to the portals of spiritual truth, and the truth opens the Individual Consciousness to the realm of intellect as opposed to sense reasoning. The Individual Consciousness begins to realize the possibilities that lie in the mind of God. However, the human consciousness can only be aware of the possibilities, because the intellectual understanding has not yet given way to spiritual knowing.

STEP 7 - PROPHET OR SEER (NAHSHON).
At this stage, there is the reception of Divine Wisdom and Knowledge into Individual Consciousness, and the imparting of religious thoughts. Nahshon (nah'-shon), in Hebrew, means, "enchanter, whisperer, prophet, or seer." When the truth is expressed more freely, the intellect is raised above the Individual Consciousness, which frees the generosity of spiritual thoughts, and the reception of Divine Wisdom and Knowledge is expressed as religion. There is still a superstitious belief in magic, as evidenc-

ed by "enchanter", or "whisperer" in the meaning of his name. However, the Individual Consciousness is learning that there is a prophet or seer, in each of us who knows the natural outcome of our thought tendencies and can foretell clearly what we are bringing to ourselves. Thus, we are shown where error thought activities lead and we can overcome them; replacing them with the good of Spirit. This is the seventh step in this level, and represents the fulfillment of the limited concepts of the I AM in the Individual Consciousness.

STEP 8 - PEACE AND PROTECTION (SALMON).

At this stage, the idea of peace and perfection become established in the Individual Consciousness and cover it with harmony, poise, strength and Truth. Salmon (sal'-mon), in Hebrew, means, "covered, clothed, strong, firm or peaceable." The intellectual thoughts under the direction of Spirit bring wisdom and intelligence to the Individual Consciousness. The Spiritual Truth gives us protection from the limited beliefs of the Individual Consciousness, and covers it with a sense of peace. Peace is the vital and vibrant quality of joyous serenity, where everything is in harmonious relationship with the Divine Mind. Peace is the indwelling Spirit that is extending God's wisdom and knowledge. As the Individual Consciousness becomes aware of this condition, the physical body is uplifted, regenerated and born again.

STEP 9 - EXTENDING PROTECTION (BOAZ).

At this stage, there is a cheerful willingness and quickness of action in the Individual Consciousness to extend protection and love to the soul in its natural state with God. Boaz (bo'-az), in Hebrew, means, "quickness, fleetness, in strength, might or in power." When the Individual Consciousness realizes the abundance and possibilities that lie in the Mind of God, it begins to see the untapped potential in Spiritual Thinking, and protection is extended to the soul. The Bible tells us that Boaz was very wealthy and extended protection to Ruth (love of the soul in its natural state). Here is richness, power of thought, and strength of character, that when established in substance and allied with the love of the soul opens the way for the birth of the Christ into consciousness.

STEP 10 - SERVICE AND WORSHIP (OBED)

At this stage, there is an active thought that pertains to service and worship. Obed (o'-bed), in Hebrew, means, "laboring, working, making, serving or worshipping." The imparting of religious thoughts plus the establishment of harmony, strength and Truth expands the Individual Consciousness to the protection of love, and results in an active thought pertaining to service and worship. When the physical characteristics of strength, might and power (Boaz) are united with love of the soul in its natural state (Ruth), it manifests in service or worship. "God is a spirit: and they that worship him must worship him in spirit and in Truth," (St. John 4:24). In other words, God is Mind; and they that worship Him must worship through thinking, or by their thoughts. Mind, in its highest aspect, and Spirit are synonymous.

STEP 11 - UNDERSTAND THE I AM (JESSE).

At this stage, man begins to understand the eternal existence of the I AM, and is firm and strong in this realization. Jesse (jes'-se), in Hebrew, means, "understanding, firm, strong, upright or Jehovah is." The root meaning of Jesse, in Hebrew, is Jah, Jehovah, or the I AM. When the Individual Consciousness is established in harmony, strength and Truth, the Individual Consciousness is expanded to the action of love, begins to think spiritual thoughts and begins to understand the eternal existence of the I AM. Out of this state of mind comes God's idea of man, the Christ. This is the shoot, or fruit, of the root idea that man is the ever living I AM of God (Isaiah 11:1). David, the son of Jesse, is representative of the Christ, or the spiritual seed from which came Jesus Christ. The Christ is the spiritual man expressed and demonstrated.

STEP 12 - LOVE INDIVIDUALIZED (DAVID).

At this stage, Divine Love is individualized in the human consciousness. David, in Hebrew, means, "beloved, loved, or well-beloved." According to Matthew 1:1, David is a Christ-type man, "Jesus (the) Christ, the son of David, the son of Abraham." Of course, this is a figure of speech and is bringing together the Christ form in body (Abraham), Mind (David), and Spirit (Jesus). In Matthew 22:42-45, Jesus confirms that the Christ existed before David.

The overcoming of Goliath, by David, illustrates the mastery of the spiritual over the material. Goliath trusted in his armor, which represents the protective power of matter and physical conditions. David represents spiritual strength and had no armor, or material protection. His power was gained by trust in Divine Intelligence. Love in Being (God) is the idea of perfect unity in all existence. When the Divine Idea is focused in man it is the Christ Love on its inner side and Jesus love on its outer. When David was in his youth and purity, he daily communed with God, and he closely reflected Divine Love. However, as king, in domination over men, he manifested the limitations of the human character. This is the twelfth step, and represents the completion of the Individual idea of the I AM, and the beginning of Spiritual understanding.

SUMMARY OF THE INDIVIDUAL CONSCIOUSNESS

The third level (Jacob to David), represents active spiritual thoughts beginning to give power to God, or the I AM. This level of consciousness gives power to the mind as opposed to the physical body. It is through the reasoning power of the intellect that the human consciousness is provided with the ability to choose. It is the choosing faculty that introduces will, which makes man individually as God. It is the function of the intellect to disclose differences and perceive similarities, but the intellect never perceives the perfect Truth. Perfect Truth is based on intelligence, which is of God, but the intellect is based on individual knowing. Intellectual knowing is always limited, because it is contaminated by the illusions of the physical world and is based on sense-perception, as opposed to the Truth. However, at this level the Truth begins to subdue the material beliefs by expressing praise. The Intellect has its foundation in Spirit, but in the unawakened man, it has linked itself entirely with the outer realm, where it reasons from the base of sense, instead of acknowledging the Divine Mind as the source of intelligence. Thus, the human consciousness grows from the intellect based on reason to the intelligence based on Spiritual Truth. The intellect grows by drawing on intuition and emotions to obtain knowledge of Divine Ideals. It is knowledge that sets the human consciousness free of the limitations of individual thinking. Thus, it is through the imagination of Jacob and his ladder that we begin the process of mental choice that allows the human consciousness to unfold at different levels of awareness as the Spiritual Truth of Wisdom and Love is accepted and embraced.

The intellect is very necessary to man, becoming truly high and exalted when illuminated by Spirit. Even though at this level there is still a superstitious belief in magic, and only a small ray of spiritual understanding, there is a prophet, or seer, in each of us who knows the natural outcome of our thoughts and who can see the path before us. As long as we accept the limits of Individual Consciousness there will always be some degree of separation between ourselves and God.

CHAPTER 20:

MENTAL CONSCIOUSNESS

The Mental Consciousness is the conscious reasoning that leaves behind the limited perceptions that everything exists for the individual, and reaches out to God, or the Divine Mind, for guidance. The human consciousness is the passive aspect of Spirit on the mental plane. It manifests itself from either the higher or the lower planes. As the spiritual consciousness descends into matter from the higher mental plane, it also rises from the lower. As the physical matter becomes full of spiritual qualities, it is fully formed and operated upon from the higher Spiritual ideals. The lower, or separated, consciousness is an illusion, since it answers to the limited nature of the Self. The consciousness itself is one, but in the material manifestation it appears as many. This apparent separation is due to the limitation of the mind that filters out much of the information that it receives. In reality, the dual consciousnesses are not opposites to each other, but are mutually helpful in bringing the Christ Consciousness into being. The Christ Consciousness is possible only as the Divine Life within itself overcomes the forms and conquers the untruths that shield its true nature. Thus, the Mental Consciousness is another phase that leads us to perfection. Figure 16 illustrates the Mental Con-sciousness, Level 4 of the Collective Consciousness Model.

STEP 1 - REACHING OUT TO SPIRIT (NATHAN)

At this stage, there is spiritual power and understanding behind

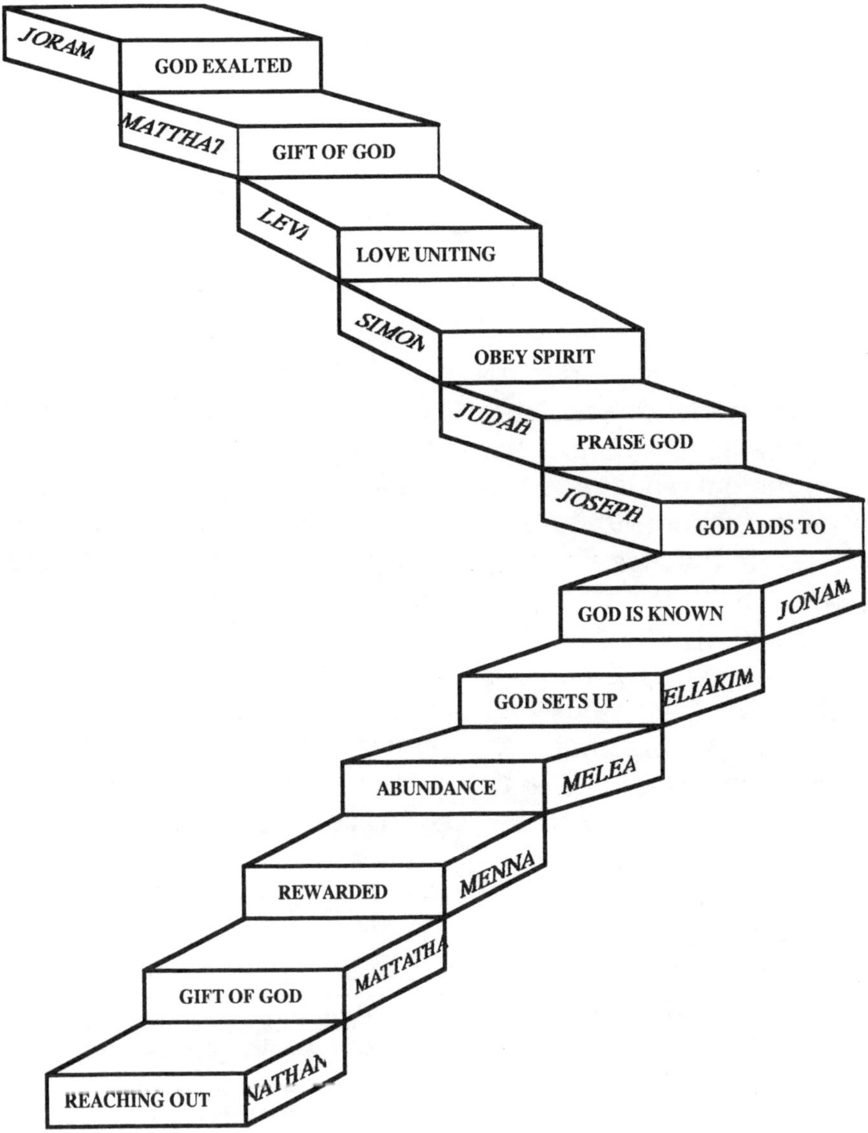

FIGURE 16 - MENTAL CONSCIOUSNESS, LEVEL 4

the words of Truth. Nathan (na'-than), in Hebrew, means "reaching out the hand, giver, give up, grant reward, or instruct." When one worships the Truth and begins to understand the I AM through Love of Spirit, there is a natural reaching out to Spirit. If we declare our word of authority without considering its spiritual relation, it will lack certain elements of stability and understanding. Instead of being related to the one Source, it will be associated with some of the many man-made thoughts. Thus, the spiritual qualities of power, foresight, and understanding must be present and active in our true words, that these words may be alive and pregnant with success and the good of Spirit. Thus, the human consciousness must reach out to Spirit for guidance and give up its attachment to the physical ways.

STEP 2 - GIFT OF GOD (MATTATHA).
At this stage, there is the perception by the ruling Mental Consciousness of the grace of God, or the possibility of attainment through the Christ. Mattatha (mat'-ta-thah), in Hebrew, means, "gift of Jehovah, or donation of Jah." Understanding the eternal existence of God, opening to spiritual understanding and reaching out for Truth brings the perception of the grace of God to the Mental Consciousness. It is the higher religious thoughts of man awakening to a realization of the Divine Possibilities of obtaining fullness of Life and Good through the Christ (gift of Jehovah). However, at this stage the individual does not seem to understand the necessity for being obedient to the Divine Law. The Mental Consciousness perceives and expects God's blessings, but does not realize the necessity for being obedient to the good in order to reap the good. It wants prophets to prophesy good to it, while it goes on in wicked and unbelieving ways. It is through the action of the higher nature that the qualities progress towards perfection in response to the aspiration and faith of the lower nature. The lower nature, of itself, cannot progress. The activities of the lower mind are ineffectual without the aid of the Spirit of Truth. This is truly the gift of God.

STEP 3 - REWARDED WITH GOOD (MENNA).
At this stage, the Mental Consciousness perceives that its good comes from God. Menna (men'-na), in Hebrew, means, "numbered, meted, or rewarded." When the Mental Consciousness reaches out to the Divine Possibilities of obtaining fullness of Life, it perceives the gifts of God, and is rewarded with only the good. The Mental Consciousness now perceives that the constantly increasing good thoughts and desires are meted (number ed) by God, and that the individual reaps greater and greater good accordingly. The nature of this authority, of being numbered, indicates that the Mental Consciousness is still being controlled by limiting beliefs. The perception is that good is a symbol of the perfect production of qualities of forms from the upper planes of being. "And God saw that it was good," (Genesis 1:10). The Truth is that good is brought about by being obedient to the Divine Laws, and the Mental Consciousness is rewarded with good experiences for the purpose of evolving to perfection.

STEP 4 - ABUNDANCE (MELEA).
At this stage, there is an inner discernment of the abundance of Spirit. Melea (mel'-e-ah), in Hebrew, means, "fullness, fully supplied, abundance or full measure." The spiritual power and understanding behind the words of Truth and the realization of Divine Possibilities through God reap the good and there is an inner discernment of the abundance of Spirit. A Mental Consciousness of abundance attracts more abundance, while fear or lack attracts limitation. Since thought produces fact, then fact must be like the thought that produced it (seeds after its kind). Therefore, abundance is identical with thought. The Mental Consciousness discerns between the good and not so good, and chooses only the good if the negative thoughts are to be cleansed away by the power of Spirit.

STEP 5 - GOD SETS UP (ELIAKIM).
At this stage, there is the will (which is of God) taking command. Eliakim (e-li'-a-kim), in Hebrew, means, "God sets up, whom God has established, God of raising judgment, or raised of God." Being obedient to the Law and reaping greater and greater good attracts more abundance to the Mental Consciousness, and allows the Will of God to be set up and take command. This command may arise out of a negative attitude of thoughts, and become positive in one's judgment. In the Mental Consciousness there are both the good and the spoiling of good (evil) until the seeming negative has been cleansed away by the power of Spirit. Yet the individual may use this power for good or for ill, according to whether he acts from the intellect or from true understanding. Thus, God set up the Mental Consciousness to receive the uplifting thoughts of Spirit to purify every error tendency and become established in Love and Truth. Truth and Love allow the Mental Consciousness to be positive in the good and use the power and judgment of God within it in righteous and constructive ways. This is similar to weeding a garden to remove what is not wanted. If the weeds are not removed, they will totally consume the garden. However, a weeded garden can be a thing of beauty and a source of enjoyment. The same is true of our thoughts.

STEP 6 - GOD BECOMING KNOWN (JONAM).
At this stage, the Spirit of love, mercy and peace are becoming known and established in the Mental Consciousness. Jonam (jo'-nan), in Hebrew, means, "Jehovah bestows mercy, Jah is gracious, Jehovah gives graciously, or mercy and compassion of the Lord". Being obedient to the Law and the discernment between productive and non-productive thoughts produces positive attitudes and thoughts, and the mercy and compassion of God becomes known to the Mental Consciousness. The Spirit can only become known to the Mental Consciousness after error thoughts of negativity have been cleansed. Removing the negative thoughts removes the confusion from the mind, and allows the concept of Spirit to return to being first in Mental Con-

sciousness. Thus God, or the Divine Mind, bestows mercy and shows compassion by providing spiritual truth to the Mental Consciousness. It is the Truth that exposes the illusions of the Mental Consciousness for what they are, nothing. Thus, they become unbelievable, and can be discarded from the mind.

STEP 7 - GOD WILL ADD TO (JOSEPH).
At this stage, there is a state of consciousness in which the Mental Consciousness increases in character along all lines. Joseph (jo'-sef), in Hebrew, means, "Whom Jehovah will add to, Jehovah will increase, or he shall increase progressively." Discernment of Truth, plus rising above negative attitudes of thought removes confusion in the Mental Consciousness, and Spirit returns to being first in consciousness. Joseph is the imaging, or increasing, power of the mind and refers to the imagination. Imagination is the power of the Word, and Will is the direction. Imagination is the Principle of Mind itself which has the capability to create. The role of the Mental Consciousness is to *direct* the power. Not to compel it, but to permit it. It is not the broader understanding that brings it about, but the belief and willingness that brings it into being. This is the seventh step in this level which indicates a fulfillment has taken place. In this case, the mental intellect has been fulfilled and is making way for spiritual knowing (intelligence). Truth plus intellect yields intelligence, and intelligence separates itself from the ignorance of the Mental Consciousness.

STEP 8 - PRAISE GOD (JUDAH).
At this stage, there is the accumulation, or increase of spiritual truth, in the Mental Consciousness through praise and prayer. Judah (ju'-dah), in Hebrew, means, "praise Jehovah, celebration of Jehovah, or laud Jehovah." As negative thoughts are cleansed away by the power of Truth, and the Spirit becomes known to the Mental Consciousness, there is an increase in vitality and substance through praise and celebration of God. All lofty ideals come from praise, and are the inspiration of everything that elevates and idealizes religion, poetry and art. It quickens and

enlarges the mind through prayer and all other forms of religious thought and worship. The Mental Consciousness is tied directly with the Father-Mind. In other words, the little self, or personal self, has been recognized and the soul approves of the spiritual forces of Truth, Wisdom and Love; there is a celebration of God ideals within the soul.

STEP 9 - OBEY SPIRIT (SIMON).
At this stage, the Mental Consciousness begins to listen and to obey spiritual guidance and instructions from God. Simon (si'-mun), in Hebrew, means, "hearing, obeying, or understanding." When Spirit becomes primary in the Mental Consciousness, the imaging power of the mind celebrates the lofty ideals, and the Mental Consciousness quickens, enlarges and is linked directly to its source. This action yields some degree of spiritual understanding. Hearing, in its higher aspect, refers to the state of mind in the devout Christian, or any other religion, who looks for and expects spiritual guidance and instruction directly from God. Hearing strictly from the physical ears yields little, because the human ear can detect only a very small range of the frequencies known to man. The hearing represented by Simon is the intuitive perception of truth that is within the soul, and is an attitude of reception of wisdom from above. God does not speak by atmospheric vibration, but by the truth itself. What we hope for and mentally see as possible in our lives materializes, and we call it substance. This is the coming of the Spiritual I AM, an unyielding, enduring consciousness of faith and strength, supported by judgment and love. "Faith is the giving substance to things hoped for," (Hebrew 11:1). In Luke 2:29 this new consciousness of the indwelling immortal life takes the place of hope, expectancy, and obedience. The results are positive activity of spiritual forces, directed by the I AM, which bring about a healing, or redeeming work, within the soul.

STEP 10 - LOVE IS UNITING (LEVI).
At this stage, love is the uniting, joining force of Divine Mind. Levi (le'-vi), in Hebrew, means, "joining, clinging, entwining, unit-

ing, or loving." Broader understanding raises the Mental Consciousness to a more spiritual knowing, and ties the Mental Consciousness directly with the Father-Mind. As a result, what we hope for and mentally see as a possibility comes into our lives as Love. Love is all that there is; the Course of Miracles says that everything is either Love or the call for Love. The Mental Consciousness connects its energy with whatever it focuses love and attention on. If the Mental Consciousness focuses love upon things of sense, things of sense become part of it and it loses the ability to enter into the realm of spirit mind. This is why the Lord commanded Moses not to make any graven images of Him. Graven images are made by mental pictures, which may be distorted by the illusions of half-truths. Love is the joining force of Spirit and is manifested differently in the body, mind and spirit. In the body it manifests as feelings, in the mind it is manifested as sympathy, and in Spirit it is love. When love is expressed through the body as feeling apart from love's dominion, violence may result instead of kindness. An example is the abuse, beating or murder of a spouse or other family member.

STEP 11 - GIFT OF GOD (MATTHAT).

At this stage, man begins to understand that God's gift to man is encompassed in the word "Grace." Matthat (ma'-that), in Hebrew, means, "gift, present, or gift of God." Praise is the inspiration of everything and raises the Mental Consciousness to a more spiritual understanding. Love connects our forces with whatever we focus our attention on, and we receive grace. In other words, we reap what we sow. The act of love makes the soul more loving. I understand the grace of God to include all things to which the human consciousness is heir through his Divine Inheritance, his Spiritual Sonship. This includes all things; unlimited attainment of spirituality and good. Thus, the gifts of God signify the total possibilities that man can attain through Spirit: fullness of life, love, wisdom and power to join with the invisible world of Spirit. We are not separate from the Divine Mind except by the perceptions of our own minds. Again, this is a choice, and this error can be corrected within the individual mind. We can trust in the redeeming grace of God, because it enables us to fulfill all righteousness.

STEP 12 - GOD EXALTED (JORAM).
At this stage, there is an elevation of the Mental Consciousness' character in power, in joy, in true success and in all good. Joram (jo'-ram), in Hebrew, means, "Whom Jehovah has set high, or Jehovah has exalted." Once love is accepted as the uniting force of God, and His gifts are accepted, the character of the Mental Consciousness is lifted to a higher level of understanding. This happens because it has accepted the Spiritual I AM, or Christ, ideals into its life. However, the kings, Jehoram of Judah, and Jehoram, or Joram of Israel, in their individual characters and reigns, were not true to the meaning of their names. As a result, evil came to them instead of the good that should have been theirs. This is the twelfth step in this level representing the spiritual fulfillment of the Mental Consciousness and indicating it is being raised to a higher level of understanding.

SUMMARY OF THE MENTAL CONSCIOUSNESS

The fourth level (Nathan to Joram), represents the beginning of Spiritual Understanding and reaching out for Spiritual Truths. These higher thoughts clear a path for increasing good thoughts, which lead to Spiritual discernment and positive judgment. As the Mental Consciousness increases in character and mental powers, it appreciates the loving power that lifts it up spiritually. In the Mental Consciousness there are both positive and negative thoughts until the negative thoughts are cleansed away by the power of Truth. Recall the Genesis story of creation in Part 1 of this book, where opposites were created to give the spiritual man choice. To evolve, the human consciousness must have the freedom to choose ideals of Spirit and to experience the manifestation of these ideals. By choosing and experiencing Spiritual Ideals and comparing them to the non-spiritual manifestation, the human consciousness obtains knowledge, which expands its mental perceptions. What the Mental Consciousness hopes for and mentally sees as a possibility in its existence comes into visibility, and is called substance. When the Mental Consciousness becomes established in Love and Truth, it uses the power of the judgment of God within it only in constructive ways. As physical matter becomes full of spiritual qualities and is fully formed and operated upon from the higher spiritual ideal, it will manifest in the highest expression of the Divine Mind. The lower, or separated, mind is an illusion, since it answers to a mind that filters out much of the informational frequencies known to man. However, the lower mind has a tremendous drawing power, because it is based on senses and desires that are extremely attractive to the human consciousness. According to *A Course In Miracles*, the Holy Spirit is the mediator between the interpretation of the physical world and the knowledge of Spirit. His ability to deal with symbols enables Him to work with the ego's, or little personal self's, beliefs in its own language. In reality, the dual consciousness' are not opposites to each other, but are mutually helpful to bringing the Christ Consciousness into being. The Christ Consciousness is possible only as the Divine Life within itself overcomes the physical forms, and conquers the untruths that shield its true Spiritual nature. Thus, the Mental Consciousness leaves behind the limited perceptions of mental percepts and enters the higher Intellectual Consciousness.

CHAPTER 21:

INTELLECTUAL CONSCIOUSNESS

The choosing faculty introduces *will*, which makes man individually as God. It is the function of the intellect to disclose differences and perceive similarities but, unaided by intuition, it can never reveal the Truth to the conscious mind. The will is the spiritual center of relative existence in the lower mind. From this center, the higher determinations of choice emanate and derive their power and direction from the mind; and the mind is of Spirit. Matter *causes* nothing at all. The forces of the physical world create only motion, but they cannot determine their own direction. There are two directive causes, one is the Divine Mind, and the other is known to us as the personal will. Thus, the problems of the lower mind are created by the personal will. In its ignorance, the unawakened mind thinks it is capable of directing its own path and ignores any suggestions from the Divine Mind. The personal will wants to do it its way. Without spiritual guidance, the personal will becomes beguiled by the things of the senses and desires of the lower mind, and it forgets the source if its being. As a result, it takes upon itself all the guilt of its finite existence and becomes a slave; but infinite will is still free. The finite will must die within itself, and affirm the Eternal Ideals of the Eternal Will. Thus, change is brought about only by choice; choosing to see things differently, and changing the personal will to receive direction only from the Divine Mind. In reality, all events that come to man in his *outward life* are nothing but the outer manifestation of the Divine fullfilling itself in him. It is the

Divine Will that man become perfect in order to work together to create only the good in the lower mind. Thus, one evolves to the Christ Consciousness by choosing Spiritual Truth; expanding the intellect to intelligence. Figure 17 illustrates the path of the Intellectual Consciousness, which is the fifth level of the Collective Consciousness Model.

STEP 1 - GOD IS HELP (ELIEZER).

At this stage, there is a belief in God as one's sustaining power. Eliezer (e-li-e'-zer), in Hebrew, means, "God of help, or God is help." Once love is accepted as the unifying force of God, the Mental Consciousness accepts the unlimited attainment of Spiritual Good and is lifted to a higher level; and the sustaining power of God is then realized. It is the power of God that relieves the consciousness in distress and assists it to better conditions and higher attainment. The rich man, Lazarus, represents the outer and inner consciousness of the average material-minded person. The outer consciousness appropriates the attributes of soul and body and expresses them through physical and mental avenues (carnal riches). The material focus starves the inner man and devitalizes the spiritual phase of the mental and physical. Thus, the asleep Intellectual Consciousness must be raised and restored. This awakening of youthful energies is necessary to the Intellectual Consciousness in the regeneration of the body. It is the understanding of the I AM that awakens it. The body cannot be made as envisioned by the Creator until all necessary thoughts are revived in it (raised from the dead). The higher thoughts must enter into sympathy and love with the Intellectual Consciousness to bring about the awakening. The stone that holds the sleeping consciousness must be rolled away through faith. The Intellectual Consciousness desires the inner life to spring forth, and to do this it must believe in the reality of spiritual powers and must exercise its faith by invoking prayer.

STEP 2 - IMAGING POWER (JOSECH).

At this stage, the Intellectual Consciousness is increasing in character through imagination. Josech (jo'- sech), in Hebrew,

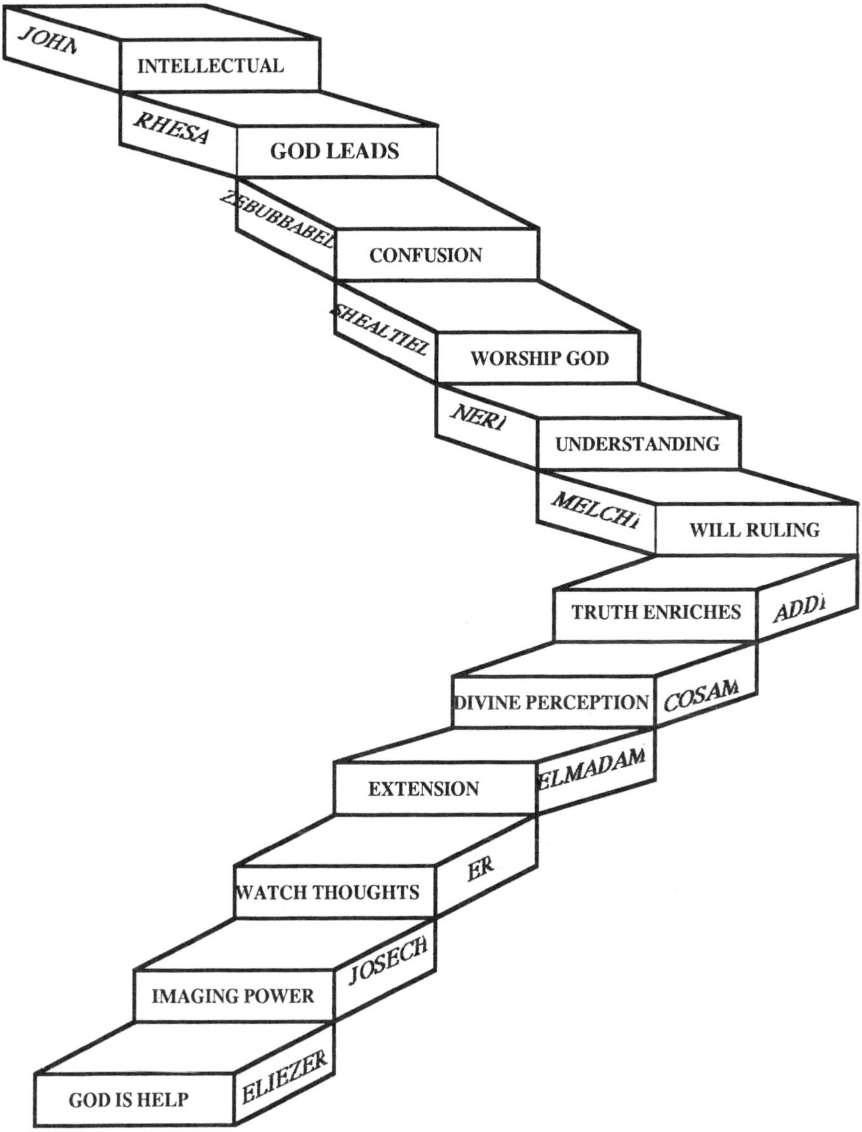

FIGURE 17 - INTELLECTUAL CONSCIOUSNESS, LEVEL 5

means, "whom Jehovah will add to, or Jehovah will increase;" and is referring to Imagination. The lifting of the Mental Consciousness to a higher level awakens the sleeping Individual Consciousness, which restores the understanding of the I AM, or God, and the imaging power of the mind is increased. Imagination is the imaging power of the mind brought into expression through association with the Word. Imagination is the molder of the flexible substance of mind. Imagination has the power to throw onto the screen of visibility substance, life forms and every idea that the mind can conceive. While the imagination is very necessary, powerful and productive, it is often belittled, derided and scorned by other faculties of the mind while functioning in the Intellectual Consciousness. At this point, the Intellectual Consciousness is unawakened spiritually. Therefore, imagination is of the intellect and is still in the process of evolving to a spiritual understanding.

STEP 3 - WATCH THOUGHTS (ER).

At this stage, there are observant, attentive and vigilant thoughts at work in the Intellectual Consciousness. Er (e'r), in Hebrew, means, "awake, watchful, or watchman." When the sleeping Intellectual Consciousness has been raised and restored through the understanding of the I AM, and the imaging power of the conscious mind is brought into expression, it becomes watchful and attentive to the thoughts in the Intellectual Consciousness. We must always be watchful of our thoughts, because we are what we think. It matters a great deal what one *watches*, or gives attention to. We cannot attain good by focusing on evil and error-thoughts. We are transformed into the Christ likeness by beholding Him, not by taking cognizance of the lesser self with its seeming limitations. "If thine eye be evil, thy whole body shall be full of darkness. If therefore the light that is in thee be darkness, how great is the darkness," (Matthew 6:23). We must vigilantly *weed* out the negative thoughts, if we are to attain spiritual knowledge and understanding.

STEP 4 - POWER OF EXTENSION (ELMADAM).
At this stage, there is an enlarging of the Intellectual Consciousness so that it may comprehend something of the immeasurable greatness of God. Elmadam (el-ma'-dam), in Hebrew, means, "God's measure, power of extension, unlimited measure, or measure of God;" and is referring to the enlarging of Intellectual Consciousness. Only by the belief in God, the visioning power of the imagination, and watching the thoughts and accepting only spiritual thoughts, is it possible to expand our Intellectual Consciousness to understand the unlimited measure of God. When the limited physical thoughts are replaced by the unlimited spiritual thoughts, the Intellectual Consciousness expands to new horizons of understanding, and the intellect is raised to a greater level of spiritual understanding. Extension is always of God and the Truth will set the Intellectual Consciousness free of the limitations of the lower mind.

STEP 5 - DIVINE PERCEPTION (COSAM).
At this stage, there is a clear, spiritual perception and insight into Truth. Cosam (co'-sam), in Hebrew, means, "diviner, divining, an oracle or a seer." When the imaging power of the mind is brought into expression, the mental thoughts are monitored and the error thoughts removed; then a clear spiritual perception and insight is brought to the Intellectual Consciousness. The human mind sees in many ways, because perception involves interpretation. Interpretations are accomplished in a mind that filters out most of the information that it receives. Therefore, it is not whole or consistent. Perceptions are temporary and are attributes of a belief in the physical world, which is always in the process of change. To know is to be certain, and certainty is of God. True perception is the basis for knowledge, but knowing is the affirmation of truth beyond all perceptions. Therefore, there begins a transition from perception to knowledge in the Intellectual Consciousness. Only through complete surrender to the higher spiritual Truth can the Intellectual Consciousness bear wholesome fruit.

STEP 6 - TRUTH ENRICHES (ADDI).

At this stage, there is the thought that in the Spirit of Truth is the ornament that enriches the soul. Addi (ad'-di), in Hebrew, means, "ornament or adorned;" which indicates the soul is enriched by the Truth. The removal of error thoughts expands the Intellectual Consciousness to the greatness of God, and there begins a transition from perception to knowledge; which enriches the soul with Spiritual understanding. Perceptions are always open to interpretation and, thus, can change, but spiritual knowledge and Truth never changes. Spiritual thinking gives man true grace and beauty and, thus, adorns the soul. The soul is the Collective Consciousness of man that has been developed out of the image and likeness of the Divine Mind. The personalized mind is identical to the Divine Mind, except for knowledge and, thus, must evolve to the perfect state of Consciousness by eliminating the illusions of the mind and accepting only the Truth. When man puts all limitation out of Intellectual Consciousness, and realizes the perfection of Spirit, his body will be perfect. This is the true meaning of being, "born again."

STEP 7 - WILL RULING (MELCHI).

At this stage, the will is ruling in man, and there is a suggestion of understanding and good judgment in domination. Melchi (mel'-ki), in Hebrew, means, "my king, my ruler, my judge, or belonging to the king." The expansion of the Intellectual Consciousness to the greatness of God, and the transition from perception to knowledge, will always enrich the soul with Truth and bring a higher Will into domination. The Intellectual Consciousness is alerted by concentrating on the mind of Christ, or the I AM. It is the innate knowing of right and wrong. This brings us to the realization of what Jesus meant when He said, "The Son of man shall come in his glory... . And before him shall be gathered all nations; and all the holy angels with him, then shall he sit upon the throne of glory. And he shall set the sheep on his right hand, but the goats on the left," (Matthew 25:31-33). Every person has within them sheep and goats. Goats are thoughts of opposition, resisting, and stubborn, while sheep, on the hand, are the most harmless of animals and represent the natural life that flows into man's consciousness from Spirit. They are pure, innocent and guiltless. The goats and sheep must be separated before the consciousness can come into the glory of the Father (Christ Consciousness). This is the seventh name in this level, and represents the fulfillment, shifting and separation of the negative thoughts of opposition from the Intellectual Consciousness.

STEP 8 - SPIRITUAL UNDERSTANDING (NERI).
At this stage, God spreads understanding and quickens the intellectual Consciousness. Neri (ne'-ri), in Hebrew, means, "Jehovah spreads light abroad, Jah is a light, or lamp of Jehovah." The transition of perception to knowledge, the Spiritual Truth enriching the soul and concentrating the Intellectual Consciousness on the I AM awakens the Intellectual Consciousness to the God light, or understanding. "Light," metaphysically, is the symbol of intelligence, and intelligence is always of God. Spiritual understanding is the knowledge that we are One with God and what is experienced is merely a reflection, or manifestation of Being. The intellectual Consciousness is now awakening to the truth that all true light, or understanding, is spiritual and exists in and radiates through the Christ Mind in man. One cannot affirm too often, "I am the light of the world," (Matthew 5:14, John 8:12: 9:5). Thus, the transition from thoughts of separation to thoughts of unity with the Divine Mind is beginning to take place.

STEP 9 - WORSHIP GOD (SHEALTIEL).
At this stage, there is activity in the Intellectual Consciousness that restores the worship of God. Shealtiel (she-al'-te-el), in Hebrew, means, "I have asked of God, or having asked of God;" which indicates that the first step to restoring the worship of God must be taken by man. When the Intellectual Consciousness has been adorned with Spiritual Truth and concentrated on the I AM, there is spiritual understanding and knowing of the one God, which restores the worship of God. It is the I AM in the Intellectual Consciousness that appeals to the divine within; mak-

ing a conscious union with Spirit. This union comes in the midst of the stress and sorrow of intellectual confusion and bondage into which the Intellectual Consciousness has drifted.This has happened as a result of not understanding the true nature of Spirit and persisting in looking to the outer world as the source of that which is real, true and worthwhile. The spiritual thought activity becomes the leading factor in putting away error illusions and restoring the worship of God and its resultant good.

STEP 10 - CONCEIVED OF CONFUSION (ZEBUBBABEL).
At this stage, there is a very strong and influential thought activity belonging to the spiritual phase of the Intellectual Consciousness. Zerubbabel (ze-rub'-ba-bel), in Hebrew, means, "sown in Babylon, conceived in Babylon, or begotten of confusion." The innate knowing of right and wrong, the intellectual Consciousness awakening to intelligence, and the conscious union with Spirit all bring about the strong, influential thought activity of Faith. Faith rejoices and triumphs even in the midst of trial, because it knows that new realizations of life and understanding; and power and glory, are at hand. This thought activity is conceived in Babel which, metaphysically, means confusion. When the Intellectual Consciousness thinks in outer, or purely mental and psychic ways that it can comprehend and contact the Divine Mind, confusion is always the outcome. This confusion is the result of a mixture of physical, sensual and mental thoughts, and results in a chaotic mental condition. These thoughts are so strong that they seem to have us in complete subjugation, symbolized by the bondage of Babylon. It is only through the inner Spirit of Truth that the Intellectual Consciousness can come in touch with and gain Truth from Spirit. This is the way it receives the perfection of poise, peace, power and all good which is of the kingdom of heaven. This spiritual thought activity becomes the leading factor in eliminating the error illusions of a confused mind.

STEP 11 - GOD TAKES LEAD (RHESA).
At this stage, the will of God is taking first place in Intellectual Consciousness. Rhesa (re'-sah), in Hebrew, means "principle,

head, chief, foremost, or will." The awakening of the Intellectual Consciousness to the Truth, the union with Spirit conceived in Faith and the Will of God begins to take its place in the Intellectual Consciousness. The Intellectual Consciousness expresses that which rules, or is enjoyed, by virtue of its own inherent movement; hence, the will. Taken in a negative sense, this same independent movement will also characterize a venomous principle, or evil desires. This is the head of the serpent of Genesis 3:15. However, because of the worship of God and faith activities of the previous steps, the inherent movement of consciousness is moving in a positive, Spiritual direction. It is the concept and acceptance of God that is the principle head, that becomes foremost in the Intellectual Consciousness at this stage of unfoldment.

STEP 12 - INTELLECTUAL PERCEPTION (JOHN). At this stage, there is a high Spiritual perception in the Intellectual Consciousness; not yet alive with Spirit. John, in Hebrew, means, "Jehovah bestows mercifully, Jah is gracious, grace and mercy of the Lord, or compassion." The union with Spirit that is conceived in Faith, allows the Intellectual Consciousness to accept God as foremost, which bestows intellectual perceptions of Truth to the unfolding Intellectual Consciousness. John the Baptist was a forerunner of Jesus the Christ and represents that attitude of mind in which we are zealous for the rule of Spirit. This attitude is not spiritual, but a perception of spiritual possibilities and activities in making conditions in which Spirit may rule. This perception of Truth leads us to strive with evil as a reality, not having discerned the truth about it's transitory character. It is the innate principle in us that always seeks to do right. It is like a crude voice in the wilderness crying for the right way. Baptism symbolizes the getting rid of the limited thoughts that encumber and darken understanding. The intellect is to prepare the way for the Spiritual Consciousness; "The least of the spiritual thoughts in man is greater than the mightiest reasoning of the intellect," (John 3:30). The intellectual concepts of things must give way to understanding that comes through the Holy Spirit. This is the twelfth step in this level and represents the completion of the intellectual and the bringing forth of Spiritual understanding, or True intelligence.

SUMMARY OF THE INTELLECTUAL CONSCIOUSNESS

In the fifth level (Eliezer to John) of the Collective Consciousness Model, Truth begins to translate the useless to the useful. The individual mind believes in solving conflicts through fragmentation, and does not perceive the situation as a whole. Therefore, it seeks to split off segments of the situation and deal with them separately. This is because the individual mind has faith in separation and not wholeness. It is the belief in separation that has enslaved the human consciousness to ignorance. The intellect must expand its beliefs to include the spiritual Truth. Thus, the Intellectual Consciousness uses symbols and words to reason and understand the nature of its existence. When the intellect is merged with Truth it becomes intelligence; and intelligence is of God. Symbols and words are physical manifestations and are always open to interpretation, while the Truth never changes or needs to be explained. This is why the illusions of the physical world are always in a state of change, because by experiencing the manifestion, the soul can determine if the experience supports its good. It is through spiritual discernment that the Intellectual Consciousness is able to choose only positive, or Truth thoughts. Truth translates the useless illusions of the physical world to useful Spiritual thoughts. Prior to this point, the human consciousness drifted to physical extremes, because of not understanding the nature of Spirit, and persisting in looking to the outer senses for its source of that which is real, True and worthwhile. Spiritual thought activity becomes the leading factor in restoring the worship of God, if the Intellectual Consciousness is to expand to the next level of Spiritual awareness. At this level, the attitude of mind is zealous for the rule of Spirit and can become destructive in its zeal for spirit. John the Baptist was a forerunner of Jesus the Christ. He signifies a high intellectual perception of Truth, but one not yet quickened by Spirit. This attitude is not spiritual, but a perception of spiritual possibilities and a prelude to conditions in which Spirit can rule. The zealous attitude of John the Baptist leads us to strive with evil as a reality, because we do not discern its transitory character. The intellect comes out of the wilderness and seeks to do the right thing. However, it is to prepare the way for the Spiritual Consciousness. The alert intellect that has been working toward the fulfillment of a divine ideal, recognizes the development of Spiritual Consciousness and acknowledges its manifestation, just as John the Baptist recognized Jesus the Christ. John the Baptist is an example of the Intellectual Consciousness that beholds the evils of civilization, condemns them, and advocates the punishment of the evildoers. This attitude of thought must fail, because it lacks a comprehension of the universal brotherhood of man with the One Mind. Therefore, the Intellectual Consciousness must die, because it is imprisoned in the magnification of the illusions of sin and evil. This is why John the Baptist says, "He that cometh after me is mightier than I, whose shoes I am not worthy to bear; he shall baptize you in the Holy Spirit and in fire," (Matthew 3:11).

CHAPTER 22:

SPIRITUAL CONSCIOUSNESS

The Intellectual Consciousness is a not a permanent state of consciousness and must make way for the Spiritual Consciousness, which is permanent. When the first enthusiasm wanes after spiritual enlightenment has occurred, there is a certain barrenness of thought and action in the mind, and it feels as if it should retire to a place where complete rest and absence of effort are available. The Bible tells us that when Jesus heard of the death of John the Baptist he withdrew into a "desert place." A desert is a place where there is a seeming lack of substance and life. In Truth, desert places do not really exist. Where God is, there is His inexhaustible resource, and God is everywhere present. From the viewpoint of Spirit, there is no such thing as lack. When the Spiritual Consciousness realizes the quickening power of the life, love and substance it makes the seeming "desert place" in its mind bloom like the rose and bring forth abundantly. However, we cannot get away from our thoughts, as illustrated by the people who followed Jesus into the desert place, (Matthew 14:13). The adverse negative states of thought remain in the body, "He hath a devil," (St. John 10:20). The son of man comes and unites His Life and substance with the appetites and passions of the subconsciousness, and He seems for a time to be of their kind. "But wisdom is justified of all her children," (St. Luke 7:35). The descent of Spirit into the body may stir up the Devil for a time, but this reign will be short if the consciousness is guided by the Spirit of truth, who will lead it into all Truth. "Except those days had been shortened, no flesh would have been saved: but for the elect's sake those days shall be shortened," (Matthew

24:22). Figure 18 illustrates the Spiritual Consciousness, Level 6 of the Collective Consciousness Model.

STEP 1 - CELEBRATION OF GOD (JUDAH).
At this stage, there is a Spiritual Consciousness tied directly with the Father-Mind. Judah (ju'-dah), in Hebrew, means, "praise Jehovah, celebration of Jehovah, or laud Jehovah," which represents the spiritual faculty that corresponds to accumulation, or increase, in the mental through prayer and praise. Faith rejoices and triumphs, even in the midst of trial, because it knows the new realization of understanding expresses the acceptance of God as foremost. The intellect prepares the way for intelligence and ties the Spiritual Consciousness directly with the Father-Mind. Prayer should be a jubilant thanksgiving instead of a supplication. The aliveness of the mind makes it draw, like a magnet, from the realm of causes which fulfills its desires. The Spiritual Consciousness gathers spiritual ideas and draws from the Universal Mind through thoughts and ideas that are absolutely true. When we pray in spiritual understanding, the highest realm of mind comes in touch with the universal and impersonal Mind, and the mind of man is joined to the very mind of God. Praise and thanksgiving multiply and increase everything that consciousness centers its attention on. Praise is the positive pole of life and keeps the soul fresh, pure and beautiful. Thus, God answers our prayers in ideas, thoughts and words, which are translated into the outer realm of form, in due time.

STEP 2 - IMAGINATION (JOSEPH).
At this stage, the higher ideals of Truth come into the Spiritual Consciousness by way of imagination, which at this stage of unfoldment is powerful and productive. Joseph (jo'-zef), in Hebrew, means, "whom Jehovah will add to, Jehovah shall increase, or he shall increase progressively;" which is referring to the imagination. With God foremost in the Spiritual Consciousness, the intellectual perception of Truth being established and the attitude

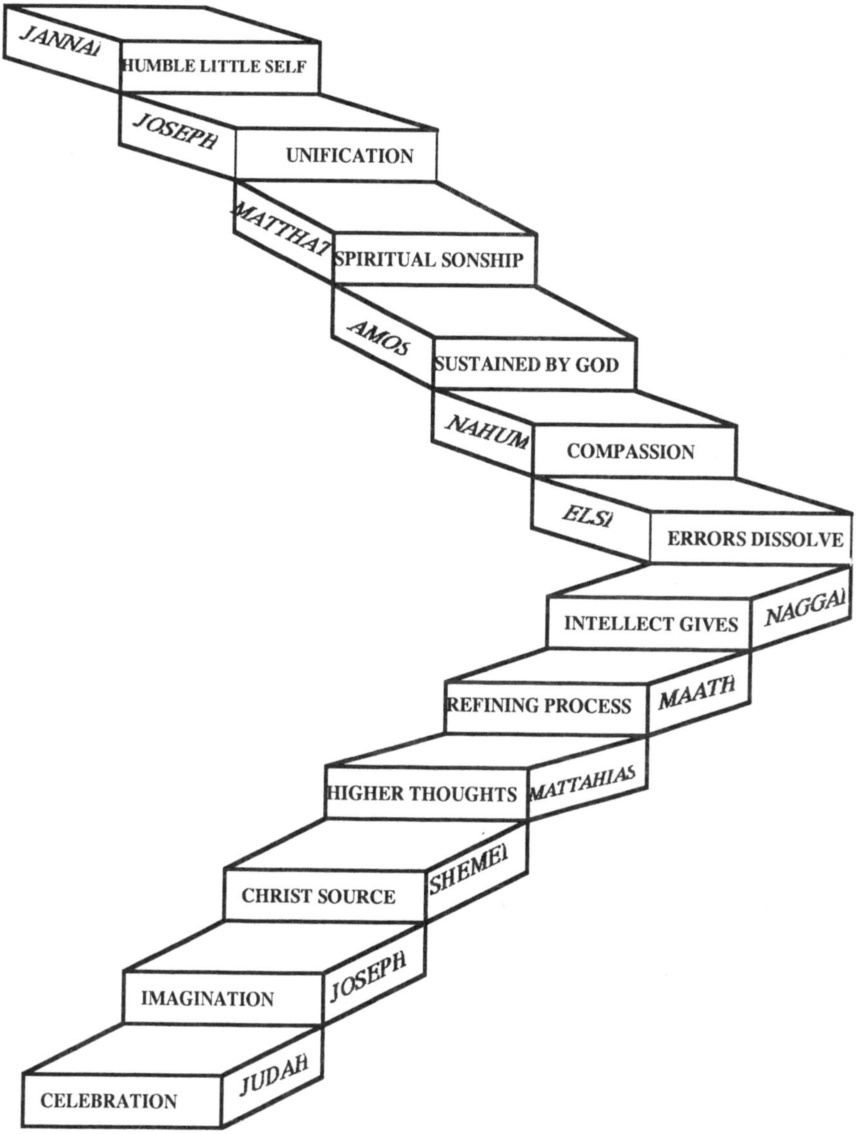

FIGURE 18 - SPIRITUAL CONSCIOUSNESS, LEVEL 6

of jubilant thanksgiving of prayer and praise, the higher ideals of Truth enter the Spiritual Consciousness as imagination. Imagination has the power to throw onto the screen of visibility substance, life forms and every idea that the mind can conceive. The involution of high spiritual ideas brings about a progressive increase of vitality and substance in the realm of forms as evolution. The substance of Truth is an abiding presence. However, this form may be lost to human sight. The Spiritual Consciousness may not seem to realize this uplifting and increase in vitality that come to it when it first begins to understand Truth, because the intellectual enthusiasm can think and talk of nothing else. Here the unification of the I AM with all the faculties of the mind and the substance of the whole man begins to take form.

STEP 3 - CHRIST AS SOURCE (SHIMEI).

At this stage, the idea of Truth becomes current throughout the Spiritual Consciousness. Shimei (shim'-e-i), in Hebrew, means, "famous, renowned, or Jah is famed;" which implies that the forces working in the Spiritual Consciousness are of a known origin. With the intelligent perception of the rule of Spirit and the Spiritual Consciousness tied directly to the Father-Mind and the previous Intellectual Consciousness being broken up, the idea of Truth becomes current in the Spiritual Consciousness. These higher Truth ideals are getting past the place of being like a "rumor" and becoming known and accepted throughout the Spiritual Consciousness through praise and prayer. Having a receptive attitude, the Spiritual Consciousness begins to hear and obey the ideas of Truth. Thus, the Christ, or the higher self, is now being understood to be the source. Christ is the fundamental principle from which the Absolute, as the Son from the Father, enters the world of manifestation and animates all things.

STEP 4 - HIGHER THOUGHTS (MATTATHIAS).

At this stage, the Spiritual Consciousness is being lifted up through the power of the indwelling Christ, or I AM. Mattathias (mat-ta-thi'-as), in Hebrew, means, "gift of Jehovah, or present of Jehovah;" which represents the awakening to the religious thoughts of the divine possibilities of obtaining fullness of life and good. With the Spiritual Consciousness tied directly to the Father-Mind, the imagination expands the character and Truth becomes current throughout all phases of Spiritual Consciousness. It is lifted up through the power of the indwelling Christ. The involution of spiritual ideas brings about a progressive increase in vitality and substance, and the Truth becomes current in the Spiritual Consciousness. It is lifted up through the gifts of God, or Jehovah. The Spiritual Consciousness is learning the necessity of eliminating all errors and limitations of the soul in order to make these high attainments and gain eternal life.

STEP 5 - REFINING PROCESS (MAATH).
At this stage, a refining process is taking place in the Spiritual Consciousness by which errors, personal and material, are removed and become small and insignificant. Maath (ma'-ath), in Hebrew, means, "smooth, polished, scraped off or removed;" which indicates that just having a perception of a Spiritual Consciousness is not enough, there must also be activity associated with the idea or thought. When man accepts his True Spiritual source, begins to perceive the gifts of God and awakens to a realization of his divine possibilities, it is natural to see the illusions of ignorance for what they are, nothing. Light is stronger than darkness, and darkness cannot survive in the light, so when illusions are brought to knowledge and understanding they just disappear. Thus, the Spiritual Consciousness "scrapes off" the thoughts that have been in bondage to ignorance, and there is a smoothing and polishing that takes place.

STEP 6 - INTELLECT GIVES WAY (NAGGAI).
At this stage, intelligence and understanding become active in the Spiritual Consciousness. Naggai (nag'-ga-i), in Hebrew, means, "giving light, shining or luminous intelligence;" which indicates that the higher religious perceptions have been polished by Spirit. When the errors of negative thought, the person-

al and material, have been made insignificant in the Spiritual Consciousness, then Truth begins to shine and luminates as intelligence. That is, the intellect begins to give way to the intelligence of Spirit. The intellect is not of God, but is from reflected light. Once the intellect has been polished of its error thinking, the Truth always shines forth.

STEP 7 - ERRORS DISSOLVE (ELSI).

At this stage, strong dedication to God, and nearness to and oneness with Him, become active in the Spiritual Consciousness. Esli (es'-li), in Hebrew, means, "God has reserved, separated from God, or reserved;" which indicates the polishing of the higher perceptions. Here the inner awareness of God is beginning to dissolve the illusion of separation between the Spiritual Consciousness and God. It is through the Spiritual Consciousness that the soul contacts God and the ideas of the One Mind begin to enter the Christ Consciousness. At this level, there is complete freedom from any ties or attraction to the desires of the lower nature. This is the seventh step in this level, and represents the fulfillment of material life and the transition to a union with God.

STEP 8 - COMPASSION AND LOVE (NAHUM).

At this stage, there is a balancing and smoothing effect of the Holy Spirit's presence in Spiritual Consciousness. Nahum (na'-hum), in Hebrew, means, "consolation, comfort or compassion;" which indicates the strong thoughts of God have converted the sympathy of the intellect to compassion and love. The refining process removes negative and error thinking from the Spiritual Consciousness and the Truth begins to illuminate the Spiritual Consciousness. The illusions of separation are dissolved and the balancing effects of Love comfort the soul. The thought of the Holy Spirit as a teacher, as well as a comforter and healer, is brought out. The Holy Spirit recognizes both God's creations and the illusions of the lower mind. Therefore, the Holy Spirit separates the Truth from the illusions by its ability to perceive totally rather than selectively. There are feelings of relief from distress that strengthen hope and cheer. The good is experienced as the Spiritual Consciousness is delivered from confusion. Now the Spiritual Consciousness enters into peace and knowing its oneness with God.

STEP 9 - SUSTAINED BY GOD (AMOS).
At this stage, the Spiritual Consciousness shepherds the natural forces of mind and body. Amos (a'-mos), in Hebrew, means, "burden, load, born up, sustained or carried;" which indicates strong thoughts of God and the adjusting effects of Holy Spirit are now sustaining the Spiritual Consciousness. According to the Bible, Amos was a Shepherd. A shepherd is a symbol of the Higher Self who leads the higher qualities upwards. Sheep represents thoughts that are obedient to the natural law, and the pure natural life of the body. This gives new meaning to Jesus' words, "Verily, verily I say unto you, I am the entrance of the higher mind above the soul (door) of the higher qualities manifesting on the mental plane (sheep). All that ever came before me are desire-nature (thieves) and sense-nature (robbers); but the higher qualities of the mental (sheep) did not hear them. I am the higher mind above the soul (door); by me if any soul (man) enter in, he shall be saved, and shall go in and out, and find transmuted emotions (pasture). The desire-nature (thief) cometh not, but for to steal, and to kill, and to destroy: I come that they might have life, and that they might have it more abundantly," (St. John 10:7 to10:10). The Christ is the higher way to truth and life, and It is the ruler of the higher qualities. The desire-nature and the sense-nature (thieves and robbers) come before the Christ and rule first in the lower nature, but the higher qualities remain latent until the Spirit stirs them from within. Through the Christ the human mind is raised. However, the Spiritual Consciousness has not as yet reached the higher qualities, so it is the Amos in us that warns us when we have transgressed the Divine Law.

STEP 10 - SPIRITUAL SONSHIP (MATTHAT).
At this stage, the Spiritual Consciousness begins to understand that God's gift to it encompasses the word "grace." Matthat (mat'-

-that), in Hebrew, means, "present, gift or God's gift;" which indicates that with the adjusting effects of the Holy Spirit and obedience to the natural laws the reward is grace, which is the gift of God. A strong consecration to God plus the balancing and smoothing effect of the Holy Spirit shepherds the natural forces of mind and body. The Spiritual Consciousness now begins to understand the grace of God. The 'Grace of God' is a symbol of the response of the Higher nature to the aspirations of the lower. It is through the actions of the higher nature alone that the soul is raised. Grace includes all to which man is heir through the divine inheritance, his spiritual sonship. Divine inheritance includes all things, fullness of life, love, wisdom, power and every spiritual quality of good. A righteous man's reward is not the result of merit. It is the Holy Spirit of God in him making itself more felt, and mingling more and more with his soul. This is because we reap what we sow.

STEP 11 - UNIFICATION OF CHRIST (JOSEPH).
At this stage, an increase in vitality and substance comes to the Spiritual Consciousness because of the broader understanding of the concept of Christ. Joseph (jo'-zef), in Hebrew, means, "whom Jehovah will add to, or he shall increase progressively;" which indicates compassion, love and God's gift of love, wisdom, power and fullness of life have been added to it. The balancing and smoothing effects of the Holy Spirit guides the natural forces of mind and body. The Spiritual Consciousness begins to understand the grace of God and begins the unification with the Christ, or the AM. This is the second Joseph in this level, and the third overall. It is clear that this Joseph was given gifts that are progressively higher in spiritual quality due to the increase in the mental imagination of Step 2 of this Level. With the unification of the Christ; the faculties of the mind, the life energies and the substance of the whole Spiritual Consciousness are raised into higher spiritual qualities of understanding.

STEP 12 - HUMBLING THE LITTLE SELF (JANNAI).
At this stage, there is the humbling of the little, or personal, self to the end that the Spiritual Consciousness may be exulted. Jannai

(jan-na-i), in Hebrew, means, "suppression, affliction, or humility." Compassion, love, God's gift and the unification of the Christ have succeeded in humbling the individualized personal consciousness that the Christ might be exulted. This is brought about by obedience to the natural law in the Spiritual Consciousness. "Blessed are the poor in spirit; for theirs is the kingdom of heaven," (Matthew 5:3). 'Poor in spirit' is a symbol of those qualities which have rid themselves of the lower desires, and are filled with the spirit of goodness and truth. "Hath not God chosen the poor of this world, rich in faith, and heirs of the kingdom which he hath promised to them that love him," (James 2-5)? In the Divine scheme of things, these qualities are free from the attractions of sense and desire, and are filled with the higher energies of wisdom and love. The desire of the little self must give up the need to control everything and release this control to the indwelling Christ. By releasing the desire "to do it my way" the little self is exalted to the Higher Self, or the Christ Consciousness. This phase signifies an unfoldment of Truth in the Spiritual Consciousness that there may be a new birth in Christ Consciousness. This is the twelfth name in this level, and represents the spiritual fulfillment of the Spiritual Consciousness.

SUMMARY OF THE SPIRITUAL CONSCIOUSNESS

In the sixth level of the Collective Consciousness Model (Judah to Jannai), we receive an active understanding of the grace of God as a Spiritual Consciousness. As we discern the truth and eliminate the false thoughts in our lives, we grow spiritually and increase in both character and in power of the mind. In so doing, we obtain an active understanding of the grace of God. These strong thoughts of God have a smoothing effect on our being. We become humble, the little personal self is decreased and the true I AM of the individual is exalted. The ideals of Truth are becoming known and accepted by the Spiritual Consciousness, and the indwelling Christ is understood to be its source. Yet at this level, the Spiritual Consciousness does not seem to understand the necessity for being obedient to the Divine Law. It is still influenced by the intellect, but is giving way to intelligence. It perceives and expects God's blessing, but does not realize the necessity for being obedient to the good, to reap good. Thus, a refining process is needed to polish the Spiritual Consciousness by removing the errors from its thought processes and beliefs. It is through the Spiritual Consciousness that contact is made with the Divine Mind, and the ideas of the One Mind enter the Spiritual Consciousness. Christ, or the Higher Self, is the fundamental principle underlying the idea of personal Godhood. It is the Divine Life which proceeds forth from the Absolute, as the Son from the Father, to enter the world of manifestation and animate all things as the Spiritual Consciousness gives way to the higher Christ Consciousness.

CHAPTER 23:

CHRIST CONSCIOUSNESS

What is the Christ Consciousness? Christ is not a person, but a principle. It is the Higher Self, and represents the divine-idea of what man can become. Christ is in everything. "The mystical conception of Christ means the Universality of Sonship, *embodied in any individual who recognizes this sonship,*" (Ernest Holmes, *The Science of Mind*). The Christ Consciousness is the unification with the One Mind. The Christ is the center of all of us, and through Its sight we are spiritual egos manifested within the outer realm. In the lower consciousness we see things not as they are in reality, but only the illusions of what we *think* they are. Therefore, we only behold the diversity and separateness which gives rise to the misconceptions of the inner and real significance of our Individuality and its ultimate re-absorption into the Infinite. Our little personality, being transitory and finite, is but a poor and partial mirroring of Its infinity. The Christ Consciousness is the door to the higher mind. It is above the soul and it alone is the Way, the Truth and the Life. Jesus the Christ was a man who experienced the manifestations of the outer world and overcame its passions and desires. Jesus was of the Spiritual Consciousness prior to his baptism by John the Baptist, at which time the dove of the Christ Consciousness descended from above. "And Jesus, when he overcame his errors (was baptized) went up straightaway out of the mental potential (water): and lo, the consciousness in which the soul and the body are in harmony with the Divine Mind (heavens) was opened unto him, and he saw the positive, energetic, forceful and formative aspects of the Divine outpouring (Spirit of God) descending like an aspiration and gently (dove) lighting upon him. And lo a voice from heaven, saying, This is my beloved Son, in whom I am well pleased," (Matthew 3:16 and 17). When the involution and evolution are accomplished, Jesus the Christ leaves the world and departs to the Father, taking with him the results of the soul-process. Jesus the Christ is the Supreme Ideal set before us to conform to, that we may become like him, and thus manifest the Christ nature that is in each of us. Jesus the Christ is the example of how we are to satisfy the commandment, "Be ye perfect as your Father in heaven is perfect." Figure 19 illustrates the last level of the Collective Consciousness Model; the Christ Consciousness.

STEP 1 - DIVINE WILL RULING (MELCHI).
At this stage, there is the Divine Will ruling in the Christ Consciousness, and a suggestion of understanding and good judgment. Melchi (mel'-ki), in Hebrew, means, "my king, my ruler or my counsel;" which indicates that the Will is beginning to be controlled by the I AM, or Christ Consciousness. When the Christ Consciousness begins to understand the gifts of God, unifies with the I AM and the little personal self is humbled, then the acceptance of the Will of God becomes known and there is understanding and good judgment. The Will rules in the active faith faculty in the Christ Consciousness and becomes discriminative to the extent of being able to counsel and advise the other thoughts of the Collective Consciousness to which it belongs. When the will begins to recognize love and to unify itself with the love thought, it becomes less dictatorial and more discriminating. A king is a symbol of a ruling quality to the soul from either the higher or the lower mind. The ideals give rise to the higher qualities, when the soul has become prepared to obey them, so that the lower qualities may be effectively ruled. To be effectively ruled requires Spiritual discipline qualities through the mental activities which control the lower emotions and desires. This then is the Divine Will ruling the passions and desires of the lower mind. Divine Mind, or God, is our eternal source and goal, which

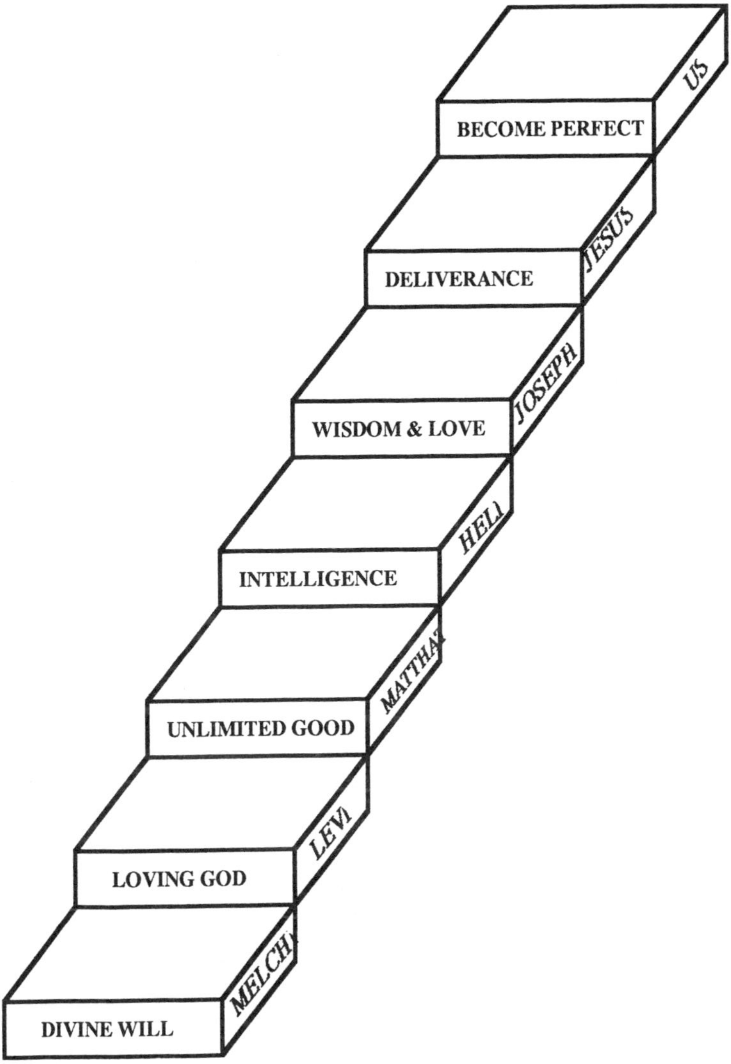

FIGURE 19 - CHRIST CONSCIOUSNESS, LEVEL 7

is love; love is self-giving; selfgivingness is joy. From the Higher Mind love is always extended, while in the lower mind it is merely projected.

STEP 2 - LOVING GOD (LEVI).
At this stage, there is the faculty of love in the human consciousness. Levi (le'-vi), in Hebrew, means, "joining, unfolding and loving;" which indicates the Divine Will has joined with the personal will of man. Unification of the I AM and the humbling of the personal self brings spiritual understanding and good judgment, which take control of the Spiritual Consciousness. There is a joining with God through the love faculty. Love is the uniting, joining force of the Divine Mind. We always connect our attention with whatever we center our love on. If we love the things of sense, they become part of us and we lose the ability to enter into the realm of the Spirit-mind. Therefore, we must overcome the strong emotions and feelings of the personal self before coming under the dominion of Divine Love. This is the equilibrium represented by Noah. All energies, or charges, must be brought into balance. Life is about integration. Integrating the physical with the spiritual. As long as there is an imbalance between the two, we will experience pain. This does not imply that the two are equal, however, because the Spiritual must always come first. The three components of LOVE (*feelings* in the body, *sympathy* in the mind, and *love* in the spirit) must all be balanced or violence may result. Balanced LOVE results in unselfishness and irresistible power for good. When love is lifted out of the intellect and personal self, the true spiritual quality is realized, and the perception of its perfection is attained. This is why the Lord commanded Moses not to make any graven images of Him. The thought that God is a great king in a place called heaven makes just such a mental image, and one grows to believe in and worship such an imaginary being instead of the true God, who is Spirit.

STEP 3 - UNLIMITED ATTAINMENT (MATTHAT).
At this stage, man begins to receive unlimited attainment of spirituality and good through the grace of God. Matthat (mat'-that),

in Hebrew, means, “present or gift of God;” which indicates that Divine Will and Love in the Christ Consciousness are extending to man all the possibilities that man has through Spirit. When the Truth unfolds in the Spiritual Consciousness and understanding and good judgment rule in the Christ Consciousness, the Collective Consciousness begins to receive unlimited attainment of spirituality and good through the grace of God. It understands that the gift of God is encompassed in the word “grace”. The ‘Grace of God’ includes fullness of life, love and wisdom. Every spiritual quality is attainable to us at this very moment. The gifts that the Wise Men of the East brought to Jesus represent qualities of mind given by divine wisdom. These Wise Men bring to the collective consciousness that which has been created as ideal by the Divine Mind. These wise thoughts from divine wisdom tell us that we have all riches; that the God-Mind in us has given us possession of the universal substance.

STEP 4 - INTELLECT ASCENDED (HELI).

At this level, there is always a seeking for spiritual progress, that is, ever-looking upward and onward to something higher and better. Heli (he'-li), in Hebrew, means, “lifted up, ascent or most high;” which indicates that the Christ Consciousness has been lifted to a most high position. When the Will is ruling in the Christ Consciousness, and the strong emotions and feelings come under the dominion of Divine Love, then there is spiritual understanding. This indicates that the Truth of Spirit has illuminated the intellect and it has ascended to the spiritual quality of intelligence. Spiritual understanding is understanding that comes from the aliveness of the Spirit of truth within man. It is knowing that you know; and knowing is always of God. Intellectual understanding cannot bring about the redemption of man's body because it does not have the intelligent principle that lays hold of the flesh with life-giving, transforming power. Only the Christ understanding can do this. It establishes a spiritual state of consciousness that will clothe itself with substance, thus, forming the imperishable spiritual body.

STEP 5 - WISDOM AND LOVE (JOSEPH).
At this stage, Wisdom and Love, which have been ideas in mind, now bring forth a manifestation of Spiritual substance. Joseph (jo'-zef), in Hebrew, means, "whom Jehovah will add to or he shall increase progressively," (perfection to perfection); which indicates that Joseph (Wisdom) and Mary (Love) are to bring forth the birth of the I AM, or the Christ Consciousness. When the strong emotions and feeling are under the control of Divine Love, the intellect is illuminated and uplifted to the spiritual quality of intelligence, then Wisdom and Love are brought into manifestation. Joseph might also be said to represent the Son of man and Mary the divine motherhood (Luke 2:40-52). Joseph was only betrothed to Mary, yet she was "great with child"; so Joseph "was minded to put her away privily." This means that we do not, in the first stages of the birth of the Christ in us, understand the process and sometimes are moved to put it away from us. The soul is heavily charged with divine life; so full that it cannot express itself intelligently, because no union has yet taken place between it and the understanding (Joseph). To me, the virgin birth is an analogy and represents a consciousness that is of God, or Spirit. Thus, this Christ Consciousness is a virgin and is new to the Collective Consciousness. Therefore, the virgin birth is not describing a physical conception, but a spiritual birth. This is not the first time that a virgin birth has been implied by the Bible. Isaac was also conceived of spirit, because Sarah was barren and past the age of bearing children (90 years old). One would do well not to place too much emphasis on the body in this case, because it will lead to great mental confusion.

STEP 6 - DELIVERANCE CHRIST (JESUS).
At this stage, the consciousness of the I AM is raised to Divine Understanding and Power. Jesus (je'-zus), in Hebrew, means, "whose help Jehovah is, salvation, Savior and deliverance through Jehovah;" which indicates that the directive power of the mind has been raised to Divine Understanding and Power. This is the I AM identity. The receiving of unlimited attainment of spirit-

uality and good and the illumination of spiritual intelligence, Wisdom and Love manifesting in the Christ Consciousness; all combined bring about the Christ. Jesus represents God's idea of man in expression and is the Christ in the absolute. Jesus the Christ was the archetypical man, which includes all the mental phases through which man passes in demonstrating life's problems. So we find Jesus passing through all the trials, temptations and mental variations of each of us, "Yet without sin," that is, not falling under the dominion of negative, or evil, thoughts. The Christ is the man that God created, the perfect-idea man, and is the real self of all men. Jesus the Christ is this self brought forth into perfect expression and manifestation. In the Christ Consciousness, the meaning of Jesus being born in Bethlehem of Judea is that the principle of Truth laid hold of the intelligent substance of Spirit (Bethlehem),and through praise (Judea) brought the Christ into manifestation. The love of the soul in man must be established in the substance of Spirit, before it can become productive of eternal satisfaction. It is wise to protect the newborn Christ Consciousness from contact with Herod, (the physical, personal sense ego). This ruling ego is temporary because it does not understand man's true origin or the law of man's being. Under the ego's rule, man does not fulfill the law of his being, and another ego must supplant the ego of sense.

STEP 7 - BECOME PERFECT (US)

At this stage, the Christ Consciousness is left for us to achieve. Jesus was the example and showed us how to accomplish this task; now the rest is up to us. In the simplest terms this transformation requires that we take three steps. *First*, discern Truth from illusion. Man must put away the error of limitation through the denial of the physical reality; that is, discernment of Truth from illusion! Denial, in this connotation, does not mean sticking the head in the sand and pretending that it is not there, but the discernment between that which is real, and the illusions of the physical world. *Secondly*, accept that we are Spirit. Man must accept the truth that his being is Spiritual. Because the Spiritual is in the realm of the invisible, it must be taken on faith. **Thirdly**, become perfect. Through understanding, we must diligently separate Truth from illusion, and begin to love the Truth, in thoughts, words and deeds. In other words, we are to become perfect and extend this perfection to the world through our actions. The Christ is the man that God created. He is the perfect man, the real self in all men. We must rise out of the limitations of the little personal self to the Christ Consciousness that Jesus demonstrated as being the way to the Father. This last level ends the journey, or Path, to the Christ Consciousness and fulfills the cycle of perfection to perfection. Once all of us have achieved the Christ Consciousness, we will all collectively join the Divine Mind.

SUMMARY OF THE CHRIST CONSCIOUSNESS

The seventh level (Melchi to Jesus), represents the God Will ruling in man, and the ideals of serving Spirit. This is the Christ Consciousness of the Collective Consciousness Model. As we choose to think only pure thoughts, we discover that Love is the uniting force behind the grace of God. The grace of God includes fullness of life, love, wisdom, power and every spiritual quality that belongs to man now and always. Joseph and Mary, the parents of Jesus, represent wisdom and love, which have been ideas of the mind, but now are to bring forth manifestation in Spiritual substance (Jesus). Jesus represents the I AM in man, the self, the directive power raised to the Divine Understanding and the power of the I AM identity. Thus, Jesus represents God's idea of man in expression. The Christ is that idea in the absolute. Jesus the Christ passed through all the trials, temptations and mental variation of each of us, "Yet without sin," (John 3:5); that is, not falling under the dominion of negative, or physical desires.

John 10:7 through 10:10 tells us that Jesus is the door to the higher qualities manifesting on the mental plane and represents the higher mind as the entrance from above to the soul. There is another way in which the lower mind is the entrance from below. From the lower mind the desires (thieves) rob us of the Truth in order to tempt and capture the soul. The thieves do not come for Truth, but to steal and to kill and to destroy. Thus, the thieves must be overcome through the process of evolution. However, this process of evolution is through the involution of Spirit. The Higher Self enters by the higher door. That is, the Divine Will opens the soul and the higher qualities respond to the voice within. The Christ is the the higher door, the way to the Truth and Life; and is the ruler of the higher qualities. The desires (thieves) that come before the Christ, rule first the lower nature, but the higher qualities remain latent until the Spirit stirs them from within. The little personal self enters the higher qualities by experience, and experience provides the knowledge by which the discernment of Truth is revealed. Through the Christ Consciousness, the mind is raised above the thieves that rob us of our True Nature. The Christ came that we might have life to become mature Spiritual Beings. The Christ laid down its human life in the involution of the prototypical human soul, in order that it might take it again in the evolution of the many souls of humanity, and so fulfill the Divine Law of sacrifice. "Now the God of peace, that brought again from the dead our Lord Jesus, that great shepherd of the sheep, through the blood of the everlasting covenant, Make you perfect in every good work to do his will, working in you that which is wellpleasing in his sight, through Jesus Christ; to whom be glory for ever and ever. Amen," (Hebrews 13:20 and 21). Death is the failure to understand spiritual values, and is the passage, as it were, of the human consciousness from the lower nature to the higher. The lower nature of the soul, centered by the personality, perishes while the victorious Christ Consciousness rises to the higher mental plane and becomes one with its Lord. The little personality is mortal; it disappears as it unites with the immortal Individuality at the end of the cycle. "But now is Christ risen from the dead, and become the first fruits of them that slept. For since by man came death, by man came also the resurrection of the dead. For as in Adam all die, even so in Christ shall all be made alive," (1 Corinthians 15:20 through 22). Thus, Christ is the way to salvation, and is the door to the Higher Mind.

SUMMARY

The Bible is a source of information at both the material and spiritual levels. As we have discussed, the traditional interpretation provides a source of understanding at a basic material level. It has been the purpose of this book to access the spiritual interpretation through a system of "decoding" the words in the texts of Genesis and Luke. This process has included a retranslatation of the Hebrew text and a reframing of these words in a metaphysical context.

The object of the Bible is to teach psychology and metaphysics, or Spiritual Truths, so that we may know how to live in alignment with the Divine Ideals. Allegories and parables are used so that everyone might receive the teaching. Without the spiritual meaning behind the story it is not possible to possess the Bible at all. The understanding of the Spiritual keys to the Bible changes consciousness for the better, and it is this rising of the consciousness that makes the higher revelations possible. The Spiritual interpretation of the Bible sets us free by teaching us how to bring health and harmony into our lives by an increasing our awareness of God.

Genesis lays the foundation, or the law, for the entire revelation given in these Holy Scriptures. It particularly deals with the creative power of thought. The other books of the Bible illustrate the way in which the law of thought works in different circumstances, but Genesis is the foundation of it all.

FIRST STORY OF CREATION

Genesis, according to Webster's Dictionary, means "coming into being, or origin." Chapter 1 and the first three verses of chapter 2 of Genesis constitute a summary of the laws that govern thought. It is, therefore, a treatise on the spiritual evolution of man and spiritual nature of man. It is not intended to be a history of the formation of the solar system or the stellar universe. It shows how humanity, as a race, and each individual, personally, come to a knowledge of the all-power, all-presence, and all-goodness of God. The treatise is divided into seven parts, or seven undestandings, and expresses the seven stages through which thought evolves to Truth.

The interpretation of the first story of creation in Genesis tells of the creation of a universal mind that is without shape and unoccupied. Divine Mind then breathes life into the presence of the illusions, which represent individualized reflections of truth, and sets up the duality in which all things are possible. It then commands that there be light to separate understanding from ignorance, and then places a firm foundation of understanding in the mental plane to distinguish the firm unwavering spiritual potential from unexpressed possibilities. This is constantly symbolized for us as the dawn of each morning.

Now the Universal Mind has the capability of Choice. Through choice the Universal Mind begins to understands that Truth yields knowledge.

The Divine Mind then gives the Universal Mind a consciousness so that it can unfold at different degrees of awareness, and commands that it bring forth the law of growth to facilitate the awareness of the Divine Mind as the source of all things. This sets the process of evolution into motion, whereby the Universal Mind can grow to the perfect state of consciousness. Life manifests as form after its own kind, and the firmness of the Divine Mind brings forth a spiritual consciouness, whose manifestation is after its kind.

This is the description of the *Law of Cause and Effect.* The cause is the thought and the effect is the manifestation. Thus, the Universal Mind is awakened to the Divine Life in the outer manifestation. It is the Divine Mind's intention to bring Spiritual I ideals and values to the unformed, darkened, material realm.

Divine Mind then brings forth the rise of intelligence, or inner knowledge, which was differentiated from the ignorance of the outer manifestation. This duality is symbolized in physical form by the sun, moon, and stars, which symbolize day, night, month, year and millennium and give the outer manifestation understanding of the intention of Divine Mind. Everything is presented in the outer manifestation as cycles, or stages, of evolution. Intelligence is then placed in the quality of understanding to distinguish intelligence from ignorance. These are signs and beacons of manifestation to know and understand the Divine Mind's intentions. Understanding yields intelligence which becomes Wisdom. Wisdom is the key to harmony in life, because wise thinking produces wise words and deeds.

Divine Mind then directs intelligence to bring forth thoughts, active and abundant, that are free to rise above the material plane. This act allows the Universal Mind to experience the effects of the thoughts and grow to be full of spiritual understanding. It brings to an end the weak and unformed thoughts in the consciousness. All weak and unformed thoughts are presented in cycles, until Intelligence purifies them and transforms them to a higher degree of awareness. All thoughts have life and are free to evolve from ignorance to full spiritual understanding.

Now all the conditions needed for evolution are in place, except for the individual spirit enity and a description of the various levels of awareness that could unfold to the perfect state of consciousess, and how it works.

The Divine Mind then establishes a spiritual enity in the image and likeness of the Divine Mind capable of reason and analysis with dominion over the unformed thoughts and conscious thoughts in the outer manifestation. This enables the spiritual enity to the realize that the Divine Mind is the source of manifestation. The Divine Mind then identifies the seven levels of awareness as: Sensual, Physical, Individual, Mental, Intellectual, Spiritual, and Christ Consciousness.

And then the Divine Mind ceases the mental effort that it had brought forth; finishes with the perfect state of physical understanding. To obtain the qualities of the Divine Mind the spiritual enity had first to reach the perfect state of physical understanding, so even the Christ Consciousness, or perfect physical understanding gives way to Spirit.

Thus, the first story of creation describes a Universal Mind created to operate in a system of apparent duality of ignorance and intelligence. The spiritual enity chooses which thought system to experience and, through choice and experience, the spiritual enity evolves to the understanding that the Divine Mind is all that there is. This natural law of growth proceeds from the outer to the inner, and consists of seven different levels of awareness terminating in a perfect state of physical understanding.

SECOND STORY OF CREATION

In the second story of creation, the Divine Source changes from God, to Lord God, a spirit form lower in manifestation than that of the Divine Mind referred to in the first chapter. The nature, or name, of the source changes to Lord God or, in its metaphysical translation, intelligence. Divine Intelligence then *forms* a spiritual soul out of the dust of the outer manifestation to work and till the Universal Mind. The soul is man's consciousness which is developed out of Spirit. The soul, at this stage, is the integration of spirit and matter and has the same qualities and likeness as the Divine Mind. However, the formed soul has both spiritual and material qualities and as such can distinguish quality differences between the two. "Whatsoever Adam called every living creature, that was the name thereof." In other words, the primitive lower mind began to perceive, and reflect upon, the different sensations, desires, and lower emotions presented to the soul, or spiritual mind. As the mind energizes the desires, each emotion is distinguished, and by experiencing the difference between things of spirit and matter the soul obtains knowledge. It is this knowledge that sets the Law of Natural Growth into operation and triggers the process of evolution. The

Summary

Divine Mind then places the spiritual body it had formed into a pleasant, harmonious, productive state of consciousness. And the vital forces of life go out of the harmonious state of consciousness to cleanse the spiritual body, and separate to becomes four principles:

The first life principle: Spirit is at work and it completely surrounds the whole Universal Mind, or Collective Consciousness. In the unfolding consciousness is the *Treasure of Spirit*: Intelligence, Wisdom and Truth.

The second life principle: The formative movement of the lower mental plane surrounding the Universal Consciousness unfolds at different levels of awareness from the darkened consciousness of body activity. Thus, the second life principle is the *mind.* The darkness of body consciousness changes as the spiritual mind perceives the Truth and holds in the mind the perfect-body idea.

The third life principle: This is the universal invigorating power of the *Holy Spirit.* The Holy Spirit is within the psychic realm of the soul and is the receiving and distributing force of Truth that gives rise to various kinds of psychic and mental action, forming the character of the soul. It is the Holy Spirit that translates the sensual passions, desires, and emotions of the body to more spiritual qualities and extends this information to the spiritual mind. Only the Holy Spirit is capable of this transformation, because it understands Spirit as well as the material realm.

The fourth life principle: The body is the fructifying cause that bears fruit and receives and distributes the nutrients for growth. Fructifying is the symbol of the Divine Life within the lower nature and is embodied through the process of involution. Spirit energizes the consciousness within the senses, and raises it to a higher level of awareness. Spirit is the cause, and the body receives the Effects. The body completely surrounds the Holy Spirit, mind, and spirit.

Thus, the spiritual body of Intelligence, Wisdom,Truth, mind, Holy Spirit, and the outer manifestation completely surrounds and protects the consciousness of the Universal mind.

THE FALL FROM THE SPIRITUAL BODY

The formed thinking spirit and its feeling helper were then placed in the spiritual body to work and observe it. Both the formed thinking component and the made feeling component of the spiritual mind were instructed to experience every mental quality connecting Spirit and the outer manifestation. The connecting link between Spirit and matter is desirable, and is part of the plan for the mind to evolve to the perfect state of spiritual understanding in the outer manifestation. However, the fruit of the connecting link of the beautiful and adverse (tree of good and evil) is undesirable, because it brings unspiritual ideals and thoughts that, if consumed, would make them unreceptive to Spiritual Truth. The Divine Intelligence knows that the beautiful and adverse is extremely appealing to the lower nature of the Universal Mind. Not being of Spirit, these thoughts confuse the spiritual mind, and upset the peace and harmony of the spiritual body. Therefore, the Divine Intelligence's *warning* is not to deny anything to that which was already perfect and lacked nothing. The fruits of the beautiful and adverse (good and evil) introduce illusions and untruths to the consciousness, and thereby create uncertainty and confusion.

Inspite of this warning, the made "feeling" component is beguiled by the Sense Consciousness, consumes of the forbidden fruit, gives the fruit to the "thinking" component and both disobey the voice of the Divine Intelligence. Having consumed of the fruits of good and evil, both discover they are naked, or without Spiritual protection; they perceive that being nude is wrong, or evil, and they hide from the Divine Intelligence. Thus, the act of disobedience manifests as Guilt and Fear.

The act of disobedience also brings confusion to the consciousness and the peaceful productive state is lost. The thinking and feeling components of consciousness must now leave this ideal state. The Divine Intelligence did not *expel* them, they *chose* to leave through their disobedience. In order to return to a perfect state of consciousness the soul must now experience the effects of the outer manifestation and exercise choice by discerning what is spiritual (good) and illuminating the illusions (errors) of the outer manifestation. Without the spiritual protection, the soul is exposed to the illusions of untruths; and because of its sensual thinking, it falls into the Sense Consciousness and is in need of a material protection to cover the soul. The Divine Intelligence gives the soul "coats of skin" for their new journey. "Coats of skin" implies a physical body, because the Sense Consciousness is the lowest form of manifestation. The physical body then becomes the mirror through which the mental thoughts are reflected, and through this reflection the body experiences the effects of these thoughts. By experiencing these mental reflections, the spiritual mind discerns which thoughts support the good. Thoughts that do not support its good can be eliminated, and in the process the fallen spiritual mind is purified. Without the involution of Spirit, the evolution to the perfect state of consciousness would be impossible. Thus signs and cycles of intelligence are continually presented to man's consciousness, or the soul, to aid it to the goal of perfection.

PATHWAY TO CHRIST

The Bible is full of signs and examples of how to achieve the goal of perfection, but none is more detailed than that presented in the Pathway to Christ. There are seven different levels in the Pathway to Christ Model. Seven, metaphysically, represents physical fulfillment, and is the sum of three and four. The number three represents the trinity of Spirit (Father, Son, and Holy Spirit), and four is symbolic of the world and nature (North, South, East, and West, for example). Therefore, the number seven is the combination, or integration, of Spiritual and material qualities. Each of the seven levels consists of twelve steps, except the first and last levels. The number twelve represents spiritual fulfillment. Twelve is a complete number in relation to conditions of the physical world. For example there are twelve divisions of life (Zodiac cycles), the twelve soul-states (twelve tribes), and the twelve soul-qualities (twelve disciples). The sets of twelve are all interrelated.

The Pathway to Christ Model addresses physical (Levels 1 & 2), mental (Levels 3, 4, & 5), and spiritual (Levels 6 & 7) components of the soul. The Pathway to Christ becomes a road map, if you will, to direct the spiritual mind to the perfect stage of physical understanding. This road map is very useful to determine where we have been, what we have accomplished, and what needs to be accomplished on the journey through life to, "Become perfect as your Father in Heaven is Perfect."

In closing, I hope that this book brings as much enlightenment to you as it has brought to me in its preparation. Hopefully, there will be many more such books in the future as I make my journey from Dan to Daniel.

"Namast'e"

Divine Spirit in me
recognizes
and salutes
Divine Spirit in you:

BIBLIOGRAPHY

Achtemeier, Paul. ed., *Harper's Bible Dictionary*. San Francisco: Harper & Row, 1985.

Addington, Jack Ensign. *The Hidden Mystery of The Bible*. New York: Putnam, 1987.

A Course In Miracles, Foundation For Inner Peace, Tiburon: 1975.

Daves, Paul. *God And The New Physics*. New York: Simon & Schuster, 1983.

Diel, Paul. *Symbolism in the Bible*. San Francisco: Harper & Row, 1893.

Eiselen, Frederick Carl, ed., *The Abingdon Bible Commentary*. New York & Nashville: Abingdon Press, 1929.

Fox, Emmet. *Alter Your Life*. San Francisco: Harper Collins, 1931.

Friedman, Richard Elliott. *Who Wrote the Bible?*, New York : Summit Books, 1987.

Gaskell, G.A. *Dictionary of All Scriptures & Myths*. New York: Gramercy Books. 1981.

Hampden-Turner. *Maps Of The Mind*. New York: Macmillan, 1982.

Hodson, Geoffrey. *The Hidden Wisdom in the Holy Bible Volumes 1,2, & 3*, Wheaton, Il: The Theosophical Publishing House, 1967

Holmes, Ernest, *A Dictionary of New Thought Terms*. Marina Del Rey, CA: Devorss & Company, 1991.

Holmes, Ernest. *The Science Of Mind*. New York: Doss, Mead and Company,1938.

The Holy Bible. Authorized King James Version. Cleveland & New York:The World Publishing Company.

Keyes, Ken. *Handbook to Higher Consciousness*. Coos Bay: Love Line Books, 1975.

Lamsa, George M. *The Holy Bible, From Ancient Eastern Manuscripts*. Nashville: Holman Bible Publishers. 1981.

The Living Bible Paraphrased. Weaton Il: Tyndale House Publishers, 1971.

Metaphysical Bible Dictionary. Unity Village, MO: Unity School of Christianity, 1931.

Murphy, Joseph. *How to Use The Laws of Mind.* Marina del Rey: DeVorss, 1980.

Shield, Benjamin, and Richard Carlson. *For The Love of God. New writings by Spiritual and Psychological Leaders.* San Rafael, Ca: New World Library, 1990.

Spangler, David. *The Laws of Manifestation*, Findhorn : Findhorn Publication, 1975.

Spalding, Baird T. *Life & Teachings of the Masters of the Far East* Volumes 1-5. Marina del Rey, Ca: DeVorss & Co., 1924.

Scofield, C.I. T*he New Scofield Reference Bible, Holy Bible Concordance*. New York: Oxford University Press, 1937

Spong, John Shelby. *Rescuing the Bible from Fundamentalism*. New York: Harper Collins, 1992.

Strong, James, S.T.D., LL.D. *The Exhaustive Concordance of The Bible*. McLean, Virginia: MacDonald Publishing Company.

Szekely, Edmond Bordeaux. *The Essene Book of Creation*. San Diego: Academy Books, 1975.

Thomas, Robert L., Th.D., ed., *New American Standard Exhaustive Concordance of the Bible*. Nashville, Tennessee: Holman,1981.

Troward, Thomas. *Bible Mystery and Bible Meaning*. Marina Del Rey, CA: DeVorss & Company, 1992.

Webster's New World Dictionary of the American Language, College Edition. Cleveland & New York: The World Publishing Company,1959.

Letter to the reader:

This Book and the associated research has had a profound affect on my Spiritual development and, therefore, my life. I hope that you have also gained by this information. I would sincerely appreciate any feedback; comments, questions or suggestions that you may have to offer. By your sharing, you help clarify difficult concepts and we grow together towards the Christ Consciousness.

May the Grace of God be with you!

Please send your correspondence to:

The Dancy Company
P.O. Box 12340
Reno, Nevada   89510-2340

Where to obtain additional copies of **LET THERE BE LIGHT.**

Check your local metaphysical bookstore. If they do not have copies ask them to order it for you.

or

Order Direct from: **THE DANCY COMPANY.**
P.O. Box 12340
Reno, Nevada 89510-2340

Send check or money order to THE DANCY COMPANY for the amount of $17.45 (book price $14.95 + 2.50 P & H) for each book. When ordering direct please provide the following information:

Full name:
Address:
City, state, & zip code:
Phone number: (optional)

Please allow 3 weeks for delivery. If you desire a faster turn around, and have a valid Master Card or Visa Credit Card; call our 24 hour voice mail at (209) 496-3899 with the following information:

Name of card holder:
Credit card number:
Expiration date:
Phone number (in case of problems):
Name and complete address where the book(s) are to be sent:

Your copy will be in the mail the next day!